STATE OF
FAILURE

STATE OF FAILURE

Yasser Arafat, Mahmoud Abbas, and the Unmaking of the Palestinian State

JONATHAN SCHANZER

palgrave
macmillan

First published in 2013 by PALGRAVE MACMILLAN® in the United
States—a division of St. Martin's Press LLC, 175 Fifth Avenue, New
York, NY 10010.

Where this book is distributed in the UK, Europe and the rest of the
world, this is by Palgrave Macmillan, a division of Macmillan Publishers
Limited, registered in England, company number 785998, of Houndmills,
Basingstoke, Hampshire RG21 6XS.

Palgrave Macmillan is the global academic imprint of the above
companies and has companies and representatives throughout the world.

Palgrave® and Macmillan® are registered trademarks in the United
States, the United Kingdom, Europe and other countries.

ISBN 978-1-137-27824-1

Library of Congress Cataloging-in-Publication Data
Schanzer, Jonathan.
    State of failure : Yasser Arafat, Mahmoud Abbas, and the unmaking of
the Palestinian state / by Jonathan Schanzer, Vice President for Research,
Foundation for Defense of Democracies.
        pages   cm
    1. Palestinian Arabs—Politics and government. 2. Palestinian
National Authority. 3. Harakat al-Muqawamma al-Islamiyya. 4. Fath
(Organization). 5. Arab-Israeli conflict—1993– I. Title.
DS119.76.S345   2013
320.95695'3—dc23
                                                        2013010358

A catalogue record of the book is available from the British Library.

Design by Letra Libre, Inc.

First edition: October 2013

10 9 8 7 6 5 4 3 2 1

Printed in the United States of America.

CONTENTS

ACKNOWLEDGMENTS

THE WRITING OF THIS BOOK HAS BEEN A JOURNEY. IT BEGAN WITH A FEW quiet meetings with Palestinians in Europe, the Middle East, and America. There was a common theme. While Palestinians are universally frustrated about Israel's policies, they are also frustrated by their own poor leadership. Intrigued, I began to write articles about the Palestinian leadership deficit, as well as the chronic abuses of power and mismanagement that have been all too common across the Arab world. The more I wrote, the more I learned from others who had similar stories to share. I soon realized that the story of failed Palestinian governance and chronic mismanagement is one that every observer of the region implicitly accepts as truth, but few have ever documented. In fact, nobody has ever produced a narrative of the Palestinian struggle for competent governance. This book is a good faith effort to do just that.

First and foremost, I must thank the Palestinians who helped me gain a better understanding of this issue along the way. Most did not wish to be named as sources, for fear of retribution. But without them, this book would not have been written.

Similarly, this book would not have been written without the support of my employer, the Foundation for Defense of Democracies. I am particularly grateful for the support of Clifford May, FDD's president, Mark Dubowitz, FDD's executive director, Bill

McCarthy, FDD's senior vice president, and Toby Dershowitz, FDD's vice president for government relations. True to their word, they helped me turn ideas into action. They were also unwavering in their support of my work, even as it came under attack from various quarters.

For fending off those attacks, I thank Nathan Siegel of Levine, Sullivan, Koch & Schulz. And for their professionalism and patience, I thank Emily Carleton, Donna Cherry, and Lauren Dwyer at Palgrave Macmillan.

I also owe debt of gratitude to David Barnett, whom I met when he was a promising student of Palestinian history at Johns Hopkins. He is now, thankfully, a full-time employee at FDD. His research and careful fact-checking were crucial to the completion of this book. FDD interns Anna Gordan, Laura Maschler, Nicole Salter, and Ari Weiss also deserve credit for reading chapters of the manuscript. They caught errors that I did not and saved me from myself. Of course, any errors herein are mine and mine alone.

I must also acknowledge Jim Prince, who has become a trusted friend and guide as my thinking evolved throughout the writing of this book. His commitment to good governance and democracy in the Arab world is incomparable.

Finally, I wish to thank my wife, Elana. She helped me, substantively and otherwise, at various stages through this journey. More importantly, she has been a steadying hand through countless other journeys along the way.

1

Collapse or Statehood?

THE PALESTINIANS ARE PUSHING FOR FULL RECOGNITION OF STATEHOOD.
They call their campaign "Palestine 194," a reference to their goal
of becoming the 194th state in the United Nations. Under the
leadership of Palestine Liberation Organization (PLO) chairman
Mahmoud Abbas, also known by his *kunya* (Arabic teknonym)
Abu Mazen, the campaign is well under way.

Critics of the campaign—notably the United States, Canada,
and Israel—said that the move was counterproductive because the
Palestinians were shirking their responsibilities, as stipulated in the
1993 Oslo Accords, to negotiate bilaterally with Israel over every
aspect of the future two-state solution. This push for the recognition
of Palestinian statehood is unilateral, critics argue, and it should
therefore be punished with aid cuts and diplomatic downgrades.

By contrast, proponents of the campaign say that Palestinian statehood is long overdue. They argue that the PLO needs
no seal of approval from the United States or Canada or Israel to
fulfill its dream of statehood. They further argue that as long as
Israel unilaterally builds settlements in the West Bank—land the
Palestinians claim for their national project—there is no reason to
negotiate. Though diplomacy with Israel resumed in July 2013,

the Palestinians made it clear they could return to this strategy at any time.

The effort officially began in September 2011, when Mahmoud Abbas stood before a buzzing UN General Assembly in New York City and announced his intention to achieve recognition of statehood for the Palestinian people. He forwarded an official request to the UN Security Council, but his bid stalled due to a lack of strategic direction on the part of the Palestinian leadership, coupled with pressure from Washington. The United States, as a permanent member of the Security Council, had vowed to veto the request, but it was unclear whether Abbas had even successfully lobbied for the requisite votes needed.

Following the defeat, the Palestinians appeared to have given up on the strategy. But in early 2012, the PLO announced that the Palestinians were gearing up for another diplomatic push. Only this time they noted that they would not seek official recognition through the UN Security Council. This time, they said, they would merely seek a "diplomatic upgrade" through the UN General Assembly, where an overwhelming majority of the states supported the PLO's initiative.

This move, Abbas acknowledged, would not lead to Palestine 194. Rather, it would grant the PLO nonmember observer state status. It would bring the Palestinians one step closer to their dream but also potentially arm Palestinians with new diplomatic weapons—such as accession to the International Criminal Court (ICC), which could enable the Palestinians to sue Israel for war crimes or establish legal claims on West Bank lands where Israel was building.

Commentators lauded the Palestinians for pursuing a legal rather than a violent approach. To be sure, Abbas deserves credit for eschewing violence after decades of terrorism perpetrated in the name of the Palestinian cause. But the real genius behind his strategy was that it marginalized the United States. No country, not even the United States, can veto a General Assembly measure at the United Nations. And the Palestinians, who had been quietly lobbying in capitals the world over for the better part of seven years, had secured the support of the vast majority of the 193 UN member states.

However, the timing of the effort was not ideal for the Palestinians, given all of the Middle East drama of 2011 and 2012: the Syrian civil war, the power struggles in Egypt, the race for nuclear weapons in Iran. Nevertheless, the Palestinians were determined to continue their quest. They continued to broadcast their intention to return to the United Nations. The United States threatened to cut off aid. The Israelis threatened to withhold the tens of millions of dollars they collect each month in Palestinian taxes. Yet Abbas was unmoved. On November 29, 2012, with the world watching, the snowy-haired Palestinian leader went back to the United Nations and secured nonmember observer state status for Palestine.

Abbas returned to a hero's welcome in Ramallah, the interim Palestinian capital just a few miles east of Jerusalem. But that was only part of the picture. On the international stage, the outpouring of support was overwhelming.

"We wholeheartedly welcome the recognition of Palestine as an observer state by the United Nations," said renowned human rights activist Desmond Tutu. "Sixty-five years after the UN recommended the establishment of a Jewish state and an Arab state side by side on former Mandatory Palestine, the world has finally taken an important step on the Palestinian part of its promise."[1]

Former US president Jimmy Carter was no less enthusiastic. "The international community now has a duty to turn this significant step by the UN into lasting peace in the Middle East. . . . The UN vote can be a catalyst for genuine negotiations between Israel and Palestine on a more equal footing," he said.[2]

Even former Israeli prime minister Ehud Olmert endorsed the move. He asserted that it was "congruent with the basic concept of the two-state solution. Therefore, I see no reason to oppose it. Once the United Nations will lay the foundation for this idea, we in Israel will have to engage in a serious process of negotiations, in order to agree on specific borders based on the 1967 lines, and resolve the other issues."[3]

Sitting statesmen also argued that Abbas's maneuver was a small yet symbolic measure to right a historic wrong. They decried the many reported Israeli injustices against the Palestinians, which have long characterized the Palestinian narrative.

Turkey's foreign minister, Ahmet Davutoğlu, stated, "We have gathered here for correcting a historical injustice against the Palestinian people. We all believe and cherish the vision of a just, peaceful, and harmonious future. For that future we should altogether have to stand behind the Palestinian bid to become a 'non-member observer state.' This is a moment of truth for all of us."[4]

China, via a foreign ministry spokesman, also indicated that the move was a way for Palestinians to recover "their national and legitimate rights and interests."[5]

Many also saw Abbas's UN upgrade as a binary equation. Supporting Palestinian rights, in their view, went hand in hand with challenging Israel or even punishing it.

The Muslim Brotherhood government in Egypt, for example, lauded the UN maneuver because it "provides the Palestinian people with the appropriate legal tools to deter and confront the crimes committed by the occupying power, and hold the perpetrators of those crimes accountable before international justice."[6]

Roger Waters, the famed vocalist for the rock band Pink Floyd and now a political activist, implored the international community to "[s]eize this historic moment. Support the vote today for Palestinian enhanced observer statehood status as a step towards full membership. And declare Israel's continued membership of the UN to be dependent on reform of its illegal apartheid regime."[7]

LOST IN ALL OF THE HOOPLA was one crucial question: Are the Palestinians prepared for this next step? Is the Palestinian Authority (PA), the interim body created in 1994 to govern the West Bank and Gaza Strip, an efficient, transparent, or financially viable authority that is prepared to function as a government for the Palestinian people? This book will explain why the answer, unfortunately, is "no." The reason: the PA and its antecedents have been beset by bad governance.

Many critics point to the consistent use of terrorism and political violence as a black mark on the Palestinian cause. This, of course, is a valid concern. Violent groups continue to litter the Palestinian political landscape. But let us for a moment suppose that the use of violence is now a thing of the past. How do the Palestinians function on a political level?

The Palestinian government, as it is currently configured, is mired in dysfunction. Not only are the Palestinian territories (West Bank and Gaza Strip) divided between two warring factions (Fatah and Hamas), it is also undeniable that both cantons have failed to function well as governments.

For the purposes of this book, we will not address the political and economic challenges associated with the Hamas government in Gaza. Hamas won the 2006 legislative elections, earning the terrorist group the right to forge a government. With Western support, the PLO and Fatah faction leaders refused to allow this to happen, ultimately prompting a civil war in 2007 that led to Hamas's violent takeover of Gaza, where Hamas has remained firmly entrenched. Although Hamas maintains an iron grip on Gaza, an Israeli and Western embargo on the tiny coastal enclave has hindered Hamas's political and economic prospects greatly. But it would be disingenuous to blame Hamas's failures on the embargo alone. Report after report indicates that the de facto government in Gaza is ruled by draconian laws, while outside actors such as Iran, Turkey, and Qatar continue to try to heavily influence decision making.

Hamas may yet declare independence for the Gaza Strip.[8] But it is unlikely to do so through diplomacy or the United Nations. The West Bank regime, by contrast, seeks to speak for all Palestinians and to press for full Palestinian independence. This book is an attempt to explain why the Palestinian government run by Mahmoud Abbas will very likely become steeped in crisis, if not fail, if and when such a state is created.

TO BETTER UNDERSTAND THE PROBLEM, one must first look back at how the PA was born. Created as a civilian caretaker government in 1994, the PA was the unlikely offspring of a terrorist organization, the PLO. The PLO, in turn, had emerged from Fatah, a terrorist group founded in Kuwait in the 1950s. Yasser Arafat, perhaps the most famous Palestinian the world has ever known, controlled both groups.

The road to the PA was not an easy one. Arafat made the reluctant strategic decision to renounce terrorism in the late 1980s, which ultimately paved the way for him to become the leader of the nascent Palestinian self-rule polity, the PA.

But even after Fatah and the PLO transitioned from terrorism to politics, Arafat obstructed outside efforts to bring transparency to Palestinian institutions as they changed shape. Under Arafat, in fact, the PA funneled untold amounts of international donor funding to a select group of insiders and did little to forge economic solutions that would create jobs or new opportunities for Palestinians in the West Bank and Gaza. As a result, the PA failed to inspire confidence among the people.

Despite all of this, the PA made some strides in the 1990s. Thanks to the determined efforts of stakeholders in the peace process, the Palestinian self-rule project gained ground in fits and starts. The PA took on increased responsibility for daily governance. But this all came to a jarring halt in September 2000 with the outbreak of the second intifada, a low-level Palestinian war marked by suicide bombings and other guerrilla tactics. While the uprising originally targeted Israel and was a response to the lack of progress toward a final status peace agreement to end all grievances with the Jewish state, it also exposed some critical fissures within Palestinian society. The most glaring of these was the lack of transparency and accountability in governance.

If there was any silver lining to the PA's challenges after the collapse of the peace process, it was the growing public support to address these problems. This paved the way for the rise of Salam Fayyad, the institution-building finance minister who succeeded in shaping a more transparent financial system and established, for the first time, a single treasury account through which all taxes and donor funds would pass.

This is not to say that Fayyad's job was easy. All along the way, the PLO and Fatah, the traditional loyalists from the two most powerful Palestinian institutions, worked assiduously to torpedo his efforts. In many ways, Fayyad was dismantling the system that had sustained these groups since 1968.

Fayyad also inspired the creation of the Palestine Investment Fund (PIF), a sovereign wealth fund intended to enrich and empower the Palestinian people. Fayyad's unenviable job was to identify, with the help of a team of accountants, the assets Arafat had amassed over years of militant activity across the Middle East and Europe and to bring them up to Western accounting standards. This was a herculean task. Fayyad's team painstakingly investigated secret holdings around the world and integrated them into the Palestinian treasury.

But Fayyad's successes were fleeting. After Arafat's death in 2004, Mahmoud Abbas rose to power, largely due to the unwavering efforts of former US president George W. Bush, who believed that Abbas was committed to peace with Israel. Abbas was

roundly lauded as the antithesis of Arafat: nonviolent and a stal-
wart against corruption.

But it soon became clear that Abbas was not the man Bush
believed him to be. From the moment he assumed office in 2005,
Abbas moved aggressively to consolidate political and economic
power. The nepotism and political patronage that characterized
the Arafat era again became the norm. Abbas undermined some
of the PA's own laws and systematically denied power to Fayyad
and other political competitors. He co-opted or weakened institutions that promoted transparency and accountability.

Unfortunately, the West further encouraged Abbas's consolidation of power after the Palestinian civil war of 2007, when Hamas
overran the PA government in the Gaza Strip. Fearing a complete
terrorist takeover of the Palestinian territories, Israel and the Western donor community, led by the United States, propped up the Palestinian leader with weapons, intelligence, and cash. The message
was clear: stay in power at all costs, and don't let Hamas take over.

With the international community overwhelmingly concerned
about the continued survival of the government in the West Bank,
Western governments abandoned all expectations of Abbas as a
leader. Discussions no longer revolved around efforts to create an
independent state with a viable public authority. The goal was
simply to keep the West Bank out of the hands of Hamas.

With the end of expectations came the decline of the nascent
political system the Palestinians had tried to build. Among other
things, Abbas ensured that Fayyad's office lacked the power to do
anything more than receive donor checks and allocate funds to
the Palestinian bureaucracy. This ultimately led to Fayyad's resignation in April 2013. Other political figures found themselves
cornered and unable to mount a challenge, let alone engage in
open political debate. Meanwhile, Abbas also detained reporters
who criticized him and shut down websites that highlighted the
alarming lack of transparency in the PA.

THERE IS A REAL AND GROWING PROBLEM in Ramallah today. To be sure, Israel's continued military presence and its accompanying restrictions have contributed to it. But the problem, at its core, is about good governance. Whatever recognition the Palestinians earn for their national project, if a viable Palestinian state is ever to emerge, its government must undergo substantial reform. Without cleaning out the ossified institutions that revolve around one powerful figure and weigh down the current system, the future state of Palestine may simply collapse under its own weight.

Right now, however, world leaders have made no such demands on the Palestinians. Too many decision makers remain dangerously silent on the problem. And that silence could smother the fledgling nation in its cradle. These leaders seek to project foreign policies that appear "pro-Palestinian." But as this book will make clear, nothing could be further from the truth.

The failure to address the issues besetting Palestinian governance is a byproduct of the way Palestinian supporters approach their cause. There is simply too little introspection. The focus instead continues to be on Israel and its policies vis-à-vis the West Bank and the Gaza Strip. In some cases, the focus tends to be on Israel as an illegitimate colonial state that must be destroyed so that a Palestinian state can be built on its ashes.

Again, this is not to deny that Israel has, throughout the course of the Palestinian–Israeli conflict, contributed to the plight of the Palestinians. It undoubtedly has. Whether through the conquest of land or the imposition of restrictive policies in the name of security, Israel has set back the Palestinian cause. This is a deeply regrettable outcome of the conflict between these two peoples.

As Hussein Ibish of the American Task Force on Palestine notes, "The occupation remains not only the most important barrier to Palestinian independence and statehood, it has also been one of the most important obstacles to successful institution building." But Ibish also notes, "Those who would argue that real institution building and practical preparation for successful independent statehood is not possible under conditions of the occupation have been proven wrong."[9]

In other words, the Palestinians must also take responsibility. They must come to terms with the fact that their ability to create a functioning state goes hand in hand with putting their own house in order. Unfortunately, Palestinian stakeholders are not there yet—not by a long shot. Such change usually arises from soul-searching, often a byproduct of journalism and scholarship that underscores the challenges and wrestles with a menu of options that could serve as solutions.

But, therein lies another problem. The Palestinian–Israeli conflict has received more mass media coverage, academic consideration, and overall attention from the world's policymakers than almost any other international issue.[10] This disproportionate focus has drawn attention away from other worthy causes, from China's Great Leap Forward to the genocides in Rwanda and Darfur. But it has also yielded a cacophony of zealous arguments from all sides, such that even the most valid arguments are lost in the noise.

However, it is more complicated than that. Access to Israel is rather open, which makes it easy to look at all of Israel's warts under a microscope. And there are many, as we have seen over the years. Yet there is a tendency to look at Palestinian politics only through the prism of the peace process. Palestinian politics seems to matter only insofar as it impacts diplomacy with Israel. Moreover, few outsiders ever gain access to Palestinian political elites, apart from the very top tier. Even fewer care to. Among those who take the time to report on what happens inside the Palestinian political system, most are dissuaded from reporting on what they find, fearing academic and political retribution, or worse.

The result is a dearth of information on the internal Palestinian dynamic. This is strange given how many activists and scholars will argue that the Palestinian issue is the most central issue in the Arab world.

IN 2011, ARAB GOVERNMENTS WERE TOPPLED across the Middle East. Repressed populations rose up against autocratic leaders, demanding new freedoms and brighter futures. The Palestinian leadership, however, remained immune to these changes. The real fight, they said, was against Israel.

But the Palestinians may be experiencing the Arab Spring in slow motion. Those in power, particularly Abbas and his circle, are finding that, despite their best efforts to change the subject, the Palestinian people wish to hold their government to account. For now, Abbas's insurance is Hamas. The international community appears content not to hold him to the same standards as some of the new governments that have been built on the ashes of fallen dictatorships for fear of a hostile takeover by the Islamist group that ripped control of Gaza from his hands in 2007.

At four years past the end of his legal term, however, Abbas needs to clear the way for new leadership. Change is long overdue. But such change will not come until Palestinian partisans recognize that the PA is broken. The Palestinian government must take responsibility for the domestic challenges it faces, allow more space for political debate, and create a self-sustaining economy to usher in a new era.

In the end, criticizing the Palestinian leadership for its ossified approach to governance is not anti-Palestinian. Indeed, it is decidedly pro-Palestinian. The sooner we begin to understand this, the sooner we can get back to the task at hand: establishing the building blocks of a Palestinian state that will help both Israelis and Palestinians get one step closer to the two-state solution.

2

The United States and the Question of Palestine

IS THE UNITED STATES INCLINED TO BE ANTI-PALESTINIAN? WE HEAR about a powerful "Israel lobby"[1] that dissuades Washington from allowing Palestinians to achieve statehood. But the history of US–Palestinian relations tells a different story. In fact, US presidents have increasingly viewed Palestinian statehood with favor and have consistently moved closer to accepting Palestine as a state with each passing administration. With each new presidency, one gets the sense that time is on the side of the Palestinians.

IN THE AFTERMATH OF WORLD WAR I and the unraveling of the Ottoman Empire, one could argue that President Woodrow Wilson supported the Palestinian quest for statehood. Columbia University's Rashid Khalidi argues that the US president was referring to the Palestinians (and perhaps the Kurds and Armenians)[2] when he stated in his famous 1918 "Fourteen Points" speech that "other nationalities which are now under Turkish rule should be assured an undoubted security of life and an absolutely unmolested opportunity of an autonomous development."[3]

Did Wilson intend to acknowledge Palestinian nationalism? It is not known. What is known is that Wilson created a commission led by Henry Churchill King, president of Oberlin College, and Charles Crane, a Chicago businessman, to survey the needs of the inhabitants of Syria, Lebanon, and Palestine. The King-Crane Commission, as it was known, visited Palestine, Syria, and Lebanon in the summer of 1919. A majority of the commission favored curtailment of Zionist emigration, reflecting the desire of the Muslim communities with whom they spoke.[4] The report was never officially published, and its findings were ultimately not considered. As historian Kathleen Christison notes, this was because Wilson suffered a stroke two months after it was written. But Christison also charges that "Wilson did not care deeply one way or the other about Palestine's political fate."[5]

True, Wilson likely did not give a great deal of thought to the demands of the local Arabs in the territory of the British Mandate. But he did not care much about Zionism, either. After World War I, US foreign policy was isolationist, fueled by a desire to avoid foreign entanglements. By design, therefore, the United States had little influence over the region, which was largely dominated by Britain and France.

Of course, Wilson supported the 1917 Balfour Declaration, which supported a Jewish homeland in Palestine, but this might be viewed more as support for an ally's decision rather than as a sign that he had any deep-rooted feelings about the issue one way or another. Christison notes that Wilson endorsed the declaration a full month after its issuance "and only upon being reminded of the request."[6] It was not until September 21, 1922, some five years after the declaration was issued, that Congress issued Public Resolution Number 73, which stated that "America favors the establishment in Palestine of a national home for the Jewish people."[7]

The roaring twenties was not a time of American involvement in the Middle East. Then, in October 1929, just two months after

riots erupted between Jews and Arabs at the Wailing Wall in Jerusalem,[8] the US stock market crashed, beginning what would become known as the Great Depression. This devastating economic
downturn lasted until the start of World War II, effectively causing Americans to turn inward and largely ignore international affairs. Under the leadership of Franklin Delano Roosevelt, who
was elected president in November 1932, Congress passed the
first of several Neutrality Acts designed to insulate America from
overseas conflicts.[9] In short, the Middle East was of little concern
to a beleaguered United States. Perhaps the one significant exception was the first oil concession granted by the Saudis to Southern
Oil of California in 1933.[10]

Whatever Americans did know about the Palestinians was
likely tainted by bloodshed. From 1936 to 1939, Palestinian Arabs fought a low-intensity war against the British and Jewish communities in protest of increased Jewish immigration. The spiraling
conflict left 5,000 Palestinians dead, 15,000 wounded, and 5,600
incarcerated.[11] Coordinating much of the violence, even amid
British efforts to recognize Palestinian demands,[12] was the mufti
of Palestine and head of the Arab Higher Committee, Hajj Amin
al-Husseini. Al-Husseini had an ongoing relationship with senior
Nazi figures, including Adolf Hitler. In a January 1941 letter that
he wrote to Hitler, al-Husseini pledged to the "great Fuhrer" that
Arabs everywhere were "prepared to act as is proper against the
common enemy and to take their stand with enthusiasm on the
side of the Axis and to do their part in the well-deserved defeat of
the Anglo-Jewish coalition."[13]

The mufti, in fact, was welcomed as an honored guest by top
leaders of the Third Reich. After meeting personally with Hitler,
he established close working relationships with high-profile Nazi
war criminals, including Joseph Goebbels, Heinrich Himmler,
and Adolf Eichmann. According to testimony at the Nuremberg
Trials, al-Husseini was among Eichmann's best friends, and he

joined Eichmann on a visit to the gas chambers of Auschwitz. In 1943, Himmler placed al-Husseini in charge of recruiting as many as 100,000 Muslim fighters to join units serving in the Balkans, North Africa, and the Middle East.[14]

Roosevelt, meanwhile, tried to distance himself from the growing controversy in the Middle East and even spurned Supreme Court Justice Felix Frankfurter's request in 1942 to meet with David Ben-Gurion, the leading political figure among the Jews in Palestine. Only after 1944—12 years after Roosevelt took office—as the death toll of the Holocaust became too much to bear, did a US president see the need for a "Jewish commonwealth."[15]

Even then, Roosevelt met with Saudi king Ibn Saud in the early spring of 1945 and promised that he would consult with the Arab leaders on any US decisions regarding Palestine. In an address to Congress on March 1, 1945, Roosevelt reportedly departed from a prepared text, stating that he had learned "more about the whole problem, the Moslem problem, the Jewish problem, by talking with Ibn Saud for five minutes than I could have learned in the exchange of two- or three-dozen letters."[16]

ROOSEVELT'S SUCCESSOR, HARRY S. TRUMAN, took office in April 1945. He felt a moral obligation to protect the Jewish people who had suffered under Nazi cruelty, believing that they had suffered "more and longer" than others affected by World War II. Many Americans also believed that "Palestine should be the haven for Jews who had survived the horrors of war."[17]

On September 26, 1947, Britain announced that it would be withdrawing from Palestine, thereby ending the mandate and leaving the fate of the territory to the international community. Two months later, on November 29, 1947, the United Nations approved a partition plan, which divided the territory up into three contiguous Arab swaths and three contiguous Jewish swaths, with Jerusalem slated for permanent trusteeship.

The White House backed partition, but Washington was not unanimous as to the merits of the plan. Specifically, the State Department's policy staff issued a paper arguing that the plan required further study. One ambassador even suggested that the entire territory come under temporary UN trusteeship.[18]

The Arab states, for their part, rejected the partition plan outright, which did little to help the Palestinian cause as the world deliberated. As Christison notes, "Far from demonstrating that they were the victims of an injustice, as they believed, [the Arabs] gave the impression around the world that they were the victimizers."[19] It was not lost on the world that the Arabs called for outright war against some 400,000 Jews living in Palestine just three years after six million Jews had been slaughtered in Europe.

In the end, Truman announced his recognition of the State of Israel at 6:11 p.m. on May 14, 1948, 11 minutes after David Ben-Gurion's declaration of independence in Tel Aviv.[20] But this did not mean that Washington did not care about the fate of the Palestinians. There was no intention to reject the creation of a Palestinian Arab state in the territory allotted by the United Nations.

Moreover, in the years following the 1948 Arab invasion and the first Arab–Israeli War, the United States showed a great deal of concern for the estimated 725,000 Arab refugees in the region. For example, in December 1948, the United States supported UN Resolution 194, which called for refugees from the conflict "willing to live in peace" to be allowed to return to their homes. The United States was also involved in devising a number of unsuccessful plans to reintegrate them.[21]

All the while, Palestinian nationalism had lost much of its momentum. The Palestinian uprisings of 1936–1939, the subsequent British crackdown, and the way in which the Arab states had exploited the Palestinian cause left the nascent nationalist movement in disarray. It would take more than 15 years for Palestinians to rediscover their desire for independence. Rashid Khalidi calls the

years between 1948 and the emergence of the PLO in 1964 the
"lost years."[22] With few nations advocating on behalf of the Palestinians, the cause was given similarly short shrift in Washington.

TRUMAN'S SUCCESSOR, DWIGHT D. EISENHOWER, assumed office in
January 1953. He was never considered to be an avowed friend of
Israel. In fact, although Israel was facing increased cross-border
fedayeen attacks from neighboring Arab states and heightened
bellicosity from the likes of Egyptian leader Gamal Abdel Nasser,
the Eisenhower administration elected not to sell arms to Israel in
an effort to avoid potential conflict with the Soviet Union.[23]

Furthermore, Eisenhower would not support the Israelis when
they captured Egypt's Sinai Peninsula (along with France and
Great Britain) in the Suez War of 1956. However, the fact that
some of Eisenhower's policies were less than friendly to Israel did
not necessarily make him "pro-Palestinian." Indeed, there was no
such paradigm. Jordan and Egypt controlled the West Bank and
Gaza Strip, respectively.

Moreover, the ideology that captured the imagination of the
Palestinians at the time was pan-Arabism. A socialist ideology
championed by Nasser, pan-Arabism was built on the premise
that the Arabs "were a single people with a single language, history, and culture." This, Khalidi notes, "obscured the identities of
the separate Arab nation-states it subsumed," including the Palestinians. And as Khalidi admits, the Palestinians were "deeply
attracted" to this ideology.[24]

Meanwhile, the United States was almost singularly concerned
with the advances the Soviet Union was making in the Middle
East. The Soviets sought to gain increased access to oil in the region, and Arab states were proving to be willing allies in exchange
for financial and military support. The US policy that emerged
from this quandary was an attempt to win back the friendship
of the Arabs.[25] Notably, Iraq, Egypt, and Syria had become client

states of the USSR. So, too, would the nascent Fatah organization, founded by Palestinian guerrilla fighter Yasser Arafat in the 1950s, sparking a new wave of Palestinian transnational terror.

AFTER EISENHOWER CAME PRESIDENT JOHN F. KENNEDY, who pledged to the Arab states that he would do more to resolve the Arab–Israeli conflict. In fact, Kennedy had called for the resettlement of Palestinian refugees while serving in the US Senate.[26]

Of course, he was also the first to call the US relationship with Israel a "special relationship," indicating that it was unshakable. Additionally, Kennedy was the first US commander in chief to sell high-tech weaponry to Israel, such as the Hawk anti-aircraft missile.[27]

Kennedy's assassination heralded the unexpected rise of Lyndon B. Johnson. Johnson, like his predecessors, was generally unaware of the Palestinian plight. As Christison notes, "By the mid-1960s, the Palestinians had drifted so far into the political background that virtually no one regarded them as a political factor of any consequence."[28] The Arab League created the PLO in 1964, but the group was largely a tool for Nasser to maintain control over the Palestinian narrative. It was not an international player.

In 1964, Fatah, the guerrilla organization under Arafat's control, began to carry out cross-border raids against Israel from Syria, Lebanon, and Jordan. However, these attacks were not of great concern to the United States. It was only when these raids increased tension between the Arab states and pushed them toward war with Israel that the United States began to take Fatah and its irredentist ideology seriously.[29]

The 1967 Arab–Israeli War was, of course, a watershed event for the Palestinian issue. The war forced Washington to deal with some new realities, as no fewer than six Arab states broke off ties with Washington in the war's aftermath. The Arab states also increasingly gravitated into the Soviet orbit. More important, American officials acknowledged that the raids carried out by Fatah had played a role in precipitating the confrontation. However, the importance of Palestinian nationalism was still not clear to the United States—primarily because no one was articulating this concept to decision makers in Washington in a consistent manner.

This changed when Arafat ascended as head of the PLO in 1968. What was once an administrative tool for Nasser's now-discredited pan-Arabist ideology became an umbrella organization for terrorist groups carrying out violence in the name of Palestinian nationalism. The drastic uptick in Palestinian violence soon became a cause for major concern for Washington.

However, this violence, coupled with Arab intransigence, continued to make it difficult for Washington to support the Palestinian cause. In the aftermath of the 1967 war, eight Arab leaders met in Khartoum, Sudan, and declared that there would be "no peace with Israel, no recognition of Israel, no negotiations with it." This became known as the "Three No's." Only as an afterthought to this rejectionist stance did the Arab leaders also call for "the rights of the Palestinian people in their own country."[30]

The nascent Palestinian cause was also marred by Palestinian immigrant Sirhan Sirhan's assassination of US senator and presidential candidate Robert F. Kennedy in California on June 5, 1968. Footage of the shooting was broadcast by the major television networks, and it was not lost on the American public that the perpetrator was of Palestinian descent.

PRESIDENT RICHARD NIXON ASSUMED THE OFFICE of the presidency in 1969 and held the office for five years, until scandal forced him to resign. Nixon's view of the Palestinians was informed early on by PLO terrorism.[31] Nixon was also forced to handle the 1970 Black September crisis, during which the PLO threatened to topple the Hashemite Kingdom of Jordan.[32] That conflict lasted until

July 1971, resulting in Arafat's expulsion to Lebanon, along with thousands of PLO fighters.

On September 5, 1972, Black September, a nascent Palestinian terrorist group (and a Fatah splinter group named after the conflict in Jordan), took 11 members of the Israeli delegation hostage at the Olympic Games in Munich. Nine athletes were subsequently killed, including David Berger, who also held US citizenship. The crisis played out on television sets across America, prompting Americans to equate Palestinian nationalism with terrorism.[33]

Six months later, another terrorist attack colored the American view of the Palestinian cause. On March 1, 1973, eight operatives from Black September stormed a party at the Saudi Arabian Embassy in Khartoum. The group took three hostages: George Curtis Moore, the American charge d'affaires at the US Embassy in Khartoum; Cleo Noel Jr., the US ambassador to Sudan; and Guy Eid, the Belgian Embassy's charge d'affaires. The terror group demanded the release of Sirhan Sirhan and a Baader-Meinhof terrorist held in Germany. The following day, Nixon announced that he would not negotiate with terrorists. That evening, Black September murdered Noel, Moore, and Eid.[34]

According to a declassified State Department cable, "[t]he Khartoum operation was planned and carried out with the full knowledge and personal approval of Yasser Arafat," while "Fatah representatives based in Khartoum participated in the attack, using a Fatah vehicle to transport the terrorists to the Saudi Arabian Embassy."[35]

A little-known footnote to this story is that Black September also plotted to assassinate Israeli prime minister Golda Meir on her visit to New York in 1973, but the bomb failed to explode. The attack was coordinated to coincide with the Black September attack in Khartoum.[36]

After these attacks, Nixon established the policy that the United States would "not pay blackmail" or give in to terrorist demands. The wave of Palestinian terrorism prompted a policy that has existed to this day: Washington does not negotiate with terrorists.[37]

But terrorism was not the only challenge for Nixon coming out of the Middle East. On October 6, 1973, the region again descended into war. On that date, the Jewish holy day of Yom Kippur, Egypt and Syria launched a surprise attack against Israel. The war ratcheted up tensions between the United States and the Soviet Union. Washington, after initially leaving Israel to fight its own battle, began to deliver critical supplies to the Israelis to fight off the Arab forces armed and supplied by the Soviets.[38]

PRESIDENT GERALD FORD ASSUMED America's highest office in the wake of the Watergate scandal in August 1974. While his top foreign policy priorities, like his predecessors', were mostly centered on the Cold War, Ford made the Middle East a key focus.

The Ford presidency was perhaps the first to recognize the need to find leaders among the Palestinians to engage in diplomacy. Secretary of State Henry Kissinger, a holdover from the Nixon administration, engaged in discussions with King Hussein of Jordan in March 1974 on the question of whether Washington would recognize a Palestinian government in exile. Later that year, Arab leaders meeting in Rabat, Morocco, officially recognized the PLO as the "sole representative" of the Palestinians.[39]

The PLO was further granted observer status at the United Nations in November of that year, and the international body passed a resolution recognizing the "inalienable rights" of the Palestinian people.[40] Speaking before the United Nations on November 14, 1974, Arafat delivered what became known as his "gun and olive branch" speech. "Today I have come bearing an olive branch and a freedom-fighter's gun. Do not let the olive branch fall from my hand," Arafat declared.[41]

Washington, for its part, was unimpressed. Kissinger responded by saying that Arafat "called for a state which really did not include the existence of Israel . . . and we do not consider this a particularly moderate position."[42]

In 1975, Senators George McGovern (D-SD) and Howard Baker (R-TN) reportedly asked Arafat whether he was willing to recognize Israel, disavow the PLO's intention of destroying Israel, and accept its 1967 borders.[43] However, Arafat would not do so publicly. Kissinger, meanwhile, promised Israel that the United States would not recognize or negotiate with the PLO unless it officially and publicly recognized Israel's right to exist.[44]

With these efforts under way, Palestinian violence continued to undermine the Palestinian cause. In 1975, the Popular Front for the Liberation of Palestine (PFLP) kidnapped Ernest Morgan, the US military attaché to Lebanon. Two other attacks inside Israel made news when they wounded one American and killed another.[45] Nevertheless, 1975 and 1976 witnessed an increase in official interest in the Palestinian cause. State Department officials began to openly opine that "Palestinian Arabs must be taken into account in the negotiating of an Arab–Israeli peace."[46] Amid ongoing terrorist attacks, back-channel talks with the PLO began.[47]

JIMMY CARTER, A FORMER GEORGIA GOVERNOR, became president in 1977. His 2006 book *Palestine: Peace Not Apartheid,* viewed by many as anti-Israeli screed, has earned him the reputation of being the most pro-Palestinian president in US history. But his affinity for the Palestinian cause began during his presidency.

On March 16, 1977, speaking at a Massachusetts town hall meeting, Carter openly endorsed a Palestinian "homeland."[48] In April, Carter met with Egyptian president Anwar Sadat to discuss the question of whether regional peace could be achieved. Sadat openly stated that he was interested in working with Carter but also stated that he would accept a peace treaty with Israel only if it included a solution to the Palestinian "problem."[49] Carter subsequently came to the conclusion that if the PLO were to accept Israel's existence by embracing UN Resolution 242, then he would work with the group directly. At the same time, Carter began criticizing Israeli building in the West Bank—a territory Palestinians were eager to claim as their own.[50]

By September Carter's State Department announced, "The Palestinians must be involved in the peace-making process." A joint statement from the United States and the Soviet Union, released in October 1977, issued "guiding principles" for Middle East diplomacy, including an Israeli withdrawal from the territories captured in 1967 and also the "legitimate rights" of the Palestinians.[51]

When Secretary of State Cyrus Vance toured the Middle East in 1977, a group of West Bank mayors sent him a letter stating that they had chosen the PLO as their "sole legal representative."[52] Vance returned with the idea to grant "trusteeship" to the Palestinians to determine whether they were prepared to live side by side with Israel in peace.[53]

In November 1977, Sadat flew to Jerusalem as an overture to make peace and inadvertently changed the subject to Egyptian–Israeli ties. But in early 1978, when Sadat and Carter met in Aswan, Egypt, they released the "Aswan Proclamation," which called for recognition of the "legitimate rights of the Palestinian people" and a Palestinian role in the peace process.[54]

However, the Palestinian cause was undermined yet again by continued violence. A PLO attack north of Tel Aviv in March 1978 killed 38 and once again drew the world's attention to the savage tactics of the organization purporting to represent the Palestinian people. As *Time* magazine noted, "The timing of the attack left no doubt about the terrorists' purpose: to sabotage any attempt by Israeli Prime Minister Menachem Begin and Egyptian president Anwar Sadat to move toward a peace that would ignore or bypass Palestinian interests."[55]

Later that year, Carter hosted Begin and Sadat at Camp David, Maryland, from September 5 to 17, to iron out a final peace accord. The last days of the negotiations dealt with a "framework for peace in the Middle East," which specifically addressed the Palestinian question.[56] On September 17, 1978, Egypt, Israel, and the United States signed the Camp David Accords. This included provisions for the Palestinians to "participate in" the negotiations surrounding their future, although the PLO remained a terrorist organization in the eyes of Washington.

RONALD REAGAN, WHO ASSUMED OFFICE in January 1981, was vocal about his distrust of the PLO. During his presidential campaign, he repeatedly identified the group as a terrorist organization that was not ready to recognize Israel. Reagan even insisted that Jordan was responsible for the Palestinians in light of Jordan's occupation of the West Bank from 1948 through 1967.

This is not to say that the Reagan administration was indifferent to the notion of regional peace. Reagan, in fact, authorized an "outside mediation effort" with the PLO to end their Lebanon conflict in 1981.[57] By the summer of 1982, the PLO, besieged in Beirut, agreed in principle to an evacuation. The PLO sought a deal that would require it only to relocate to refugee camps, not leave Lebanon altogether. US (and Israeli) opposition nixed that plan.[58] One could argue that this opposition was anti-Palestinian, but Reagan notes in his memoir that he sought to expel all outside actors—the PLO, Israel, and Syria—from Lebanon to ensure permanent calm.[59] US diplomat Philip Habib negotiated the PLO withdrawal from Beirut, allowing Arafat to escape from Lebanon.[60] Reagan dispatched the marines to supervise the evacuation.[61]

In his 1983 book *Fateful Triangle,* Noam Chomsky alleges
that the Israeli "invasion of Lebanon . . . was predicated on
American support."[62] But it is undeniable that Reagan's perspective changed after the Sabra and Shatila bloodshed, during which
a Christian militia engaged in a brutal massacre of Palestinians in
two Palestinian refugee camps. That event prompted him to focus
on saving PLO lives and subsequently on resolving the Palestinian
problem.

On September 1, 1982, Reagan introduced a peace plan that
affirmed US support for Israel but also sought to address "the
legitimate rights of the Palestinians." The Reagan plan departed
from previous American efforts in that it made specific recom-
mendations on how a compromise might be reached. The recom-
mendations included a five-year "peaceful and orderly" transition
in which the Palestinians would gain autonomy in the West Bank
and Gaza. However, because the PLO was not named in this plan
(in keeping with the US policy of not negotiating with terrorist
organizations), Arafat and his lieutenants rejected it outright.[63]

Reagan's plans suffered another blow on October 23, 1983,
when an Iran-backed suicide bomber attacked the US Marines
barracks in Beirut, killing 241 marines. The attack prompted Reagan to lower America's profile in the Middle East. By February
1984, the United States had left Lebanon.[64] Despite this setback,
Reagan continued to stand behind his plan for Palestinian autonomy. His plan called for a settlement freeze, with the clarification
that "America will not support the use of any additional land for
the purpose of settlement."[65]

Amid a tumultuous year of continued Palestinian terror attacks,[66] along with Israel's October 1985 bombing of the PLO
headquarters in Tunis,[67] the Reagan administration launched yet
another initiative designed to create a Jordanian–Palestinian fed-
eration in the West Bank.[68] The United States insisted that the PLO
not be directly represented as part of its continuing policy not to

negotiate with Arafat's terrorist group until it accepted Israel's existence. The Jordan initiative broke down in February 1986. The PLO charged the United States with attempting to "delude" the Palestinian people and blamed it for the failure of the peace process.[69] A rash of Palestinian terrorism soon followed. From Fatah's bombing of a TWA flight over Italy in March 1986[70] to the September 1986 Abu Nidal (a Fatah splinter faction) hijacking of a Pan Am flight from Pakistan that led to the killing of 22 hostages,[71] the damage to US–Palestinian relations was significant. By 1987, the United States had closed the PLO office in Washington, and a Senate bill called for the PLO to reveal its investments in the United States.[72]

Ties between the PLO and United States were at their nadir at the outbreak of the first intifada in December 1987. After the uprising began, however, the Palestinian issue became one of national—even international—concern. Until this point, the United States had not been satisfied that the PLO was prepared to renounce violence and negotiate with Israel. However, amid the chaos—the rise of the violent Islamist Hamas faction, Jordan's decision to renounce all claims to the West Bank in 1988, and Arafat's assurances that he could end the violence—Washington's policy on the Palestinians was about to change.

In January 1988, Secretary of State George P. Shultz called for US-sponsored negotiations with a three-year transition period of autonomy for the Palestinians in the West Bank and Gaza, with the end result being full control.[73] Despite strenuous Israeli objections, Shultz also met with two Palestinian-American professors (both members of the Palestinian legislature): Edward Said and Ibrahim Abu-Lughod.[74]

On December 14, 1988, Arafat openly and publicly affirmed his recognition of UN Resolution 242, the US precondition for dialogue, and, in the process, declared an independent Palestinian state.[75] After this, the United States opened relations with the

PLO, with encouragement from world leaders.[76] This chain reaction of events marked the official beginning of the US-led peace process that has endured to this day.

WHEN FORMER CIA DIRECTOR George H. W. Bush entered office in early 1989, polls indicated that 64 percent of Americans approved of contact with the Palestinians.[77] Secretary of State James Baker called on both Israel and the PLO to negotiate; however, neither side appeared particularly ready to do so.

A new window for diplomacy opened in August 1990, when Iraqi leader Saddam Hussein's forces occupied oil-rich Kuwait. The United Nations quickly condemned the invasion, as did the Arab League.[78] Getting these Arab states to join an international military coalition was a more difficult task. As historian Charles D. Smith notes, as an enticement, the Bush administration promised to "sponsor an international conference to consider the Palestinian question."[79]

By the end of 1990, even as the United States prepared to invade Iraq with a multinational force from Saudi Arabia, Saddam declared that his army would leave Kuwait only if Israel withdrew from all Arab lands in an unsuccessful bid to divert public opinion.[80] In January 1991, on the eve of the first US war with Iraq, Arafat met with Saddam in Iraq. A former treasurer for the PLO reportedly saw Saddam hand Arafat a $50 million check for supporting him.[81] Arafat soon announced that the Iraqi president remained confident that he would prevail over the US-led forces.[82] Moreover, Arafat announced that the PLO would side with Iraq.[83] On January 17, 1991, the United States led the attack against Iraqi installations in Kuwait, and within days, Saddam's army was decimated.

In the wake of the Gulf War, Arafat was clearly discredited. Yet the United States continued to pursue the notion of Middle East peace and even championed Palestinian nationalism. In May

1991, Baker stated that Israel's policy of building in the West Bank was an obstacle to US peace efforts.[84] Later that year, he sent a "letter of assurance" to the Palestinians, affirming US commitment to the concept of land-for-peace negotiations with Israel, recognizing "how much importance Palestinians attach to the question of East Jerusalem" and underscoring the "legitimate political rights of the Palestinian people."[85]

On October 30, 1991, the first conference of the nascent Arab–Israeli peace process began in Madrid.[86] Informal contacts grew between Israel and the PLO. The Palestinians were undoubtedly emboldened by this recognition of their national aspirations, which was endorsed primarily by the United States. The importance of supporting Arafat gained acceptance internationally, particularly as the terrorist group Hamas began to amass power in the West Bank and Gaza Strip.

PRESIDENT BILL CLINTON BEGAN HIS PRESIDENCY with the peace process well under way. By the summer of 1993, secret talks were being held between Israelis and Palestinians. The result of the talks was an agreement to move forward with a "Declaration of Principles on Palestinian Self-Rule," which was signed by Arafat and Israeli prime minister Yitzhak Rabin on September 11, 1993. The two men then famously shook hands on the White House lawn.[87]

Parallel to the diplomatic progress and the plans to create the PA, Washington took steps to ensure a strong Palestinian economy. The State Department hosted a gathering of several hundred Jewish and Arab-American businessmen, who committed to a joint effort to invest in the Palestinian territories.[88] As the peace process progressed, the United States also agreed to support Palestinian industrial zones in the West Bank and Gaza with duty-free status on goods exported from those areas.[89]

But even then, Palestinian violence against Israel continued to undermine the process. It also took the lives of Americans. For example, an April 1995 Palestinian Islamic Jihad bus bombing killed a young girl from New York. In August 1995, Hamas carried out a bus bombing that killed one American. In 1996, another Hamas bus attack killed 26, including three Americans. A suicide bombing in 1996, carried out jointly by both Hamas and Islamic Jihad, killed another two Americans.[90]

But Palestinian violence was not the only challenge to peace. Rabin was assassinated in 1995 by Israeli extremist Yigal Amir, bringing to power Likud's Benjamin Netanyahu. The new Israeli leader was less enthusiastic about the concept of "land for peace," however. In 1996, eight former high-ranking US officials sent a letter to Netanyahu, pushing him to make further concessions to the Palestinians.[91] For the next two years, it was apparent that Clinton believed Netanyahu was the problem. The White House criticized Netanyahu's plan to extend the municipal boundaries of Jerusalem and expressed further frustration that the Israelis would not commit to more redeployments from the West Bank.[92] Although Netanyahu signed the Wye River Memorandum, an addendum to the existing peace structure, the Clinton administration actively worked to derail Netanyahu from getting reelected. Clinton even sent a team of political consultants to Israel to undermine his electoral bid.[93]

In December 1998, Clinton addressed the Palestinian National Council (PNC) and other Palestinian groups in Gaza, becoming the first US president to address an audience of Palestinians in a Palestinian city. After the address, the PNC voted, almost unanimously, to remove from the PLO's Palestinian National Charter the articles calling for the destruction of the state of Israel. Clinton promised the Palestinians that "America is determined to do what we can to bring tangible benefits of peace. . . . I am pleased to announce we will also fund the training of Palestinian health care providers, and airport administrators, and increase our support to Palestinian refugees. And next year I will ask the Congress for another several hundred million dollars to support the development of the Palestinian people."[94]

The Oslo Process culminated in a final push for peace as the Clinton presidency came to a close. Clinton believed that he had earned the trust of Israeli prime minister Ehud Barak, who succeeded Netanyahu, thanks in part to the efforts Clinton had put forth to ensure that Netanyahu fell. But Arafat remained another story.

The Camp David II peace summit took place from July 11 to July 25, 2000. In short, it failed. Multiple accounts indicate that Arafat was unhappy with what he was offered, and that he ultimately chose violence over continued negotiations. Somewhere around halfway through the summit, Clinton proposed to Arafat a state with 92 percent of the West Bank and all of Gaza, as well as compensation for land lost to Israel, the removal of the majority of the contentious settlements, and Palestinian sovereignty over the Muslim and Christian Quarters of Jerusalem. Arafat refused. To this, Clinton reportedly replied, "You are leading your people and the region to a catastrophe."[95]

Even after Arafat launched the Al-Aqsa Intifada, a low-level war, against the Israelis in late September 2000, Clinton did not give up. In late December, he presented to Arafat the Clinton Parameters, calling for roughly 94 to 96 percent of the West Bank to become a Palestinian state. Clinton also suggested a bifurcated Jerusalem (including the Old City) and offered US assistance in leading an international commission to address the issue of refugees.[96] Arafat rejected this offer, too. Frustrated, Clinton left office in January, and war continued to rage.

PRESIDENT GEORGE W. BUSH, who assumed office amid the second intifada in early 2001, pressed Arafat repeatedly to condemn the violence,[97] but Arafat would condemn only specific attacks and only did so under duress.[98] With the understanding that even

Clinton's generous proposals were met with violence, Bush declared that all previous proposals were off the table. He indicated that he would not deal with the Palestinians until they renounced violence. Al Qaeda's attacks against America on September 11, 2001, reinforced this decision. In the wake of the attack, Reuters captured footage of Palestinians dancing in celebration.[99]

To be sure, in the aftermath of the 9/11 attacks, there was a lower threshold on the part of Bush administration officials for tolerating Palestinian violence. From the White House spokesman[100] to Secretary of State Colin Powell[101] to President Bush himself,[102] the message to the Palestinians was consistent: curb the violence. By June 2002, the United States was openly looking for an alternative to Arafat's leadership, claiming that he continued to encourage terrorism.[103]

With the PA in crisis, Bush began to tout a new policy of promoting Palestinian economic and political reform.[104] As one State Department spokesman noted, "The focus is really on working with people who can make a difference, who can be effective leaders, spokespeople, for the Palestinian community."[105]

In what is now known as the "Rose Garden Speech," Bush called on the Palestinians "to elect new leaders, leaders not compromised by terror. I call upon them to build a practicing democracy, based on tolerance and liberty. If the Palestinian people actively pursue these goals . . . the United States of America will support the creation of a Palestinian state." Bush used the term "roadmap" to describe his way forward out of the Middle East crisis.[106]

In 2003, the president officially unveiled his roadmap, delineating specifically what was needed to achieve peace and Palestinian independence.[107] He did so after the spring appointment of Mahmoud Abbas as the first Palestinian prime minister, which was seen as a position created and engineered by the West to create new institutions, dilute the power of the presidency, and perhaps directly challenge Arafat's authority.

Bush's roadmap had three phases: (1) ending terror and violence, normalizing Palestinian life, and building Palestinian institutions; (2) transition; and (3) permanent status agreement and end of the Palestinian–Israeli conflict.[108] At a May commencement speech at the University of Southern California, Bush stated, "If the Palestinian people take concrete steps to crack down on terror, continue on a path of peace, reform and democracy, they and all the world will see the flag of Palestine raised over a free and independent nation."[109]

The Bush administration worked almost singularly with Abbas thereafter, highlighting his importance to the project of Palestinian reform and development.[110] But Arafat marginalized Abbas, ultimately prompting the new premier to resign in September 2003.[111] The move was a blow to Washington, given how much US leaders had cited him as an alternative to Arafat.

On November 11, 2004, Yasser Arafat died. Initially, his death appeared to be a blessing, particularly for an administration seeking political reform. However, Arafat's grip on power had been all encompassing; his death left a leadership vacuum. The territories soon fell into disarray.

Although none of Fatah's leaders seemed to know how to regain control, the United States continued to express full confidence in Abbas to weather what was termed a "difficult leadership transition." The State Department pledged to "continue to provide a substantial overall package of assistance for Palestinians, which in 2004 has totaled about 200 million dollars." Washington further pledged an additional $3.5 million for elections and election monitoring, plus another $20 million in "direct budgetary support to the Palestinian Authority, reflecting our confidence in the direction of the PA's reform program."[112]

On January 9, 2005, the Palestinians held elections for their new president. Bush lauded the elections, which were basically free and fair, and affirmed that the United States stood "ready to help the Palestinian people realize their aspirations."[113] Bush was further heartened that the winner of the elections was none other than the man he had personally endorsed as an alternative to Arafat.

Amid continued promises for assistance to Palestinian reform and growth, Bush met with Abbas in May 2005, five months after the elections. "We will stand with you, Mr. President, as you combat corruption, reform the Palestinian security services and your justice system, and revive your economy," Bush said. He also announced a $50 million aid package to help build homes in the Palestinian territories.[114] The two men met at the White House again on October 20, and Bush reiterated his confidence that Abbas was an advocate of peace, political reform, and economic growth.[115]

Sandwiched between these two cordial presidential visits was the Israeli withdrawal from Gaza. After more than 38 years of control there, the last Israeli tanks left the area on September 12, 2005.[116] The move was seen as a victory for Hamas and, in retrospect, likely bolstered the group's standing ahead of the legislative elections scheduled just four months after the pullout.

Secretary of State Condoleezza Rice, however, welcomed Sharon's decision to allow for Palestinian elections in January 2006, including Hamas's participation, citing it as a first step in the "[d]evelopment of a Palestinian democracy based on tolerance and liberty."[117] Hamas won the election by a landslide. The Islamist faction, best known for acts of violence against Israel, claimed 76 of 132 seats (74 under the Hamas banner, plus 2 independents), granting it the right to form a government. It had been a free and fair election.[118]

Despite the Hamas electoral victory, Rice insisted, "[t]he Palestinian people have apparently voted for change, but we believe

THE UNITED STATES AND THE QUESTION OF PALESTINE

that their aspirations for peace and a peaceful life remain unchanged."[119] Rice seemed to imply that it did not matter who led the Palestinian government, and that the United States would support statehood as long as there was hope for a two-state solution.

Sharon suffered a stroke on January 4, 2006, bringing his deputy Ehud Olmert to power. Olmert's government worked with Congress to isolate Hamas.[120] However, the United States never ceased providing aid to the Palestinians. Rice announced in April 2006 that humanitarian aid to the Palestinians would increase by 57 percent, to $245 million, but because the new Hamas-led Palestinian government failed to accept the basic nonviolent principles of the Middle East Quartet, a diplomatic body consisting of the United Nations, the United States, the European Union, and Russia, "the United States is suspending assistance to the Palestinian government's cabinet and ministries."[121] Still, other aid reportedly flowed through temporary mechanisms to PA institutions that did not have Hamas ties.[122]

In December 2006, Bush invoked the ire of Palestinians when he signed into law the Palestinian Anti-Terrorism Act. The bill sought to: (1) support a peaceful, two-state solution to end the conflict with Israel; (2) oppose those terrorists and terrorist groups that thwarted peace; (3) promote the rule of law, democracy, the cessation of terrorism and incitement, and good governance; and (4) urge members of the international community to avoid contact with and refrain from supporting Hamas until it agreed to renounce violence against Israel.[123]

In the meantime, Rice continued to work with the Palestinian leaders who were not overtly committed to violence in the hopes of getting back to peacemaking with the Israelis. To that end, she met with Abbas and Olmert and affirmed the US commitment to the creation of a Palestinian state, as long as it was not "born of violence and terror."[124] Bush extended further support to Abbas in June 2007, when he authorized extended direct aid to the

PA to pay for Abbas's administrative and personal security costs, saying that it was "in the national security interest of the United States."[125]

As it turned out, Abbas needed more security. Between June 7 and June 14, 2007, Hamas launched a military offensive against his PA and seized control of the Gaza Strip. The group took command of major arteries, commandeered the media, and took over PA government buildings and installations. The PA's security compound fell to Hamas after fighters burrowed a tunnel beneath the building, detonated deadly explosives, and breached the building.[126]

The coup was unquestionably a setback for the Bush administration, which had been advocating for the spread of democracy throughout the Arab world. As Bush stated,

> The alternatives before the Palestinian people are stark. There is the vision of Hamas, which the world saw in Gaza—with murderers in black masks, and summary executions, and men thrown to their death from rooftops. By following this path, the Palestinian people would guarantee chaos, and suffering, and the endless perpetuation of grievance. They would surrender their future to Hamas's foreign sponsors in Syria and Iran. And they would crush the possibility of any—of a Palestinian state. There's another option, and that's a hopeful option. It is the vision of President Abbas and Prime Minister [Salam] Fayyad; it's the vision of their government; it's the vision of a peaceful state called Palestine as a homeland for the Palestinian people. . . . By following this path, Palestinians can reclaim their dignity and their future—and establish a state of their own. Only the Palestinians can decide which of these courses to pursue.[127]

With these words, the president effectively affirmed that the United States still sought to support a peaceful Palestinian state, even as chaos had enveloped the Gaza Strip. The president then announced on November 20, 2007, that he would host a peace conference in Annapolis, the coastal state capital of Maryland, to "signal broad international support for the Israeli and Palestinian leaders' courageous efforts" that would lead to "the establishment of a Palestinian state and the realization of Israeli-Palestinian peace."[128]

When the Annapolis Conference was launched on November 27, Bush announced that a steering committee, led by Washington, would work to implement the roadmap for peace, with the goal of establishing a Palestinian state by 2008.[129] As Rice later recalled, it was "the first major Middle East peace conference in 16 years, and the only one of its kind to be held on U.S. soil. Representatives of more than 50 countries, including 14 Arab states, sat with the Israeli prime minister, foreign minister, and defense minister to pursue a different future for the region."[130]

While an atmosphere of cynicism cast a cloud over the conference, the White House launched yet another initiative on behalf of the Palestinian people. In early December 2007, Rice asked Congress to approve $400 million in aid for the Palestinians for 2008 while also calling for US companies to fund Palestinian projects.[131]

Within months, the aid was released, and the loans began to be issued. Bush continued to promise the Palestinians that he sought a "viable state . . . a state that provides hope."[132] In addition, Rice announced in June 2008 that the United States had spent $86 million to train and equip Palestinian military forces and requested additional funds to continue the program.[133]

Despite these efforts, the Bush administration came to an end without tangible results for the Palestinians. The civil war between Hamas and Fatah remained an obstacle, as did the lack of progress toward a comprehensive peace. Nevertheless, Bush arguably left office as the president who had gone further than any other to promote Palestinian independence.

PRESIDENT BARACK OBAMA, who came to office in January 2009, continued Bush's policy of promoting a two-state solution, but he seemed ready to support Palestinian statehood, even without the backing of the Israeli government. Obama sought "to do things differently in the region."[134] The new president was more forceful in his insistence that the Israeli government stop all construction settlements in the West Bank and even in contested lands in Jerusalem, indicating it was territory that would become part of a Palestinian state.

After the February 2009 election of Benjamin Netanyahu to a second tenure as prime minister, Secretary of State Hillary Rodham Clinton started discussions surrounding "the creation of a Palestinian state despite opposition from the incoming Israeli Government."[135] Thus began what appeared to be a US foreign policy that tilted in favor of the Palestinians and against the wishes of the Israeli leadership.

In a much-anticipated global address, Obama delivered what became known as the "Cairo Speech" on June 4, 2009. The president declared, "Now is the time for Palestinians to focus on what they can build. The Palestinian Authority must develop its capacity to govern, with institutions that serve the needs of its people."[136]

By early 2010, mention of Palestinian statehood had become a somewhat commonplace occurrence among Obama administration officials. Speaking in February 2010 at the US-Islamic World Forum in Qatar, for example, Clinton voiced her support for a diplomatic solution that "reconciles the Palestinian goal of an independent and viable state. . . . We have encouraged the Palestinians to pursue their homegrown plan to build their institutions, end incitement, improve security, to lay the foundation for a future stable, democratic Palestinian state. We are supporting President Abbas and Prime Minister Fayyad in their efforts to build, train, and reform their security forces."[137]

Meanwhile, new tensions emerged between Israel and the United States. During a planned visit to the region in March 2010, Vice President Joseph Biden slammed a decision by the Israeli government to announce construction in Ramat Shlomo, a town that lay outside Israel's traditional 1967 borders. Although the area was technically North Jerusalem, not East Jerusalem, which the Palestinians claim will be their future capital, Biden "condemned the action." He further stated that the Obama "administration is fully committed to the Palestinian people and to achieving a Palestinian state that is independent, viable, and contiguous."[138]

This stormy encounter set the stage for returning Prime Minister Benjamin Netanyahu's visit to Washington later that month. At the meeting between the two leaders, Obama presented the Israeli premier with a list of demands, including an extended freeze on development in East Jerusalem and the West Bank. Obama then left the prime minister and the Israeli delegation by themselves, withdrawing from the meeting to have dinner with his family and conduct other business.[139] The president's move was viewed internationally as a snub to the Israeli leader.

Stories soon began to surface about the White House position on Palestinian statehood. *Haaretz* quoted Arab reports that Obama had promised the Palestinians a state by 2011.[140] This came on the heels of a *Washington Post* piece positing that Obama was even considering a Palestinian unity government that could include Hamas—a position that challenged US policy dating back to Nixon, who stipulated that the United States would not negotiate with terrorist groups.

In July 2010, Obama upgraded the diplomatic status of the PLO mission in Washington to general delegation. The president then announced the formal resumption of peace talks in September 2010, with the goal of achieving a viable state, living in peace with Israel, by 2011.

OBAMA'S PEACE PLAN FAILED and so did his vision for a settlement freeze. But the latter inspired Abbas, along with scores of other countries, to pursue a new policy. It remains the cornerstone of an international campaign in place today to help the Palestinians lay claim to all lands on the Arab side of the 1949 armistice lines. According to Abbas, "It was Obama who suggested a full settlement freeze. . . . I said OK, I accept. We both went up the tree. After that, he came down with a ladder and he removed the ladder and said to me, 'Jump.'"[141]

Obama clearly climbed down from this metaphoric ladder. He ceased to focus on Israeli settlements and appeared to have improved his ties with Netanyahu during his trip to the Middle East in March 2013. Obama also staked out a rather permanent position against Abbas's ongoing attempts to gain recognition of a Palestinian state at the United Nations. In July 2013, his administration initiated a new round of peace talks to help the Palestinians achieve statehood through diplomacy.

But whether a given American president supports the Palestinian statehood initiative is less important than whether the initiative deserves American support. From a political perspective, the instinct is to simply say "yes." After all, the Palestinians have been waiting for six long decades to declare their state, and president after president has seemed to grasp this with increasing urgency.

But from a governance perspective, many questions remain. Former peace negotiator Aaron David Miller asks, "Do we have a stake in creating the conditions for a failed state?"[142] Unfortunately, it appears that we do.

3

Guerrilla Governance

THE EVOLUTION OF THE PROBLEMS SURROUNDING PALESTINIAN GOVER-
nance, particularly those tied to financial mismanagement, is not
an easy one to track. The antecedents of the PA are guerrilla organizations—first the Fatah faction and then the PLO—that were
decidedly not interested in employing the services of Ernst &
Young. Nor were they interested in making their books open to
the public.

It would be wrong, however, to suggest that Palestinian political culture is inherently corrupt or prone to corruption. In reading
the histories of pre–World War I Palestine or the British Mandate
period, one gets no indication that corruption was any more of
a problem among Palestinian Arabs than it was anywhere else in
the region. For one, fully functioning Palestinian governments did
not exist during these historical periods. It is therefore not a fair
comparison. Moreover, the locally based Palestinian leaders during these periods presided over a system that looked nothing like
the system in place today.

The problems addressed in this book are decidedly contempo-
rary. Their history begins a half century ago. And while pessimists
might argue that this represents virtually all of the modern history

of Palestinian nationalism, it might also be argued that 50 years is not so much time elapsed that the problem is irreversible.

THE CORNERSTONE OF TODAY'S PALESTINIAN LEADERSHIP is the Fatah faction, which was founded in the mid-1950s in Kuwait by Yasser Arafat. Fatah is a reverse acronym for *Harakat al-Tahrir al-Filastiniya* (the Palestinian Liberation Movement). While *hataf* means "doom" or "death" in Arabic, *fatah* means "conquest," "victory," or "triumph."[1] And this is exactly what its members sought: the conquest of Israel, the Jewish state established in 1948.

For at least a decade after the creation of Israel, the Palestinian nationalist movement was in disarray, if it was not fully defunct. Rashid Khalidi, reportedly a former PLO spokesman[2] and now a professor at Columbia University, cedes that there was a "hiatus in manifestations of Palestinian identity for a period after 1948."[3] But this began to change when the members of Fatah established a clandestine network of paramilitary cells designed to attack Israel. The leader of Fatah at the time, Yasser Arafat, raised funds throughout the Middle East for this very purpose.[4]

It should be noted here that Arafat claimed to have been part of a successful construction company during his time in Kuwait.[5] However, as biographer Said Aburish notes, Arafat "did not create a construction company or become partner in one."[6] Andrew Gowers and Tony Walker, authors of another book on Arafat, say that although the Palestinian leader was involved in a contracting business, he was notorious for "exaggerating the scale of his business career and of the wealth it generated."[7] As it turns out, Arafat appears to have had a yearly salary of approximately $30,000 while in Kuwait, "which allowed him to give money to Fatah," among other activities.[8]

Arafat, at varying points in his life, may have had the backing of wealthy patrons. Aburish notes, for example, that during the 1960s, Arafat targeted "wealthy Palestinians who resided in

Kuwait and other oil-rich countries," such as Qatar, for financial support.[9]

Whatever the sources of Fatah's income, for completely understandable reasons, donors and accounts were kept secret. Fatah was, after all, a violent revolutionary group. For this reason, most of its political activities were shrouded from the public eye. The secrecy of Fatah in Kuwait marked the beginning of a decades-long process in which the Palestinian leadership kept secret its finances and decision making.

In 1965, the clandestine group embarked on a campaign of terrorist attacks launched out of Syria.[10] By the end of the following year, Fatah reportedly executed 41 raids into Israel. In the first half of 1967, Fatah launched another 37 attacks.[11]

While the attacks did not pose an existential threat to Israel, they were part of an overall trend: Israel was increasingly getting drawn into conflict. On May 15, 1967, Egyptian president Gamal Abdel Nasser ordered the United Nations to withdraw from the Sinai Peninsula on Israel's border and positioned two Egyptian divisions there. Days later, he denied Israeli vessels access to the Red Sea port of Eilat. Fatah exacerbated these tensions by carrying out five additional attacks against Israel.[12]

To preempt an Egyptian attack, the Israelis struck first on June 5, 1967, and in the process wreaked havoc on the Egyptian, Syrian, and Jordanian armies. In just six days, the Israelis captured from those three states significant territory, including East Jerusalem (Jordan), the West Bank (Jordan), the Gaza Strip (Egypt), the Sinai Peninsula (Egypt), and the Golan Heights (Syria).

While these defeats were crushing across the Arab world, the country most significantly affected was Egypt. Nasser had been the unquestioned regional leader entrusted by the Arabs to "liberate Palestine." With the fall of Nasser, the region was forced to look elsewhere. The Arab world looked to Arafat and his band of Palestinian guerrillas for answers.

Soon thereafter, in 1969, Arafat ascended as the head of the PLO. This umbrella organization of Palestinian groups was not well known. Nor was it particularly effective. It was created by the Arab League in 1964 as Arab states postured and crowed about destroying Israel. But with Arafat's leadership, the PLO became an infamous, secretive, and lethal organization that had a jarring impact on world security. The guerrilla leader initiated an epidemic of airplane hijackings.[13] Subsequent high-profile terrorist attacks included the 1972 slaughter of Israeli athletes at the Olympic Games in Munich; the 1973 attack on the Saudi embassy in Sudan, which led to the murder of the US ambassador and his deputy; and the 1985 assault on the cruise ship *Achille Lauro*, where an elderly American Jew was shot dead and dumped into the ocean.

The PLO established its first real headquarters in Jordan. Indeed, the Fatah-led PLO built a state inside the state of Jordan, a country that had already absorbed many Palestinians fleeing the 1948 and 1967 wars. The resulting power struggle between Arafat and King Hussein was Black September, a bloody war within Jordan in 1970 that resulted in thousands of Palestinian casualties and the reemergence of a free Jordanian state.

From there, Fatah and the PLO again attempted to create another ministate, this time inside Lebanon. This effort in the late 1970s and early 1980s contributed to violence that ultimately led to the Lebanon civil war. In response to Palestinian violence launched against it from the north, Israel invaded Lebanon in 1982 and waged war against Arafat's PLO. When Israel gained the upper hand, the Palestinians were again forced to abandon their ministate. Documents left behind, later translated by scholar Raphael Israeli, demonstrate that the PLO's training and weaponry came from the Eastern Europe Soviet bloc and the former Soviet Union.[14]

Based on anecdotes, the PLO's financial well-being in Lebanon depended significantly on illicit activity. Khalidi notes that "cronyism, corruption, and the absence of discipline" were among the problems that "marred the PLO's performance in Lebanon."[15] The PLO also reportedly resorted to crime. On January 20, 1976, PLO members robbed the British Bank of the Middle East in Beirut and took "anywhere from $20 million to $50 million worth of gold bars, Lebanese and foreign currency, stocks, and jewels."[16] And while Arafat personally opposed the drug trade, some PLO members were said to be involved in the trade of hashish that was harvested in Lebanon's Bekaa Valley.[17]

Over time, the corruption had a corrosive effect. In 1979, one PLO member found the state of affairs within the organization so bad that he quit because of the "intolerable corruption within the ranks of the revolution. . . . Leaders and commanders didn't maintain the modest lifestyles they once had. They turned into merchants, each looking after their own interests. They are opportunists to a greater extent than can be imagined."[18]

Perhaps the most damning portrait of the bloated and ossified "Abus"—those with a *kunya,* as was common among the PLO leaders in Lebanon—comes from political scientist Fouad Moughrabi, writing in the *Arab Studies Quarterly:*

An obese and comfortable elite began to emerge. The gap separating them from the majority grew severe. The Abus sent their children to camps in Europe, while the others sent their children to *Ashbal* (young cubs) camps in Lebanon or Syria. The Abus had chauffeured cars (a Mercedes or a BMW represented high status) and heavy billets of guards. Above all, each Abu had the backing of one or two millionaires. At National Council meetings, caucusing often took place in the suites of the millionaires where the Abus could escape the throng of the mob. Each Abu has his system of patronage and his

own budget. Nothing may be done by one Abu to encroach on the
turf of the other.

As a result, Moughrabi notes, "the Palestinian movement
suffered."[19]

This did not deter Arab states from donating to the cause,
however. During the 1978 Baghdad Summit, Arab states agreed to
provide $250 million to $300 million per year to the PLO. Most
of this money would be spent on "arms, wages of fighters and
their families, and representatives abroad."[20] Saudi Arabia agreed
to provide $85.7 million, UAE $34.3 million, Algeria $21.4 mil-
lion, Iraq $44.6 million, Qatar $19.8 million, Kuwait $47.1 mil-
lion, and Libya $47.1 million.[21] While in Damascus, Arafat said
that he had personally received $67 million that year.[22] The fol-
lowing year he reportedly received an airplane from Saudi Arabia's foreign minister.[23]

Following its ouster from Lebanon, the PLO leadership found
itself in Tunisia in the mid-1980s. Khalidi notes that during this
period, the PLO's "institutions in exile became ossified and lost
most of whatever vitality they once had."[24]

But whatever the PLO lacked in vitality, it made up for by buy-
ing influence. The *Wall Street Journal* reported in 1986 that Arafat and his associates were known to "distribute smaller bundles
of money to ensure political support in sensitive areas." In 1986,
for example, the PLO gave $150,000 to the *Al-Quds* newspaper
in Jerusalem. Shortly after the paper received the money, pro-PLO
editorials reportedly began to appear in the traditionally pro-
Jordanian outlet.[25] Author Jillian Becker asserts that "PLO money
was handed out directly to Palestinians in the camps [in Leba-
non]."[26] As one analyst explained, "The PLO's far-flung bureaucracy and military . . . represents a huge patronage network."[27]

As the *Wall Street Journal* reported, the PLO had become an
economic juggernaut, with assets ranging from $2 billion to $14

billion. It was, inter alia, "the largest producer of eggs in Guinea, an exporter of pineapples to France and the Soviet Union, distributor of $52 million in social security payments a year, co-founder of an airline in the Maldive Islands, and a partner in the duty-free shop in Tanzania's international airport."[28] Sources of its income were murky, but the Saudis alone paid the PLO some $86 million per year, with another $40 million coming from taxes paid by Palestinians living in Arab states. Reports also suggest that the PLO received "material assistance" from China,[29] as well as military and political assistance from the Soviet Union.[30]

Among the PLO's biggest cash cows was the Palestine National Fund (PNF). Donations from PLO supporters, in particular the Arab states, as well as the revenue from the "liberation tax," went to the PNF. Indeed, the PLO exacted a "tax of between 5 and 8 percent on Palestinians' wages throughout the Arab world" each year.[31] According to Neil Livingstone and David Halevy, the tax "generated between twenty-five and thirty million dollars" each year.[32] In 1978, it reportedly generated closer to $50 million.[33] There was also the Palestine Martyrs' Work Society (SAMED), which was designed "to create the nucleus for a Palestinian revolutionary economy, to develop economic self-sufficiency for the revolutionary and the masses, and to lay the foundation for the economic structure of the future Palestinian soviet."[34] In 1982, SAMED, which was under the control of Fatah,[35] had gross revenue of $45 million[36]; it averaged approximately $40 million a year.[37] SAMED operated at least 35 factories in Lebanon as well as numerous endeavors abroad, including farms and shops throughout Africa and the Middle East.[38]

The Wall Street Journal estimated that PLO annual expenditures amounted to some $220 million, with line items for health care and diplomatic missions. The PLO's social welfare system, on which some 60,000 Palestinians depended, was among the larger budget items.[39]

In other words, from Jordan to Lebanon to Tunisia, the PLO
was operating like a bloated government bureaucracy without actually governing a territory of its own.

THE ROAD TO PLO SELF-GOVERNANCE began on December 8, 1987,
when an Israeli military vehicle truck crashed into a car filled with
Gaza Palestinians returning home from work inside Israel, killing
four. The funerals turned into angry demonstrations, which rap-
idly erupted in the West Bank, too. This was the start of the first
Palestinian uprising, or intifada.[40]

Without question, the intifada was a direct challenge to the
Israeli government's control of the territories captured in 1967.
It was undeniably a political awakening and a watershed moment in the history of the Palestinian quest for statehood. But
the intifada also led to a Palestinian unraveling. For one, it
crippled the Palestinian economy as business owners both shuttered their shops in protest of Israel and boycotted goods that
were critical to daily life.[41] Moreover, the violence against Israel
prompted reprisals, including the Israeli government's decision
to bar entrance to Palestinians, thereby denying them an opportunity to earn a living.[42] Israel added to the economic devastation
by destroying the homes and property of numerous Palestinian
agitators.[43]

And while most of the violence was directed at Israel, internecine violence became all too common, particularly in the form of
attacks against suspected Palestinian collaborators.[44] The Israeli
human rights group B'Tselem noted 121 cases in which Palestinian factions carried out punitive actions against fellow Palestinians for collaboration.[45] One historian observed that much of this
often had "nothing to do with collaborators and much to do with
local feuds and blood debts."[46] The Palestinians used the uprising
as a pretext to settle scores with personal enemies or to attack
foes in rival clans and families. In the end, Palestinians in the West

Bank and Gaza Strip killed at least 800 of their own for allegedly supplying Israel with intelligence.[47]

The devastating effects of the intifada would become evident only years later, after the establishment of the PA in 1994. For one, the uprising left in its wake a culture of violence that did little to encourage successful state building. One could also argue that the economy took such a hard hit that Palestinians were simply unprepared for the massive investment from the international community that would soon come their way.

While these issues bubbled beneath the surface and would require years to be viewed in their proper perspective, Palestinians rightly viewed the intifada as a significant moment for their nationalist cause. This was the first time since the 1948 war that Palestinians had gathered in significant numbers in the name of independence.

Meanwhile, from its headquarters in exile in Tunis, the PLO was disconnected from the uprising. Arafat and his inner circle attempted to assert leadership, but it was difficult to do so from a distance. Various grassroots factions took control on the ground, representing a broad array of political factions. Among those to emerge, in 1987, was the violent Islamist group *Harakat al-Muqawamma al-Islamiyya,* which means the "Islamic Resistance Movement," whose acronym HAMAS means "zeal" in Arabic. Through leaflets and grassroots organizing,[48] this splinter group of the Muslim Brotherhood[49] immediately sought to establish itself as a leader of the intifada. In doing so, Hamas posed a direct challenge to the PLO as the voice of the Palestinian people.

The PLO leadership quickly recognized that because it was in exile and not directly part of the uprising against Israel, it was ceding leadership to Hamas and other factions. Arafat scrambled to regain leverage. Ironically, he did so by positioning himself as the man who could bring an end to this Palestinian nationalist awakening.

With Washington and other Western capitals in dire need of a way to contain this destabilizing uprising, Arafat indicated that he would tacitly recognize Israel by accepting the November 1947 UN General Assembly Resolution 181 that called for a partition of Palestine into a Jewish and an Arab state. In doing so, he pried open a window of opportunity for the United States to broker a long-needed peace agreement between Israel and the Palestinians. All the while, the notorious guerrilla leader positioned himself as the rightful heir to the leadership of the new Palestinian government in waiting.

Troublingly, while Arafat began to rebrand himself and the PLO as bedrocks of good governance, Hamas continued to foment unrest in the West Bank and Gaza, where many Palestinians began to lose faith in Arafat as their leader. Some Palestinians interpreted Arafat's recognition of Israel as a sign of weakness or even an unwillingness to fight. Some questioned why Fatah and the PLO had not succeeded in ousting Israel from the territories, particularly if Fatah and the PLO had been leading the charge during the uprising as it had claimed. While the PLO slowly relinquished its traditional role of guerrilla fighters, Hamas eagerly filled the vacuum.

Finally, in November 1988, Arafat called for a peace conference based on the PLO's acceptance of UN resolutions 242 and 338, which for the first time in the group's history tacitly accepted the existence of the state of Israel. This laid the foundation for diplomacy and also elicited strong reactions from the international community in favor of Palestinian autonomy. Within two weeks, at least 55 nations recognized Palestine's independence,[50] transforming the PLO almost overnight into a quasi government.

From there, a whirlwind of diplomacy and statecraft ensued. Led by Washington, the international community courted the Palestinians and facilitated back-channel discussions with the Israelis to iron out a series of understandings that laid the foundation for a diplomatic process. That process culminated in a celebrated photo opportunity on the White House lawn on September 13, 1993, when Israeli prime minister Yitzhak Rabin and Arafat agreed on the basis of Palestinian autonomy in the West Bank and Gaza Strip. The Declaration of Principles[51] led to the creation in 1994 of the PA (*Sulta al-Wataniyya al-Filastiniyya*), an interim administrative organization staffed primarily by Fatah and the PLO, to govern parts of the West Bank and Gaza Strip.

Lost in all of the fanfare was the question of who could run the PA's institutions with competence. Indeed, while the PLO had no shortage of ambitious figures fit for politics, it was not brimming with seasoned bureaucrats with extensive experience in state building. Unfortunately, it would take the better part of a decade for the international donor community to understand this.

4

The Oslo Years

REVELING IN HIS NEW POSITION AS THE UNQUESTIONED RULER OF THE
Palestinian people, on July 1, 1994, Arafat made his official return as *ra'is* (president) by motorcade via Egypt's Sinai Peninsula
into Gaza, where throngs of celebrating Palestinians greeted him.[1]
Concurrently, some 1,500 members of the Palestinian Liberation Army, a paramilitary force cultivated jointly by the PLO and
the Arab states, crossed the bridges linking Jordan and the West
Bank, forming the backbone of the PA's security apparatus. Their
ranks would balloon to 17,000 by 1995.[2]

The creation of the Palestinian security forces was a relatively
easy task. What proved more difficult was the establishment of
the other key institutions of a Palestinian state while Israel was
still in control. As former peace negotiator Aaron David Miller
recalls, "The real challenge, which is unique in modern history,
was to end the [Israeli] occupation through negotiation, but at
the same time build institutions of governments within the limits
defined by [the Oslo] agreement."[3]

In addition, it became clear that, despite decades of insisting on
the need for Palestinian independence, the Palestinian leadership
was unprepared for the task of governance. Nathan Brown notes

that, among other things, the Palestinians were charged with the daunting task of stitching together "a disparate set of institutions that had grown up in different settings"[4]—meaning the institutions created in the West Bank (both under Jordan and Israel); in the Gaza Strip (both under Egypt and Israel); in pre-Mandatory Palestine under the Turks; in Mandatory Palestine under the British; not to mention those in Jordan, Lebanon, and Tunisia, where the PLO had created ministate infrastructures after the creation of Israel.

But this problem likely paled in comparison with the troubling Palestinian political culture that had evolved as a result of the mainstream Palestinian faction's long-standing involvement in both clandestine and violent activity. As Rashid Khalidi observed, "The deviousness and subterfuge that were indispensable for a weak PLO in dealing with the predatory mores of the states that dominated Arab politics . . . were much less well adapted to, or completely unsuitable for, other arenas," such as running a government. He further asserted that, "given the backgrounds of most of [the PLO] in clandestine, underground, and military activity, few had the requisite training, experience or disposition for the routine tasks of governance and administration that awaited them." As a result, "most of the leaders of the PLO, from Arafat on down . . . proved to be poorly suited for the task of state building, for transparent governance, or for a stable structure of governance based on law."[5]

Not surprisingly, the PA ran its governing operation the way it had run Fatah and the PLO—as a politically centralized system with Arafat sitting at the top. Most of the Palestinian officials were also members of Fatah, which meant that they were loyal to Arafat. Political opponents were not tolerated; they were subjected to scare tactics or even arrests.

BUT THE CONCERNS DIDN'T END with politics. The lack of transparency—particularly financial transparency—was an early concern for the nascent PA. While the PA was created virtually overnight, its many assets were not brought out into the light of day. To be sure, a budget was made public. But the subterranean financial sources—the funds not provided by the international community to assist in state building—remained opaque.

As noted in the previous chapter, analysts had long observed that Palestinian finances were a black box. Arafat biographers Janet and John Wallach commented that "Fatah's secret assets are known only to three or four people, and Arafat's signature must appear on all of Fatah's checks."[6] Authors Neil Livingstone and David Halevy noted in 1990 that it was "difficult to put together a balance sheet for the PLO since it does not make any of its finances public."[7] A 1993 *U.S. News & World Report* article quoted a Palestinian official as saying, "The day Arafat dies, may God forbid, it will take the organization at least 50 years to get its act together. . . . Only Arafat knows all the exact details concerning the finances." The same report stated that "much of the PLO's financial picture, particularly Mr. Arafat's management of the organization's secret Fatah budget, remains murky."[8]

Concerns also emerged about the way in which this new government was run. In the summer 1994 issue of *Foreign Affairs,* Israeli analyst Amos Perlmutter warned that a Palestinian state ruled by Arafat "will likely be authoritarian, non-inclusive, and undemocratic. Such a state will be controlled by Arafat's security services, which will do all that is necessary to keep themselves in power. . . . It does not augur well for political pluralism, participation, and, above all, institutionalization, that is, the creation of a democratic and stable Palestinian state."[9]

According to Dennis Ross, Middle East envoy during the Clinton years, there was always "tension between peace building and what would be the state building." As Ross noted, "We were dealing in a world where in the Middle East, leaders make peace, publics don't. The irony, of course, is publics make real peace."[10]

To be fair, the PA did not look much different from the other patriarchal states in the region, such as Egypt or Tunisia, which maintained reasonably good ties with Washington. But, as Khalidi stresses, the PA's political structures "also closely reflected his [Arafat's] personal characteristics, notably in terms of his indomitable desire to be in charge. As the preeminent founding leader . . . Arafat left his mark on styles of authority, forms of organization, and structures that have endured."[11] In other words, he was no Hosni Mubarak, and he was no Zine al-Abedine Ben Ali, who both helped create lasting institutions despite their autocratic regimes.

Arafat was a force to be reckoned with. As Khalidi notes, in the early 1990s, "there remained virtually no one within the Palestinian leadership who could stand up to *al-khityar,* the 'old man.'" To maintain his power, Arafat emphasized the "personal over the organizational, his notorious tendency to create duplicate lines of authority . . . his systematic undermining of administrative routine, and his general preference for controlled chaos over order." In addition, Arafat "worked tirelessly to keep all the strings controlling Palestinian politics, particularly the financial ones, in his hands alone."[12]

As scholar Hillel Frisch notes, "The omnipotence of one leader and the absence of any role for the most important collective bodies in the PLO [was] exacerbated by the way PA officials [were] chosen." Fatah leader Marwan Barghouti, now imprisoned for his role in killing Israelis during the second intifada, complained in 1995 that officials were chosen "based on the desire to co-opt families and extend clans and strengthen their roles."[13] Frisch contends that Arafat engineered a "neopatriarchy" in which one man provides stability and security through control of virtually every aspect of the political system, but at the cost of that system's "long-term decline in the capacity to govern due in part to the increasingly stringent control and co-optation of the civil society."[14]

With most of the levers of power at his fingertips, it should come as no surprise that Arafat easily captured an electoral majority in 1996 and became the first elected leader of the PA.[15] It should also come as little surprise that the problems associated with transparency and governance continued. Part of the problem with Arafat arose because one never knew which hat he was wearing: Was he the chairman of the PLO, the president of the PA, or the leader of Fatah? These varying roles made it difficult to firmly establish his accountability. And as long as the peace process continued, Washington was generally not interested in pressing the issue. Neither were the Israelis, as long as Arafat kept a lid on violence in the West Bank and Gaza.

Ross recalled, "Every time we pushed forward issues related to rule of law, we would get pushback from the Israelis, saying 'Don't apply those kinds of standards to [Arafat]. We want him to be able to arrest people.'"[16]

Aaron David Miller adds, "State security courts and human rights abuses? Terrible. But you've got to keep the peace process alive. Corruption? Terrible. But you've got to keep the peace process alive." The hope was that if Washington could "get to an agreement, which was a transactional act, that would produce transformation."[17]

There was a price to pay for turning that blind eye, however. The PA's finances were beset with corruption and unaccountability. In 1997, a Palestinian report found that "$326 million of the Palestinian autonomy government's $800 million annual budget had been squandered through corruption or mismanagement."[18] Additional findings revealed that "serious financial and administrative violations were committed by most of the Palestinian Authority's ministries and other institutions." At least $223 million had been lost.[19] As Brown observes, most of the infractions were "personal use of ministry cars, unaccounted international long distance calls, padded expense accounts. A few were more significant, such as use of border controls to divert business to relatives of senior officials."[20]

Brown, however, felt that the corruption was not the real story. Rather, he wrote that the exposure of the story was "far more remarkable" because it was "unprecedented in Arab politics."[21] Among other things, the Palestinian report prompted calls for dismissing members of the Palestinian cabinet, including Minister of Planning and International Cooperation Nabil Sha'ath and Minister of Civil Affairs Jamil al-Tarifi. Both ministers, however, kept their positions.[22] Moreover, once the furor died down, "Arafat ordered future audits to be kept secret."[23]

But if Arafat's aim was to shroud illicit finances from the public eye, he was unsuccessful. In April 1997, Israeli journalists Ronen Bergman and David Ratner exposed Arafat's secret bank account in Tel Aviv. The account, believed to be accessible to Arafat and his financial adviser Mohammed Rachid, was said to have received at least 500 million shekels [$1.25 million] and was not under the supervision of the PA. Rachid insisted that the account was not secret, and it was one in which "Israel deposits money in it, and a day later it is transferred to Gaza."[24]

Additional questions about monopolies also dogged Arafat's political elite. According to the US State Department, there were at least 27 monopolies in the PA's territories. Reportedly, at the time the PA was created, the leadership "decided to control several essential economic sectors through monopolies; and the rights to operate the monopolies were given to several of the Authority's senior officials." According to Bergman and Ratner, the Palestinian monopolists bought products from Israelis and sold them in the Palestinian territories at a higher price. The profits reportedly lined the pockets of high-level Palestinian figures.

The revelations prompted Palestinian outrage. Hussam Khader, a Fatah official, charged that "every honcho got himself a fat slice of the imports into the Authority. One got the fuel, another got the cigarettes, yet another the lottery, and his crony the flour. Gravel is a monopoly belonging directly to the security apparatuses, and they earn a fortune from it that finances their operations." Khader called these crony capitalists a "mafia" that undermined the Palestinian Legislative Council. "These men will do everything they can to continue their activities unsupervised and unmonitored," he said. Haider Abd a-Shafi, a principal figure in the early diplomatic exchanges with Israel, charged that, "without the monopolies, the economy could be in much better shape."[25]

Dr. Hisham Awartani, a Palestinian academic, lamented the sorry state of the PA's nascent market economy. He stated,

> We, the Palestinians, have a tendency to blame Israel for all our economic problems. That is a major mistake. We have to blame ourselves as well. First of all, I think we have to get rid of the Authority's entire economic leadership. . . . They have all failed. They must all go home.[26]

IN FEBRUARY 1997, EDWARD ABINGTON, a former American consul general in Jerusalem who was often viewed as an unwavering ally of the PLO, surprisingly voiced his displeasure with the PA's record on human rights. "Security is important, but it cannot come at the cost of human rights," he said. "Too many Palestinians have died while in PA custody, but Palestinians must not suffer at the hands of other Palestinians. . . . All of these problems may be part of the growing pains of a new democracy, but left untreated they represent a serious threat to the eventual establishment of truly representational government for the Palestinians."[27]

One component of the PA's human rights problem stemmed from the stifling of political dissent. But another component was the response to Hamas's attempt to challenge the legitimacy of the PA. Encouraged by Washington and Jerusalem, the PA began to conduct operations against Hamas and arrested many suspected

Hamas sympathizers without charge. Paradoxically, according to one Palestinian commentator, such operations "contributed to Hamas' popularity as the political underdog and spokesman for the marginalized and forgotten."[28] The PA's heavy-handed measures also laid the groundwork for the internecine conflict that eventually erupted in 2007.

At the time, however, countering Hamas was deemed to be in both the national and international interest. The Israelis needed Hamas violence kept to a minimum if they were to continue to maintain the support of the Israeli public for the peace process. The United States, too, needed Hamas pinned down if it were to preside over the completion of the process set in motion by the Oslo Accords, as President Clinton so clearly intended to do. Famously, US vice president Al Gore publicly lauded the PA's legal system in 1995.[29]

But as Brown noted, "It is difficult to conceive of a court that would violate more judicial principals."[30] Yet none of the parties involved—the United States, Israel, or the PA—actively challenged the Palestinian legal system or the security services' lack of oversight or legal framework, as long as the overall security environment was tolerable, meaning that Hamas remained contained.

Meanwhile, charges were accumulating against the PA. In April 1997, the *Guardian* contended that Arafat "and his coterie of unofficial economic 'advisers' have thrown up a ramshackle, nepotistic edifice of monopoly, racketeering, and naked extortion which merely enriches them as it further impoverishes society at large."[31] According to Bloomberg, between 1995 and 2000, Arafat "diverted $900 million of the authority's tax and business income to personal bank accounts."[32] Another report from Bloomberg revealed that, between 1997 and 2000, the Palestinian leadership had transferred $238 million to Switzerland without notifying its donors.[33]

In June 1999, a report on Palestinian governance, penned by Palestinian academics Khalil Shikaki and Yazid Sayigh and released under the names of American activist Henry Siegman and former French prime minister Michel Rochard, noted that the PA needed to implement "reforms that are within the present powers of the Palestinian Authority."[34] Two months later, Arafat signed a decree to create a committee to follow up on the Rochard and Siegman report as a means to "strengthen Palestinian institutions." Later that year, the Palestinian government reported that tax revenues were appropriately flowing to the treasury, as required, and that steps were being taken to halt the troubling practice of diverting funds to public companies without proper oversight.[35]

But the perception of corruption continued to dog the PA. In October 1999, Azmi Shuaibi, a member of the Palestinian Legislative Council and chairman of the Budget Committee, lamented that "Palestine, at such an early stage, already resembles the rest of the Arab countries in its traits of corruption." He compared PA corruption "to the corruption that exists in the rest of the Arab countries' governments. It is similar in its abuse of power by those in public positions."[36] The following month, a manifesto signed by 20 prominent Palestinians slammed Arafat and the PA for corruption. The manifesto, known as the *bayan al-ashrin* or the Statement of Twenty,[37] stated that Arafat had "opened the doors to the opportunists to spread their rottenness through the Palestinian street." In addition, it charged that the Oslo Accords had led to the "bartering of the homeland for the enrichment of the corrupted and corrupting in the PA." Finally, it called on Palestinians "to sound the alarm against the PA's misrule in every town and village, every camp and corner of the land."[38] Such a move was unprecedented in Palestinian society, let alone in the Arab world. The response, however, was mass arrests.

With pressure mounting for greater transparency, in July 2000, the PA released substantial information about its financial holdings. According to the *New York Times,* a statement sent to the International Monetary Fund (IMF) detailed how "Palestinian Commercial Services Company, which is owned by the Palestinian Authority but not supervised by its legislature or finance ministry, [controlled] large minority stakes in a Jericho casino, a Ramallah Coca-Cola bottler, a Bethlehem convention center, and myriad other private businesses, plus full ownership of a cement plant that had long enjoyed a government-protected monopoly."[39]

The report further revealed that Palestinian Commercial Services was the

> direct recipient of sales taxes—more than $500 million in the past two years alone—collected by Israel but owed to the Palestinian Authority under the 1993 Oslo peace accords. The tax receipts had been deposited in a Tel Aviv bank account controlled by Mr. Rachid and Mr. Arafat, a practice ended by Israel in April after persistent complaints by the World Bank, the International Monetary Fund, and other institutions. . . . Some of the tax money was used by Mr. Arafat for undisclosed official expenditures, but most went to the Palestinian Commercial Services Company, according to Palestinian officials.[40]

The *New York Times* also noted that the report contained "a few unexpected oddities, like small joint investment funds with the government of Qatar and the Peres Peace Center, a Tel Aviv foundation started by Shimon Peres, the former Israeli prime minister." The report further found that Palestinian Commercial Services "put $9 million into a small biotechnology company in London, Ontario, Bioniche Life Sciences, its only disclosed investment outside the Palestinian territories."[41]

Shortly after these blockbuster revelations, Arafat had little choice but to call for the creation of a sovereign wealth fund by presidential decree. The Palestine Investment Fund (PIF) would soon be created as a means to consolidate all of these assets and more.

DURING THE 1990S, PALESTINIAN-ISRAELI SECURITY COOPERATION and diplomacy were the dominant narratives in the West. The issue of Palestinian governance was a mere sideshow. But the problem was no less important to the Palestinians. By the time the Americans, Palestinians, and Israelis were gearing up for the final push for peace in the summer of 2000, a poll by the Palestinian Center for Policy and Survey Research found that 76 percent of Palestinians believed that corruption existed in PA institutions.[42] It had become glaringly apparent to West Bankers and Gazans alike that throughout the 1990s, during the endless process of diplomacy and confidence building, the world had neglected to closely examine the economic and political culture of the nascent Palestinian polity. As Brown observed, the PA "could be oppressive and corrupt in ways unconnected with the Oslo Accords."[43]

Thus, after nearly a decade of world leaders turning a blind eye to these problems, the Palestinian people had plenty of reason to doubt the peace process. Of course, this was not the primary reason for their rejection of the deal that Israeli prime minister Ehud Barak put on the table with Clinton's blessing. But the bitterness that the West Bank and Gaza populations must have felt about the mismanagement over their national project could not have helped matters.

In 2000, the Palestinian people plunged into the second Palestinian uprising, now commonly known as the Al-Aqsa Intifada. As Khalidi notes, the circumstances left the "Palestinian polity drifting like a rudderless ship, without any recognizable strategy at a time of supreme crisis."[44] At this point, Washington realized its own shortcomings. As Dennis Ross recalled, "We should have been focused on the state-building enterprise. . . . We didn't really focus on that until, in effect, after the collapse of Oslo and the beginning of the second intifada."[45]

5

The Al-Aqsa Intifada

AT THE START OF THE SECOND INTIFADA IN LATE SEPTEMBER 2000, after seven years of attempted peacemaking with Israel, Arafat elected to turn his back on diplomacy. In essence, the longtime PLO leader also turned his back on the PA. As violence erupted throughout the West Bank and Gaza, the quasi government began to crumble and, with it, Arafat's standing as an international leader.

Although his choice of "resistance" initially resonated on the Palestinian street, Arafat soon began to lose the hearts and minds of his people at home. As the campaign of violence stretched from weeks to months, the rival Hamas organization ascended as the driving force of the attacks against Israel. As one Palestinian analyst observed, the new uprising had produced an "unknown, faceless generation of leaders, and nobody knows where they are going."[1] Arafat's Fatah and PLO were increasingly less relevant.

But that was not where the bad news ended for Arafat and the Palestinian ruling elite. The Palestinian people, frustrated by the end of an optimistic era, began to demand that the PA account for the reports of corruption and mismanagement that mounted during the lead-up to the second intifada. Thus, as the PA struggled to function in a war-zone environment, it also came under fire from its own people.

IN RETROSPECT, IT IS SOMEWHAT SURPRISING that accounting for financial mismanagement was a priority for the Palestinians, given the many hardships that they endured at the time. For one, the fatalities during this conflict were staggering. An estimated 2,647 Palestinians were killed in the West Bank and Gaza Strip from September 2000 through August 2003, with more than 36,448 injured.[2]

With the renewal of violence against Israel, Palestinians also began to attack each other. Some Palestinians charged others of "collaboration" with Israel. And according to Nathan Brown, the PA's State Security Court "proved an efficient and ruthless device for meting out punishments to suspected collaborators."[3]

Additionally, to reassert his control over the Palestinian territories, Arafat cracked down on rival factions and attempted to neutralize his political foes. His rivals responded to these attacks with violence. In November 2000, some 3,000 Islamist protesters clashed with PA police over the arrest of Mahmud Tawalbi, a popular Palestinian Islamic Jihad leader. In February 2002, Palestinian police battled with more than 200 demonstrators outside a jail in Hebron, from which 60 Palestinian Islamic Jihad and Hamas prisoners eventually escaped. These repeated clashes prompted one Israeli official to predict that the PA would "disintegrate" and Arafat would be "replaced by Hamas and Islamic Jihad."[4]

The PA experienced a bruising financial crisis, too. According to some reports, the quasi government's revenue plummeted from more than $600 million (at its peak) to just $27 million by 2001.[5] According to another report, the PA's total worth was down by more than two-thirds after the first year of conflict, thanks to widespread corruption, a steep drop in productivity, and the reluctance of international donors to give additional foreign aid.[6] These financial woes forced the PA to cut administrative salaries. The Palestinian newspaper *al-Hayat al-Jadida* reported that senior PA figures began to desert their posts.[7]

Along with the depletion of its human and financial resources, the PA also lost its physical infrastructure. Although Arafat was not directly responsible for all the violence against Israel, the Israelis held him accountable. In April 2002, the Israel Defense Forces (IDF) carried out a large-scale military campaign known as Operation Defensive Shield, which hammered key PA security and government buildings. The damage to PA infrastructure was catastrophic.

ARAFAT, MEANWHILE, COULD NOT ARTICULATE a clear vision for the outcome of this crippling conflict. On the one hand, he embraced Islamism and violence. His Fatah faction created the al-Aqsa Martyrs Brigades (AAMB), which co-opted Islamic symbols and slogans. By 2002, the Brigades had claimed responsibility for dozens of headline-grabbing attacks in which Israeli civilians were killed. The group rivaled Hamas in this respect. On March 21, 2002, for example, an AAMB suicide bomber detonated himself in the middle of a crowded street in Jerusalem, killing 3 and injuring 86. Less than three weeks earlier, another AAMB suicide bomber killed 10 and injured 50 at a bar mitzvah celebration.[8] The Brigades openly admitted their allegiance to Arafat. One commander in Tulkarem acknowledged, "We receive our instructions from Fatah. Our commander is Yasser Arafat himself."[9] Documents subsequently seized by the Israeli military from PA offices further demonstrated that Fatah (the dominant faction of the PA) bankrolled nearly every aspect of the Brigades' terrorist operations—from explosives to guns and gas money.[10]

Yet at other times, Arafat embraced secularism and talked of peace. For example, Arafat jumped at a proposal made by the

Middle East Quartet (the US, the EU, the UN, and Russia), known as the roadmap for peace, which promised a de facto Palestinian state, with final borders to be set by 2005.[11] Having accepted the Quartet's plan, in an attempt to regain control over Palestinian territories, Fatah requested that Hamas cease attacks against Israel. But with the PA unable to gain the upper hand, interfactional clashes spilled over onto the streets.[12] Fatah responded by burning a Hamas press office and shooting at the homes of two Hamas leaders.[13] The two factions exchanged blistering public barbs. A Fatah leaflet released on December 10, 2002, warned Hamas, "Anyone who wants to challenge [Fatah], his end will be in our hands."[14]

While political tensions between these two factions existed since the launch of Hamas in 1987, and those tensions had certainly increased during the 1990s, the intifada exacerbated the Hamas–Fatah conflict. In many ways, the armed conflict against Israel set the stage for the decline of Arafat's faction and the rise of Hamas.

ISRAEL, MEANWHILE, HAD COMPLETELY GIVEN UP on Arafat as a peacemaker. Alongside the military efforts to weaken him, the Israelis also began to expose the corruption that had thrived under his rule. In November 2000, the Israeli newspaper *Yediot Ahronot* issued a story that referred to one PA account totaling some 1.6 billion shekels, composed of "tax returns on gasoline." It concluded, "[Mohammed] Rachid claims that everything was transferred to the Palestinian Finance Ministry. Israeli officials heard from Palestinian ministers that most of the money was never transferred. Joseph Saba, director of the World Bank in the territories, said, 'We have no idea what happened with this account.'"[15] Rachid denied the story and added that revenues never exceeded $500 million.

Between the violence with Israel and the accusations that continued to fly, many Palestinian investors were scared off. In December 2000, a Palestinian American businessman said that he was unwilling to invest in the Palestinian territories because of the rampant corruption: "To invest in gasoline, steel, telephones, electricity, or cigarettes, you have to go to the same guy [Mohammad Rachid]. Smart people won't go into a situation like this. Small businesses have been run out."[16]

More broadly, the Palestinians simply did not trust their own government. A July 2001 poll by the Palestinian Center for Policy and Survey Research found that 83 percent of Palestinians believed that corruption existed in PA institutions.[17] In December 2001, the number had decreased to 74 percent but still reflected a crisis in confidence that the PA had created.[18]

By the following year, the Israelis began to sense that Palestinian corruption was an issue they could exploit. In April 2002, the *Jerusalem Post* editorial board wrote that "evidence of high-level Palestinian corruption and misuse of donor nation funds, as well as PA repression of human rights and basic civil liberties, [must] be made available for all the world to see. . . . Israel has little choice but to send the PA leader packing."[19]

One month later, with the intifada still raging, the Israeli government released a detailed report based on evidence obtained during Operation Defensive Shield that stated:

> Corruption is rampant in the PA, it includes irregularities in the administration, management of the Palestinian economy by monopolies which enable the financial rewarding of senior PA officials and their families. In addition, the distribution of PA money amongst the Palestinian population was characterized by inequality and created large gaps between the majority of the Palestinian population and senior PA officials who enjoy a high standard of living, the expropriation of lands, and altering verdicts by bribery and threatening the lives of judges.[20]

The report was specific about the conspicuous wealth of certain PA officials. It alleged that "senior PA officials enjoy a high standard of living."[21]

The report also noted "forceful contributions and false arrest of businessmen by the PA security forces and their release in exchange for money and bribes. A senior businessman from Tulkarem was forced to pay $100,000 for the release of his brother who was arrested by the security apparatuses for collaboration with Israel. A Christian businessman paid $5,000 for the release of his brother arrested by counter-intelligence apparatus personnel."[22]

The Israelis were clearly using the report as a means to galvanize international support for their military response to the Palestinian uprising. Of course, that did not mean that the report was untrue. As one EU diplomat admitted, the world had been turning a blind eye to Palestinian corruption. The diplomat was quoted as saying, "Everybody has known for quite some time now that money ended up in the wrong hands."[23]

Even Arafat realized that he would need to tackle the problem before it tackled him. According to Brown, in May 2002 "Arafat responded to the growing domestic and international pressure by convening the Palestinian Legislative Council to deliver a speech vowing to launch a reform program and hold new elections." Brown observed that this speech was "greeted cynically by many in the PLC whose experience with years of unmet or overly vague promises had convinced them that true reform was not likely to be forthcoming from the existing leadership, even as modified. And the decay of Palestinian institutions and lack of clear leadership during the intifada undermined the argument that supporting Arafat aided national unity."[24]

US president George W. Bush was equally unimpressed with Arafat's gestures. Granted, Bush was more concerned with Arafat's support for terrorism. Nevertheless, the following month, he declared that Palestinian reform required "new and different leadership." As Brown observed, in the president's view "reform without replacing Arafat would not be deemed reform."[25] In the months that followed, Bush continued to push for Arafat's exit but would never succeed. He did, however, succeed in promoting Mahmoud Abbas to the newly minted position of prime minister. The president's message was clear: Arafat would no longer remain unchallenged as the leader of the Palestinian people.

Meanwhile, the PLO continued to suffer from a crisis in confidence. An August 2002 poll by the Palestinian Center for Policy and Survey Research found that 85 percent of Palestinians believed that corruption existed within PA institutions.[26] This poll came on the heels of reports by Agence France-Presse about former PLO financier Joweid al-Ghossein.[27] Al-Ghossein, who served as secretary-general of the Palestinian National Fund until 1996, charged that Arafat had transferred some $8 million of international donations to one of his personal accounts.[28]

Arafat, for his part, finally appeared to understand the pressures he faced. Or perhaps others within the Palestinian leadership forced his hand. As Brown noted, the Palestinian Legislative Council in September 2002 "accomplished what other parliaments in the Arab world have been shut down for even discussing; it brought down the cabinet and forced a decree for new elections."[29]

6

Fayyadism

IN JUNE 2002, SALAM FAYYAD WAS NAMED FINANCE MINISTER OF THE
Palestinian Authority (PA).[1] A quiet and unassuming bureaucrat,
Fayyad was serious about reform. He stood in stark contrast to
the Palestinian figures who had dominated the political scene during the Arafat era. And it was his approach to governance that
provided hope to advocates of the Palestinian national project after Arafat was gone.

IN 1996, SHORTLY AFTER THE PA WAS CREATED, Arafat assigned
Salam Fayyad, a Palestinian who holds a doctorate in economics
from the University of Texas at Austin, to be his representative to
the International Monetary Fund (IMF). Just three years into the
creation of the PA, Fayyad was convinced that a focus on building
strong institutions and fighting corruption was the key to success.
As James Prince, a former adviser to Fayyad, recalls, "Fayyad believed that although the newly minted Palestinian economy was
absorbing billions of dollars in assistance, the average person was
not feeling better. In fact, all the financial indicators and quality
of life factors began a steady decline upon the establishment of
the Palestinian Authority. Only [through] effective institutions . . .

would the PA ever move into a legitimate, popular, and durable public administration able to gain support from its constituency."[2]

However, at the time, Fayyad was largely overshadowed by the brash leadership style of Yasser Arafat. As Prince noted, "He had a point of view that couldn't compete with Arafat's role as a Nelson Mandela figure."[3]

Of course, nobody could compete with Arafat's larger-than-life personality in the early years of the PA. But Fayyad was not trying to compete with him. He was focused on the economic viability of the Palestinian national project. To this end, in 1997, just after joining the IMF as the Palestinian representative, Fayyad reportedly penned a rather bold letter to IMF official Stanley Fisher (who went on to become Israel's Federal Reserve chief), asserting that even if the Israelis and Palestinians were to find a way to sign a peace agreement, the final status of Palestinian statehood was doomed because of Palestinian public administration challenges. To say the least, this was a minority position at a time when optimism over the peace process was in full bloom. The memo was suppressed,[4] but the thinking behind it was the basis of what became known as "Fayyadism": Palestinian nationalism would only succeed in the creation of a state if the proper effort went into institution building.

By 1999, it was getting harder to ignore Fayyad. With the mishandling of international donor funds, financial indicators were deteriorating. But one particularly jarring incident in 1999 involving the Palestine International Bank (PIB) shook the international community's faith in the Palestinian system. As the former chairman of the bank, Issam Abu Issa, relayed in the pages of *Middle East Quarterly*:

> Arafat issued a decree dissolving the Palestine International Bank's
> board of directors. The state-controlled Palestine Monetary Authority [PMA] took over the bank, and with Arafat's blessing and written

approval, formed a new supervisory board of directors, including at least one convicted and Interpol-wanted felon. The unlawful takeover was a confiscation of my own, my shareholders', and my clients' private assets for Arafat's personal use. At the date of seizure, PIB total assets amounted to $105 million.[5]

At the time, Prince, who worked for the multinational accounting firm PricewaterhouseCoopers (PwC), "had been repeatedly trying to convince Arafat and his adviser Nabil Shaath of the need to reform the financial systems of the PA in order to keep donors from cutting off funds and to win back the hearts and minds of the increasingly frustrated Palestinian population who had not yet felt the benefit of any peace dividend. When the PIB threatened to become a significant international incident, Arafat, with advice from Mohammed Rachid and Shaath, compromised." The PA retained PwC to conduct a fraud investigation based on international standards. According to Prince, the subsequent "PwC report concluded by recommending prosecution of Abu Issa in a court of law and the public dissemination of the investigative work product." However, Prince notes that Arafat "missed the opportunity to do what was right and he cut a deal by which Abu Issa could safely leave the country, [with] his assets firmly controlled by Arafat and the Palestinian Monetary Authority."[6]

Abu Issa's version was significantly different. He alleged that

The PMA altered, hid, or destroyed bank records in their campaign to demonstrate malfeasance on my part retroactively. They supplied false information to the PricewaterhouseCoopers (PwC) group leading to a faulty audit . . . As they seized the bank, Arafat's security services harassed me. I fled to the Qatari mission in Gaza. Arafat's staff confiscated my private belongings, including my car, which Arafat took for himself. My brother Issa accompanied a Qatari Foreign Ministry delegation to Gaza in order to resolve the stalemate. But, upon his arrival, Palestinian police acting on orders from Arafat arrested him. The PA said they would trade his freedom for mine. Only after the State of Qatar threatened Arafat with financial sanctions and severing of diplomatic ties did the PA give us free passage to leave Gaza for Qatar.[7]

It became clear to the international donor community that the Palestinian financial system was insufficiently regulated. The Palestinian leadership had little choice but to shift its focus away from the glamor of international diplomacy and toward the significantly less sexy realm of institutional development. In a mid-1999 meeting in Gaza, according to Prince, Arafat told a delegation from PwC that he was "determined to implement reform." He asked PwC to help design a "methodology and concept for the reform effort." Arafat pledged that he would go to the forthcoming Tokyo donor summit in October 1999 to read the statement committing to reform.[8] To be sure, none of this was called "Fayyadism" at the time. But there is no denying that Fayyad's ideas had won the day.

There was also no denying that the international donor community wanted economic reform and did not trust Arafat to implement it. This is why the PA turned to outside auditors and accountants. With their assistance, Fayyad would soon push the PA toward political reform and institution building and away from neopatriarchy.

THE BASIS FOR THE PALESTINIAN REFORM PLAN was somewhat simple. The Palestinians, in the interest of creating a viable state, needed to get a handle on a few key sectors. For one, the PA needed to consolidate its security forces. After the outbreak of the second intifada in 2000, too many factions were undermining domestic security (not to mention regional security).

Another challenge was to wean the Palestinians off a cash system and to bring workers onto a formal payroll system. This would help the Palestinian leadership get a better handle on the economic health of the territories while also cutting down on opportunities for corruption or financial mismanagement. Along these lines, the PA also needed to consolidate its revenue generators that were controlled by Arafat or elements of the Palestinian Authority but were not included in the Palestinian budget. Indeed, the government truly lacked any solid sense of what its debits and credits looked like at any given time. Finally, the PA needed to establish a better-functioning bureaucratic system, which also meant the decentralization of presidential power. To put it another way, the office of the president was too strong, whereas the other offices that were essential to the daily governance of the PA were simply too weak. All of this needed to change.

While the challenges were great, there appeared to be genuine interest among the Palestinians to effect this change. But the timing could not have been worse. The move toward better governance came right as President Clinton's time in office was ending. And Clinton's goal was to finish what he started. The president sought to push the Palestinian leaders to make painful compromises at the negotiating table with the Israelis while they were still scrambling to make sense of the economic challenges that faced them. As a result of the economic challenges (admittedly much of their own making), the Palestinian leaders were weak and less sure-footed going into final-status talks in 2000.

For this reason, along with other domestic and broader strategic considerations, Arafat spurned Clinton's offer of a Palestinian state on some 95 percent of the West Bank and 100 percent of Gaza. Inexplicably, soon after that, Arafat launched a new round of violence against the Israelis rather than returning to the negotiating table.

Not surprisingly, the figures in Arafat's inner circle most closely associated with corruption reportedly supported the peace plan. They likely understood that they had the most to lose if peace was not achieved. Arafat apparently did not understand this. His decision to embrace violence at this time was, in retrospect, a strategic mistake. To be sure, the violence launched out of the West Bank and Gaza had a deleterious impact on Israel, which was the primary goal. But it was also clear that some of the Palestinian violence and frustration stemmed not only from hatred for Israel but also from the fact that the quality of life in the territories had never really improved for a great many Palestinians despite massive donor aid year over year. This fact was not lost on the average Palestinian.

The intifada began in late September 2000, and the violence raged for about four months before the inauguration of a new US administration under President George W. Bush, who immediately made it clear that Arafat was part of the problem and would not likely be part of the solution. Bush did not see the utility of investing his presidential credibility in a process where Arafat, a former terrorist who had returned to terrorism, was a key player.

Arafat reportedly was aware of his reputation in the West. He was also aware of the PA's significant cash shortfall, brought on by a steep drop in donor assistance. He began to undertake efforts to rein in the violence. He also continued to promise reform. However, he lacked the credibility to do so. That's when he turned to Salam Fayyad.

As Bush noted at the time, the appointment of Fayyad was a "positive development, because one of the things that worries us is spending any international aid on an authority that might not keep good books; that the money might not actually get to help the Palestinian people, but might end up in somebody's pocket."[9]

WHEN FAYYAD, THEN A REGIONAL MANAGER for Arab Bank, was named finance minister in June 2002, the intifada was still raging. Palestinian terror groups continued to attack Israel with frequency, and the Israeli military responded with harsh retribution. Under these difficult external circumstances, Fayyad went to work.

Fayyad's approach was simple. He was less worried about the violence and more concerned with the troubling political culture that had overtaken the PA. It did not bother him that he was appointed by Arafat. He undoubtedly knew that he represented the upstanding image that Arafat sought to project to the international donor community as he struggled to salvage what was left of the PA. But it is unclear whether he understood that he would serve as a convenient straw man for any shortcomings in the reform program. He also may not have realized that, despite the fact that Arafat needed him to instill confidence among the donor community, Arafat could still oppose the economist domestically, which would play well on the Palestinian street.

Fayyad wrangled with Arafat over security reform and payroll reform, which was effectively a direct challenge to Arafat's control over the PA's estimated 120,000 employees. In retrospect, Fayyad's greatest point of leverage was the *Karine A* Affair. In January 2002, Arafat had been caught red-handed trying to smuggle in weaponry from Iran by sea, and the Israelis intercepted the shipment.[10] This discovery only served to reinforce the perceived need for a single treasury account as a means to ensure that Palestinian finances were spent on governance, not on illicit ordinances. It also reinforced the need for reform in the security sector. Bush administration official Elliott Abrams recalls that "13 security agencies had to become three agencies and report to the prime minister, not the president. I think we made progress."[11] Dennis Ross also lauded Fayyad's reforms in this area, which enabled the PA to "stop paying the security guys from paper bags in cash, and letting them skim off the top."[12]

The Israelis, however, had written off Arafat. In many ways, they had written off the entire PA. In May 2002, the Israeli Foreign Ministry weighed in, charging that "corruption is rampant in the PA," marked by "monopolies which enable the financial rewarding of senior PA officials and their families," not to mention the "expropriation of lands, and altering verdicts by bribery and threatening the lives of judges."[14]

But the Israelis were also part of the problem. In December 2002, former Israeli intelligence official Uzrad Lew exposed in the pages of *Maariv* that PA tax and customs revenues had been transferred in 1997 to a Swiss bank account in the name of an offshore holding company called "Ledbury Global Inc."[15] Lew went on to publish a full book titled *Be-tokh ha-kis shel ha-Ra'is* (*Inside Arafat's Pocket*) in 2005 alleging how Palestinians and Israelis alike benefited from corruption during the Arafat era. Yossi Ginnosar, a former Israeli security official and back-channel envoy to the Palestinians who died in 2003, took the brunt of the criticism.[16]

"Ginnosar was the key player. Not one Israeli had access to Arafat the way that Ginnosar did," Lew recalls. "Ginnosar began to take cuts of deals the Palestinians made with Israel. . . . We're talking about millions of dollars here. This goes on for many years, even through the *intifada,* while the Palestinians were at war with Israel."[17]

IN AUGUST 2002, WITH ARAFAT'S BLESSING, Fayyad announced the formation of "a fund to oversee all money handled by the Palestinian Authority, in response to pressure on the leadership to clean up its finances."[18] The Palestine Investment Fund (PIF) was officially founded in 2003, and its primary aim was "to safeguard and consolidate the Palestinian people's investments and property, both in Palestine and abroad."[19] The idea for PIF, according to

Prince, was born in 2001, when PwC "was engaged by Arafat to animate Fayyad's vision in developing an appropriate investment holding vehicle by which to manage public investments and stimulus programs."[20]

As Fayyad stated in 2002, "There is something liberating about full transparency, it helps you sleep better at night."[21] The fund helped the international donor community sleep at night as well. As Abbas later ceded, the fund was created "in response to calls from the United States government (USG) and the European Union (EU) for increased transparency and accountability within the Palestinian Authority institutions and affiliates."[22]

The creation of the fund was no easy task, however. The PLO had amassed a huge investment portfolio over the course of four decades. In some cases, little was known about the investments. As such, bringing them into the newly revamped Palestinian Treasury brought a certain amount of risk. Fayyad's goal was to lower the risk profile and include only transparent and clean investments.

Fayyad spearheaded the investigation of money and assets controlled by Arafat or anyone else connected to the PA. Dozens of consultants and accountants, including Jim Prince, were assigned to the task of investigating some 80 enterprises around the world.[23] Once they determined where the assets of PA or PLO were hidden, their job was to "clean" and take control of them.

In January 2003, initial media reports began to reveal where Arafat had squirreled away millions of dollars in PLO money over the years. The reports indicated that the PLO had lucrative deals with Israeli figures, among others, with assets held in Switzerland, Africa, and America, to name a few. The reports created a splash in the international media. Locally, they sent shockwaves through the Palestinian economy as monopolies were exposed and sometimes shattered. The timing was less than fortuitous. The intifada continued to wreak havoc on the Palestinian economy. The exposure of these secret businesses often exacerbated the instability.

As Prince notes, the companies brought into the fund were only part of the story. The holdings that Fayyad elected not to include in the PIF were deemed not "clean enough." Many of those assets were never revealed. It is unclear whether they are still held by Palestinian interests today.[24]

In the end, Fayyad settled on a model based on a German public investment fund. By all accounts, it was a successful endeavor. In 2003, the PIF had a net income of $40.1 million on revenue of $85.1 million.[25] Moreover, by forcing the sale of assets not related to economic development or in competition with the private sector, hundreds of millions of dollars were put back into the Palestinian Treasury—up to $700 million.[26]

The *New York Times* summed up the venture nicely. In short, Fayyad had tracked down "assets in 79 commercial ventures, from Canadian biopharmaceuticals to Algerian cellphones, and hired Standard & Poor's to examine them for their value and ownership structure. He published the results as they came in, identifying the officials involved, centralizing the investments under a new supervising agency and laying plans to sell them off."[27] The result was that Fayyad had earned his first big success.

In 2004, Mohammad Shtayyeh, managing director of the West Bank–based Palestinian Economic Council for Development and Reconstruction, announced that "[a]ll the Palestinian money [$799 million] has been consolidated in the Palestine Investment Fund."[28] By the following year, the IMF valued PIF assets at $1.3 billion.[29]

FAYYAD'S WORK DID NOT END with the PIF, however. He continued to crusade for transparency.

"This will no longer be a guessing game. No more rumors and innuendo about where the money is and where the money went,"[30] he promised in early 2003. With the help of foreign diplomats, Fayyad struggled to gain a handle on the international donations as well as the money flowing through PA businesses.[31]

The reasons for his efforts were clear, and Fayyad continued to speak publicly about the need for them. "The systems were not mature or sufficiently developed in the management of public funds," he said. "[T]here is an 'anything goes' type of environment. . . . When you have that environment, it would be naive to assert there was no corruption. Of course there was. You have a system that's totally loose. No controls. No audit. Extrabudgetary spending taking place all over the place. It's wrong and it needs to be fixed."[32]

But, while Fayyad was busily working to reconstruct the Palestinian economy, political turmoil had enveloped the PA. The violence of the intifada had not receded, and relations with the United States were at an all-time low. Arafat, now viewed as an obstruction to peace by Bush, faced pressure to appoint a new prime minister. According to reports, the decision came down to a number of figures, one of whom was Fayyad. Fayyad, however, rejected the idea. "I'm a newcomer to the Palestinian Authority. There's no doubt in my mind there are others who have been there in public service who are more suitable for the job,"[33] he said.

Fayyad removed himself from the running and stepped aside for Mahmoud Abbas in order to continue to pursue economic reform and capacity building for the PA. This only added to his credibility.

In May 2003, the *New York Times* noted that Fayyad was making new strides: "Acting through the Palestinians' monetary authority, [Fayyad] ordered all banks in the West Bank and Gaza to block checks written on those funds by other ministries. And he told the banks to transfer the money to the treasury."[34]

But it didn't end there. As the *New York Times* noted, "Fayyad stripped authority over the civilian payroll from the Palestinian civil service bureau and brought it to his own ministry; this meant that the bureau in charge of hiring no longer also distributed checks, and it enabled Fayyad to obstruct a patronage system that was annually adding 10,000 to 15,000 people—many with less than sterling résumés—to the payroll."[35]

In a move that was unheard of in the Arab world, Fayyad also "issued the first detailed, public Palestinian budget, of $1.28 billion, and he posted it on the web (www.mof.gov.ps)."[36]

But perhaps the most brazen of Fayyad's initiatives was simply "ignoring many of the slips that arrived bearing Arafat's signature, the ones requesting a job for someone or help with bills or students' fees. Fayyad now had an all-purpose answer for requests he deemed unworthy: there was no allocation in the budget for them, so he was powerless to act."[37] By December 2003, the Associated Press reported that "Palestinian corruption and mismanagement, initially a major donor complaint, have become less of an issue."[38]

THIS IS NOT TO SAY THAT FAYYAD had finished cleaning up the PA. An April 2003 poll by the Palestinian Center for Policy and Survey Research found that 81 percent of Palestinians believed corruption still existed within PA institutions.[39] In some ways, Fayyad's good work exacerbated their concerns because it shed light on the problem.[40] In a general investigation of the Petroleum Authority in 2003, for example, Fayyad discovered many inconsistencies in the paperwork. He declared, according to a December 2003 report, "the documents related to the revenues from oil products— or how the money was used—can't be found. They have disappeared from the ministry."[41]

In September 2003, the IMF issued a damning report that cast light on the problem of nepotism within the PA, with a focus on

Arafat's budget. Among other things, the report noted, "The [Palestinian] President assumes the prerogative of providing aid to various organizations and individuals . . . other claimants and organizations are part of politically favored networks who should not be getting such grants. . . . This inevitably raises questions and suspicions which are inconsistent with accountable and transparent public finance systems."

The report further noted that "lucrative monopolies on cement and petroleum . . . started generating substantial profits which were also being diverted away from the budget." The exact numbers were difficult to tally, but the authors estimated that there was "about US$300 million in profits channeled outside the budget" between 1995 and 2000, whereas "tax revenue and profits from commercial activities diverted away from the budget may have exceeded US$898 million."[42]

Two months later, in November 2003, CBS News's *60 Minutes* ran an investigative piece on Arafat's wealth. The findings were nothing short of sensational. According to the report, "Yasser Arafat diverted nearly $1 billion in public funds to insure his political survival, but a lot more is unaccounted for." In addition, "U.S. officials estimate Arafat's personal nest egg at between $1 billion and $3 billion." The CBS report also noted that funds from a Swiss bank account (likely the one mentioned by Uzrad Lew) closed in 2001 could not be found.[43]

FAYYAD CAME UNDER FIRE in 2004 when Lew claimed that money the PA invested in Switzerland was used to finance attacks carried out by violent factions associated with Fatah, and that the funds were right under Fayyad's nose. "I can prove that money from the Swiss accounts of the PA is financing terror and that Salam Fayyad is not doing anything to prevent it,"[44] Lew charged. The funds, which Lew estimates totaled in the "hundreds of thousands," were channeled to the Tanzim, which was one of the primary violent groups under Arafat's control at the height of the intifada. Lew later added, "There were hundreds of checks given to Marwan Barghouti, Hussein al-Sheikh, and Zacharia Zubeidi, all Tanzim commanders, from the Palestinian Treasury. There is no way Fayyad did not know."[45] In his defense, Fayyad, who became finance minister in June 2002, did not control all of the accounts until 2003, and it would be nearly a year before Fayyad was able to establish a single treasury account under his control.

But such criticisms of Fayyad were not common. The unassuming economist was generally viewed as a bright spot amid a seemingly endless stream of bad news coming out of the PA.

And the bad news kept coming. For example, in July 2004, amid an investigation into corruption allegations surrounding the cement industry, Palestinian legislators alleged that "wealthy associates of Mr. Arafat . . . facilitated the sale of cheap Egyptian cement to Israeli contractors building the hated security wall in the West Bank."[46]

The following month Arafat ceded, "Some mistakes have been made by our institutions and some have abused their positions and violated the trust placed in them."[47] A September 2004 poll by the Palestinian Center for Policy and Survey Research found that 88 percent of Palestinians believed corruption existed within the PA.[48]

Poor governance was the least of Arafat's problems, however. The Israelis, who still held him responsible for launching the intifada, had surrounded his presidential compound in Ramallah with tanks and troops. The Palestinian leader was physically pinned down, and his political infrastructure was eroding beneath his feet. He remained in his compound until shortly before his death on November 11, 2004.

But even after he died, the financial accusations continued to fly. Bloomberg reported that "Citigroup Inc., the world's biggest financial services company, invested $6.8 million for Yasser Arafat," through managers "who set up accounts under other names."[49] Additionally, *Time* raised questions about whether his wife received large sums from the PA and further reported that auditors of PA finances claimed "Arafat was guilty of skimming $2 million a month from the gasoline trade in the territories."[50]

Elliott Abrams recalls, "When Arafat died, we undertook an effort to find his money. We did it in conjunction with a couple of other European governments, much in the way you do when any dictator dies in Africa, Asia, or Latin America. My memory is that we found hundreds of millions of dollars."[51]

WHILE ARAFAT WAS REVERED by his people for almost single-handedly focusing the world's attention on the Palestinian cause from the 1960s until his death, the problem of corruption would, to some extent, define his legacy. As a result, Palestinians were hungry for new leadership.

Arafat, ever the lone patriarch, had been loath to appoint a successor. Against his wishes, Bush had succeeded in promoting Mahmoud Abbas as a leader in waiting.[52] Thus, when Arafat died, Abbas's ascension was virtually guaranteed. On January 9, 2005, Abbas was elected *ra'is* of the PA.[53]

7

The Rise of Abu Mazen

FOR A WORLD LEADER, MAHMOUD ABBAS IS LITTLE KNOWN OUTSIDE OF his public persona. An authoritative English-language biography has never been published about him. This fact is, to say the least, remarkable particularly because he has been in power since 2005. Of course, journalists and policy analysts have written much about him since he ascended to power—and even before he became a public figure. But even then, none of what has been written could be considered an insightful narrative history of the man's life.

Abbas has contributed to this blind spot. He has not gone to great lengths to share much about his life with the public. He has written several books—the most famous was his memoir *Through Secret Channels*, about the process leading up to the signing of the Oslo Accords[1]—but they reveal little to nothing about him. His presidential website offers up a short biography, but it reveals very little about him that was not previously known.[2]

This dearth of information is not cause for alarm, but it is curious. Given the centrality of the Palestinian–Israeli conflict to the security of the rest of the Middle East, why don't we know more about the man who speaks on the Palestinians' behalf?

According to some Palestinian insiders, Abbas never saw himself as a leader. He was apparently quite happy acting as a midlevel functionary within the PLO. As such, he rarely took risks and rarely stood out among the hundreds of other cadres from the PLO bureaucracy. Thus, for years, observers may not have seen Abbas's life as particularly worthy of documenting.

"He was never even second or third tier," one Palestinian activist recalls. "He became the leader of the Palestinians by the process of elimination—literally. He was not considered worthy of being shot by the Israelis."[3]

To say the least, Abbas's road to leadership was a surprising one. And when he finally reached the top political spot in the Palestinian hierarchy, he appeared entirely unprepared. Still, he approached the job earnestly; for the first few years, he appeared to be genuinely committed to regional peace. However, a half-decade of political blood sport seemed to take its toll. Having learned the limitations of his position, Abbas appeared to be more interested in holding on to power than in leading. The result was a decline in Palestinian governance and a resurgence of the problems that Palestinians endured during the Arafat years.

MAHMOUD ABBAS WAS BORN in the town of Safed on March 26, 1935.[4] He was born at a particularly tumultuous time in Palestinian–Israeli history. It was at this point that both the Palestinian Arabs and the Jews began to engage in discernible campaigns of violence on behalf of their respective nascent nationalist movements. Abbas was born between bouts of violence in Mandatory Palestine—the Palestinian riots of 1929 and the Arab revolts of 1936–1939.

According to Abbas, until 1948, he lived in Safed with his parents and six siblings. His father worked in trade with the Bedouin tribes.[5] At the start of the 1948 Arab war against Israel, when Abbas was 13, the family fled to Syria.[6]

Whether the Abbas family was forced out of Safed or whether they left in fear of the growing violence is a matter of debate. In 2011, in an op-ed in the *New York Times,* Abbas claimed he "was forced to leave his home."[7] But in 2009, he provided another account in which fear of "Zionist terrorist organizations" was the motivating factor for his family's departure. He claimed that the Arabs of Safed "could feel that there was [Jewish] vengeance for the 1929 uprising. . . . When they felt that the balance [of power] had shifted, they decided to leave. The city in its entirety left, in order to protect their lives and their women's honor."[8]

Abbas contradicts himself yet again on his own website, noting that

> there was no worry in our minds at all that we would emigrate from our country, until the village Ain al-Zaitoun near our city fell to the Haganah gangs. They closed the western gates to the city, and there was not another way out, so the people of our city began considering taking out the children and women out of fear that they would be subjected to massacres. So my father decided to remove the children of the family, and I was the eldest of them. My two eldest brothers stayed with weapons, and my mother refused to leave them, so she decided to stay.[9]

Eventually, the whole family arrived in Syria, where, according to Abbas, they "took up shelter in a canvas tent provided to all the arriving refugees."[10] Abbas's website claims that they arrived in the "Syrian village of al-Batiha" in the Golan Heights but then traveled onward to Damascus where the family "did not know anyone." From there, they moved on to Irbid, Jordan, where a relative on his father's side hosted the family for one month. The family soon returned to Syria and lived briefly in the village of al-Tell near Damascus, "where the people donated housing, schools, and mosques to us." When the family ran out of money, they moved back to Damascus and rented a two-room house in a poor Kurdish neighborhood in northern Damascus. "We lived in one room with our parents, and my oldest brother, who was married, lived in the other with his children."[11]

Young Mahmoud Abbas joined the workforce to support his family—"all of us, without exception, because if we didn't work, we would not eat and we would not live."[12] He found a job laying floor tiles,[13] which included "carrying tiles and mixing cement and sand, and doing everything necessary to make one Syrian lira per day." He later found employment as a waiter.[14]

In 1954, at the age of 19, Abbas claims he helped found Syria's first Palestinian organization. According to Abbas, "We began working in the shadows, starting from the basic principle that the Arabs were talking about liberating Palestine, and this work could not be done without the participation of the Palestinians themselves." Abbas and his cohorts began to seek military training for Palestinians. In 1956, Abbas joined a Syrian military academy near Homs but apparently only stayed there for one month.[16]

In 1958, he earned a BA in law at Damascus University.[17] He also married his wife, Amina, that year.[18] Abbas then went "to work at an oil company" in the Persian Gulf (exactly where is not clear). Here, his life intersected with that of a young revolutionary named Yasser Arafat.

IN 1959, ABBAS JOINED FATAH, only one year after the group's founding in Kuwait. In the early years, Arafat and his cohorts created secret cells to carry out attacks against Israel. By 1965, Fatah began to carry out attacks. From a military standpoint, most of Fatah's early attacks were unimpressive.[19] Nevertheless, the guerrilla group continued to organize and was soon able to launch operations from every state bordering Israel. By the end of 1966, Arafat's faction claimed to have carried out 41 raids into Israeli territories.[20] A small war was under way.[21]

What role did Mahmoud Abbas play in these attacks? The long-standing narrative is that he did not take part in terrorist activities against Israel. But it must be noted that Fatah existed for one reason in the late 1950s and early 1960s: to carry out attacks against Israel.

Abbas's exact role within the Fatah faction remains something of a mystery, but there can be little doubt about the role that Fatah played in the Middle East. By 1967, the guerrilla group had carried out dozens of attacks against Israel. These attacks exacerbated regional tensions, as Egypt and Syria taunted the Israelis and threatened to invade Israel.

Seeking to gain an edge in what seemed to be an inevitable clash, the Israelis launched a preemptive attack on June 5, 1967, that both surprised and decimated the Egyptian, Jordanian, and Syrian militaries. In six days, Israel took control of East Jerusalem, the West Bank, the Gaza Strip, the Sinai Peninsula, and the Golan Heights. For the Arab world, Egypt's defeat was devastating. Egyptian president Gamal Abdel Nasser had been a heroic figure. His brash challenges to Israel were an inspiration to the region. But after Egypt's colossal failure on the battlefield, the Arab world began looking for new inspiration. The Palestinians, in particular, began to look to their own *fedayeen* (freedom fighters). Specifically, they began to look to Fatah.

In 1968, Arafat gained control of the PLO, a group that had been created by the Arab League in 1964. The PLO became an umbrella organization for a number of Palestinian guerrilla groups that rose from the ashes of the Arab defeat in 1967. The global Palestinian violence that followed, directed primarily by the PLO, was unprecedented.

AMID THESE SIGNIFICANT REGIONAL CHANGES, Abbas decided to make "resistance" a full-time profession. He recalls, "In 1969 I resigned from my job in Qatar and joined the brothers in Amman [Jordan], where my family and I lived, and assumed the tasks of mobilizing and organizing."[22] Little is known about him during this time. According to a brief biography published by the BBC, Abbas was known for his "clean and simple living."[23]

Jordan, at that time, had become the new headquarters for Arafat and the PLO. But it would not be for long. The Palestinian guerrillas were not welcomed there, particularly as they attacked Israel from Jordanian territory, eliciting Israeli reprisals. Increasingly, the Palestinians operated as a state within a state. Jordan's King Hussein had lost control of his own territory. The monarch attempted to rein in the group but found that Arafat was unwilling to yield. The result was the Black September war of 1970 that resulted in a victory for the monarchy but also in an estimated 3,000 Palestinian casualties.[24]

After Black September, Abbas returned to Damascus, although the majority of Palestinian guerrillas fighting under Arafat had moved to Lebanon, where they prepared for the next phase of the Palestinian struggle. Why Abbas chose not to remain with the bulk of the movement is not known. But he later recalled that his time in Syria allowed him to learn more about the enemy: "I devoted much of my time to learning about Israeli society. There had been a general phenomenon in the ranks of the Palestinian revolution, from the leadership to the [foot soldiers], which was a lack of attention paid to the composition of Israel, which we were fighting."[25]

But Abbas was not simply reading about Israel. During the early 1970s, by his own admission, he also raised funds to sustain Fatah's campaign against the Jewish state.[26] This is important to note because it marked a rather gruesome period of Palestinian violence, which included the 1972 massacre of Israeli athletes at the Munich Olympic Games and the 1973 attack on the Saudi embassy in Sudan that led to the murder of the US embassy's chief of mission. Years later, Mohammed Daoud Oudeh (Abu Daoud), the mastermind of the Munich Massacre, suggested that although Abbas did not know what the money was being spent on, he was responsible, in part, for raising the funds that financed the Munich Massacre.[27]

BY THE LATE 1970S, it appeared that Abbas had assumed a somewhat more important role within the PLO. News reports from that time period suggest that amid the PLO's drive for greater recognition, he was an interlocutor with Iraq, Syria,[28] Qatar,[29] Tunisia,[30] Morocco, Libya,[31] Saudi Arabia,[32] Yemen, and Kuwait.[33]

His diplomatic activity extended beyond the Arab world to the Soviet bloc, with documented meetings in Moscow[34] and Prague.[35] In February 1980, he visited Moscow, where he met with officials from the USSR Committee for Solidarity with the Countries of Asia and the Soviet-Palestinian Friendship Society.[36]

From what we can tell, he served as a bridge between the USSR and the PLO. In this capacity, he put a Palestinian imprint on the Soviets' anti-American propaganda. In 1980, he wrote in a Russian newspaper, "The USA is counteracting any plan directed at allowing the Palestinians to create their own independent state and acquire sovereignty," and he made sure to note that the Palestinians had a "reliable and faithful partner in this struggle—the Soviet Union."[37]

Among other initiatives, Abbas advocated for closer ties between Saudi Arabia, a patron of the Palestinians, and the Soviet Union.[38] This marriage was unlikely given that the Saudis already were heavily invested in sending mujahedin to fight the Red Army in Afghanistan.

Abbas also forged closer ties with Cuba, signing a "five-year work agreement on solidarity and cooperation" between Cuba and the Palestinian resistance. In fact, Abbas was once described as the president of the Cuba-Palestine Friendship Association.[39]

Although Abbas was never identified as a top leader of the PLO during this period, he could be described as a rising figure. He was a member of the Fatah Central Committee and later joined the PLO Executive Committee.[40] As Abbas notes on his presidential website, "I was not present at the national council meeting that chose me. . . . When I was consulted about it while in Moscow, I told them I refused. But when I returned to Damascus I found myself a member of the committee, and I did not participate in its work for two full years, until the [Israeli] invasion of Beirut."[41]

The Israelis invaded Lebanon in June 1982 in an effort to flush out the PLO. In his capacity as a PLO official, Abbas called on the Arab states to provide aid to Palestinian groups fighting against Israel.[42] When the Arab states sat out the war, Abbas began to prepare for the flight of the PLO from Lebanon to Tunisia. According to Abbas, "When the Israeli invasion happened and they imposed a blockade of Beirut, I realized that a phase had ended, and that a new phase was coming. I moved to Tunis, as the Tunisian government agreed to receive the [Palestinian] leadership, and it was a lifeline to the Palestinian revolution, which lived a fertile period of its life [there]."[43]

THE YEAR 1982 WAS AN IMPORTANT ONE for Abbas for other reasons. He defended his PhD in history at the Institute of Oriental Studies of the Russian Academy of Sciences in Moscow.[44] Abbas's scholarship, however, has long been a subject of controversy.

Abbas's thesis, titled "The Connection between the Nazis and the Leaders of the Zionist Movement 1933–1945," was published as a book in Amman in 1984: *The Other Side: The Secret Relationship Between Nazism and Zionism.*[45] According to Abbas, "The Zionist movement led a broad campaign of incitement against the

Jews living under Nazi rule, in order to arouse the government's hatred of them, to fuel vengeance against them, and to expand the mass extermination."[46] Additionally, Abbas wrote, "Following the war, word was spread that six million Jews were amongst the victims and that a war of extermination was aimed primarily at the Jews . . . The truth is that no one can either confirm or deny this figure. In other words, it is possible that the number of Jewish victims reached six million, but at the same time it is possible that the figure is much smaller—below one million."[47]

In addition, Abbas asserted that a "partnership was established between Hitler's Nazis and the leadership of the Zionist movement. . . . [the Zionists gave] permission to every racist in the world, led by Hitler and the Nazis, to treat Jews as they wish, so long as it guarantees immigration to Palestine."[48]

Finally, Abbas's book touted "a scientific study" of French Holocaust denier Robert Faurisson, who "denies that the gas chambers were for murdering people, and claims that they were only for incinerating bodies, out of concern for the spread of disease and infection in the region."[49] Notably, in February 2012, Iranian president Mahmoud Ahmadinejad—a public Holocaust denier—presented Faurisson an award for "courage, strength, and force."[50]

In later years, as Abbas was subject to increased Israeli and Western media scrutiny, he disavowed his own work. In 1995, Abbas told the Israeli daily *Maariv*, "Today I would not have made such remarks."[51] In 2003, as Bush touted him as Arafat's successor, he went a step further, saying, "The Holocaust was a terrible thing and nobody can claim I denied it."[52] In July 2011, as PA president, Abbas told a Dutch newspaper, "If they say six million, I say six million. . . . I do not deny the Holocaust."[53]

Remarkably, despite this record, he emerged as one of the PLO figures responsible for outreach to the Israelis and the Jewish

Diaspora. Beginning in the early 1980s, he began to engage with left-leaning Israelis.[54] As he later stated, PLO policy was "to create relations with Jewish forces inside Israel . . . who recognize the PLO and our right to self-determination and an independent state."[55] In March 1983, for example, Abbas led a Palestinian delegation that met with members of Israel's Communist Party in Prague.[56]

As Abbas later recalled, "We hoped that our meetings with the Peace Now movement and other Oriental [Sephardic] Jews as a group could form a bridge between Arabs and Israelis." Three major meetings took place, according to Abbas. The first took place on November 6, 1986, in Romania. The second was in Hungary on June 12, 1987, and the final meeting took place in Spain on July 5, 1987.[57] These were the building blocks for what eventually evolved into the peace process.

THE MEETINGS THAT ABBAS CONDUCTED with the Israelis and world Jewry did not take place in a vacuum. In the early 1980s, even as its cadres continued to carry out grisly terrorist attacks around the world, the PLO engaged in strategic outreach. As Abbas told *Voice of Palestine* radio, the goal was to reach out to "the peoples of Western Europe—and to the American people, and convince them of the justice of our cause. We must not leave the arena empty and let the Zionists and Western imperialism have their say in this arena. . . . Pressure must be applied to public opinion and this applies to America in particular."[58]

The Jewish outreach portfolio was, to say the least, one of the least coveted portfolios a PLO official might have, given the organization's animus toward the Jewish state. As one Palestinian insider notes, "He was a pioneer of this area. But it was a terrible portfolio. That said, it helped him gain a foothold in the leadership."[59]

In his own way, Abbas continued to advance within the Palestinian system. His rise was by no means meteoric. In 1983, he was selected to be a part of Fatah's financial supervision committee,[60] and in 1984, he was appointed head of the PLO's Arab and international relations portfolio (a position he held until 2000).[61] There was no doubt that Arafat still ran the show, while Abbas merely contributed to the cause when and where he was asked.

Abbas typically refrained from engaging in activities that tied him to Palestinian terrorism, but he did engage in some rare violent rhetoric. In October 1985, he told the Egyptian newspaper *Al-Gomhuria*, "The Palestine revolution would embark on a campaign of attacks against US interests wherever they might be, because the USA was not seeking peace but the capitulation of the PLO."[62] But relative to the rest of the organization, as Arafat biographers Janet and John Wallach noted, Abbas maintained "a low profile."[63]

MAHMOUD ABBAS'S PROFILE GOT A BOOST with the launch of the Palestinian–Israeli peace process. The process began on December 14, 1988, when the Tunis-based Arafat accepted UN Security Council Resolutions 242 and 338 and recognized Israel's right to exist.[64] This was the result of a series of direct and indirect meetings over the course of several years, during which Western powers sought to convince the PLO to renounce violence and begin serious negotiations for a two-state solution. Once Arafat relented, US secretary of state George Shultz announced that Washington was "prepared for a substantive dialogue with PLO representatives."[65]

Abbas was named as a representative to the United States to convey the official PLO view.[66] But his role in the Oslo process was far more complex. In 1989, he traveled from Jordan[67] to Moscow[68] to Toledo, Ohio,[69] in a diplomatic capacity. Judging from the press reports, it appeared that Abbas barely stayed in the same place for more than a night or two all year. Throughout this flurry of activity, he maintained his position on the PLO Executive Committee[70] and continued to serve as Fatah's first assistant secretary in charge of international affairs.[71]

By 1991, Abbas was leading the PLO's negotiating team with Israel.[72] This provided him significant influence with regard to the PLO's strategy.[73] As he recalls in his memoir, he soon "noticed that many Israeli officials wanted to meet [him], specifying [him] by name."[74] With his new and elevated profile, Abbas continued to travel frenetically around the globe, building support for the PLO's position in Moscow,[75] Egypt,[76] Prague,[77] and beyond.

But his diplomatic post did not mean that Abbas was predisposed toward a diplomatic solution. He began to draw lines in the sand before the negotiations even began. The Associated Press quoted him as saying, "Palestinians from East Jerusalem must participate in peace negotiations. . . . There can be no concession on this."[78] He also told the Egyptian newspaper *Al-Wafd,* "We shall not go to the peace conference unless the USA gives us guarantees about Jerusalem and settlements."[79]

The Palestinians and Israelis soon began to negotiate a framework for a two-state solution. And Mahmoud Abbas was a central player in this historic process. However, this did not translate to increased power for Abbas within the Palestinian matrix. This was confirmed when Yasser Arafat's plane went missing in a sandstorm in 1992.[80] As speculation raged over who would possibly succeed the PLO chief, Abbas was described in the Associated Press as having "little backing among the movement's hierarchy and military commanders.[81] Canada's *Globe and Mail* viewed him "more as a technocrat than [as] a leader."[82]

But such talk was premature. Arafat emerged from the wreckage and returned to center stage. He, along with Abbas, signed the Oslo Accords in September 1993. However, Abbas was not the first choice. Indeed, he signed the Declaration of Principles (DoP) because Palestinian foreign minister Farouk Kaddoumi refused to do so.[83] Nevertheless, Abbas was seen by some to be the brains behind the Oslo process. The *Guardian* described him as the one who had "engineered the deal."[84] Several Israeli figures believed Abbas should have received the Nobel Prize. It was Arafat who reportedly was adamant that Abbas not receive the honor alongside the longtime PLO leader.

During his speech at the signing ceremony on the White House lawn, Abbas proclaimed that the Palestinians had "come to this point because we believe that peaceful coexistence and cooperation are the only means for reaching understanding and for realizing the hopes of the Palestinians and the Israelis. The agreement we will sign reflects the decision we made in the Palestine Liberation Organization to turn a new page in our relationship with Israel."[85] He followed up with promises that as a result of the agreement, "terrorism will disappear from the Middle East."[86]

In 1994, with the peace process in full bloom, Abbas became the head of the PLO's Negotiating Affairs Department, a position he held until 2003.[87] In this capacity, in the eyes of the West, Abbas appeared as a reform-minded bureaucrat. He criticized Arafat for making decisions in an undemocratic fashion[88] and even called for the integration of a younger leadership.[89]

In March 1995, Abbas was appointed head of a committee to monitor the ongoing peace talks with Israel.[90] A few months later, Abbas signed, on behalf of the PLO, the Interim Agreement with Israel, also known as Oslo II.[91] However, as the Associated Press noted, Abbas "gradually disappeared from the political scene. . . . Insiders say he is avoiding involvement with Arafat's self-rule government, criticized for corruption and incompetence, in order to remain untainted in a future leadership bid."[92] Abbas apparently sought to establish himself as independent of Arafat's autocratic leadership style.

In *Through Secret Channels,* Abbas noted, "Leadership is not just status, privileges, and perks. It consists basically of a mixture of courage, an ability to sense the wishes of the masses, vision, and self-denial in serving the cause. Leadership does not mean self-preservation, consolidation of personal position, and basking in the comforts of a closed circle, but venturing out to do what is right."[93]

Whatever issues he may have had with the Palestinian leadership under Arafat, Abbas kept them out of the public eye and remained a key player in the evolution of the peace process with Israel, working side by side with Israeli politicians.[94] In a quiet and workmanlike manner, however, Abbas continued to fulfill various roles within the Palestinian bureaucracy. He also emerged as an unequivocal Palestinian voice opposed to violence against Israel.[95] This position, while popular in Israel and the United States, earned him enemies at home. In February 1997, three men were arrested for plotting his assassination.[96]

Abbas increasingly came to be viewed as the heir apparent. In January 1998, Arafat reportedly told President Bill Clinton, "When my time will come I will be replaced by my brother Abu Mazen."[97] This perception was held internationally, too. As French analyst Jean-François Legrain noted, "If the policy of negotiations with Israel and the United States continues, Abu Mazen . . . will undoubtedly have the best chance of succeeding Arafat as PLO chairman."[98]

Not surprisingly, Abbas was part of the official Palestinian delegation at the Middle East Peace Summit at Camp David in July 2000. But surprisingly, after all of the work he had invested in the bilateral talks, Abbas expressed his misgivings about even attending the summit.[99] One former Palestinian negotiator believes that this was more about Abbas's personal rivalries than his position regarding a permanent peace with Israel. He was perceived as adopting a position that was diametrically opposed to that of his political rivals, Mohammed Rachid and Gaza strong-man Mohammed Dahlan.[100]

IN JULY 2001, AFTER THE COLLAPSE of the peace summit at Camp David, when the prospects of peace with Israel had all but evaporated and the second intifada was still raging, Abbas was quoted as saying, "We did not miss an opportunity at all [at Camp David], but rather survived a trap which was laid for us." Central to his position was his refusal to relent on the "right of return" for Palestinian refugees displaced by the wars of 1948 and 1967. Abbas stated,

> We made our position clear: [Israel] must take historical responsibility and accept the right of return and [responsibility for compensation for both those who wish to return] and those who do not. For those who wish to return—compensation would be for the use of their property, and for those who don't wish to return—the compensation [will be for] the value of their property and sufferings. Additionally, [Israel] must pay compensation to the countries who host the refugees; this was all that we demanded.[101]

In rejecting the Israeli offer at Camp David, Arafat and Abbas appeared to be of one mind. However, it soon became clear that the two men were at odds with each other on other scores. In early 2001, after Abbas reportedly traveled to the United States to be treated for prostate cancer, he met with Secretary of State Colin Powell in Foggy Bottom and apparently did so without authorization from Arafat, who subsequently "froze" Abbas out. One Fatah official admitted that "Abu Mazen is sick of Arafat. . . . He has lost hope of any progress."[102]

Such reports seemed to imply that Abbas was the reformer, seeking to change the ossified and corrupt regime that Arafat had fostered in the West Bank and Gaza. Accordingly, Western officials began to hold up Abbas as a logical alternative to Arafat, who ultimately was responsible for spurning the US-brokered peace deal at Camp David. What appeared to be most important to Western decision makers were his calls for an end to military operations in the second intifada.

"What happened in these two years, as we see it now, is a complete destruction of everything we built,"[103] he said. He also condemned the Al-Aqsa Martyrs Brigades, the armed wing of his own Fatah faction, saying, "The position of the Palestinian leadership and the Fatah [movement] is that we are against the operations claimed by the Brigades."[104]

With the violence of the intifada raging and world leaders growing desperate to find a way out of the current impasse, Abbas, after years of fulfilling the role of a dutiful functionary in the shadow of Arafat, soon emerged as the viable alternative. Abbas had credibility among Palestinians because he had been with Fatah from the early years. But he also had credibility in the West because he was seen to have kept a distance from Fatah's terrorist activities. In addition, as the *New York Times* noted, Abbas had "good contacts with both Israelis and Americans."[105]

Something else helped pave the way for the rise of Mahmoud Abbas. As a result of widespread Palestinian nepotism, poor governance, and destructive behavior, donor states (led by the United States) pressured the PA during the intifada to bring in a prime minister for some oversight. Here again, due to the widely held perception that he stood against Arafat's ossified political machine, Abbas was a logical choice.

In March 2003, amid an American campaign to sideline Arafat due to his continued involvement in terrorism against Israel, the *New York Times* reported that diplomats were actively "pushing for the appointment of Mr. Abbas as part of an Israeli and American initiative to strip Mr. Arafat of his executive powers."

By mid-March, despite opposition from Arafat and his inner circle, Abbas was nominated as prime minister of the PA.[106]

IN APRIL 2003, ABBAS WAS SWORN IN as prime minister and interior
minister of the PA. Shortly thereafter, President Bush said he was
"pleased with the new leader of the Palestinian Authority."[107] But
this did not mean that Arafat was defeated; the longtime PLO
chief, using all of the formidable political tools at his disposal,
did whatever he could to ensure that Abbas was sidelined when it
came to foreign policy, negotiating with the Israelis, or Palestinian
security issues.[108]

Not surprisingly, given Washington's ongoing feud with Arafat, the Bush administration openly threw its weight behind Abbas. As Powell noted, the White House believed that a stronger
Abbas would pave the way for "a much more active American
engagement" in the Middle East, specifically peace talks between
Israel and the Palestinians.[109] To this end, on April 30, 2003, the
Bush administration officially launched a formal policy designed
to put the peace process back on track: the roadmap.[110]

In June 2003, the New York Times editorial board declared
that Abbas was "the most important reason there is renewed hope
for progress in the Middle East." As a result, the paper called on
the Arab states to "strengthen the new Palestinian prime minister,
Mahmoud Abbas."[111] This seemed all the more wise as Abbas
continued to call for an end to the intifada, explicitly calling for
a cessation of Hamas and Islamic Jihad attacks against Israel.[112]
As former Palestinian official Ghaith al-Omari recalls, "The anti-
Arafat thing was serious. There was good reason to be optimistic
about him [Abbas] at the time."[113]

The Bush administration rewarded Abbas's calls for an end to
the intifada with plans for new financial packages to bolster the
prime minister's authority.[114] In July 2003, Abbas met with President Bush, who declared him to be a man of "vision and courage

and determination."[115] Abbas's visit to the White House was the highest-ranking visit by a Palestinian official under the Bush administration. Arafat never received an invitation.

Arafat refused to tolerate this challenge. He turned the PLO power structure against his prime minister, making it virtually impossible for Abbas to achieve anything short of drawing praise from the West. As a result, in July 2003, Abbas resigned from the Fatah Central Committee, and a few months later, in September, he resigned as prime minister.[116] Ahmed Qurei, aka Abu Ala, widely regarded as an Arafat loyalist, succeeded Abbas.

In the months to come, Abbas was clearly sidelined. Arafat ensured that he was blocked from any major PLO decisions. As al-Omari recalls, "He had no allies during his time out of office."[117]

The *New York Times* reported that Abbas's decision to resign "stunned Bush administration officials . . . and raised fresh questions about the administration's strategy of trying to marginalize Yasser Arafat."[118] One administration official conceded, "We knew that this process could lead to a train wreck, but it's the only path worth pursuing."[119] But as Bush later stated, "Prime Minister Abbas was undermined at all turns by the old order—that meant Mr. Arafat."[120]

BUT ARAFAT WOULD NOT OBSTRUCT Abbas for long. As the intifada dragged on, and Arafat continued to have a hand in the violence, the Israelis pinned him down in his presidential Muqata compound in Ramallah. He remained there, surrounded by Israeli tanks and troops, from September 2002 to October 2004. The standoff ended when Arafat fell gravely ill and required medical attention. He was taken to Paris for medical treatment in late October 2004 and died there of mysterious circumstances on November 11, 2004.

Following Arafat's death, Abbas was elected head of the PLO. In addition, the Fatah Revolutionary Council endorsed him as

Fatah's presidential candidate. He was certainly not the most popular man among the Palestinian leadership, but he was the logical
choice. Now that he headed the PLO, it seemed only natural that
he become the official leader of the Palestinians' caretaker government. On January 9, 2005, Abbas was elected as president of the
PA, winning 62 percent of the votes.[121]

Reports, however, suggest that "the election was plagued by
inconsistent voter lists, limited media access, and curbs on freedom
of movement."[122] Nevertheless, the election was widely viewed in
the West as a victory for peace and better Palestinian governance.
Bush affirmed that the United States stood "ready to help the Palestinian people realize their aspirations" and was heartened to see
Abbas, the man he had backed as an alternative to Arafat, win
at the polls.[123] In his victory speech, Abbas committed himself to
Bush's vision: "Let us start implementing the roadmap . . . and in
parallel let us start discussing the permanent-status issues so that
we can end, once and for all, the historic conflict between us."[124]

Abbas addressed the question of violence head on. But doubts
about the PA's governance lingered. After all, it was the same PA.
As Elliott Abrams recalls, after Abbas was elected, there was not
a sense in Washington that "now is when to go to [Abbas] and say
'Let's root out the corruption.' That was not the stance of the US
government. . . . On corruption we never had a program. We did
not have a five-point plan."[125]

While that may have been a lost opportunity, Washington's
concerns about Abbas's ability to lead may have trumped concerns
about governance. Filling the void left by Arafat was no easy task.
Arafat had established almost absolute control over every aspect
of the PA.[126] He had created short chains of command that all
reported to him directly. He had bought the loyalty of his subor-
dinates through a patronage system which ensured that his people
were paid well for their allegiances. Moreover, he had created an
intricate network of rival security and intelligence operations that

competed for power and budgets that only he could bestow.[127] This pyramid scheme of corruption, fostered over nearly four decades, began to crumble without the man at the top. It was virtually impossible for Abbas to step in and make sense of the mess that his predecessor had created.

But the problems weren't only financial. Abbas was still working to bring all of Fatah's violent factions, spawned during the intifada, back under his control. The younger generation of Fatah fighters, who for more than a decade had sought to share the power and patronage systems, was difficult to rein in. Abbas was also forced to contend with disgruntled old-guard members who had lost power and prestige with the collapse of the Oslo peace process.[128]

As part of the Fayyad program, the PA had already successfully consolidated a number of the security forces. Following the death of Arafat, the Bush administration created the office of US Security Coordinator (USSC) for Israel and the PA to help reshape the security forces that had been operating under, and were largely loyal to, Arafat and Arafat alone. The USSC was at first headed by Lieutenant General William "Kip" Ward and then by Lieutenant General Keith Dayton, whose name became the most closely associated with the effort. "Dayton's Army," as it was known, was widely regarded as another successful reform within the PA. These forces were trained in Jordan and deployed in the PA.[129] The overall effort satisfied Fayyad's reformist agenda while also yielding a benefit to the Israelis and the United States, who were working to clamp down on the violence of the intifada and the war on terror, respectively. This also served to strengthen Abbas.

ABBAS, HOWEVER, STRUGGLED in other areas. Arafat had been a revolutionary figure who inspired his people and embodied the Palestinian cause. He wore military fatigues to business meetings, along with his signature *keffiyeh*, which when draped over his shoulder took on the shape of pre-1948 Palestine. He was "Mr. Palestine." By contrast, Abbas was mild-mannered. He wore a suit and tie and carried with him the air of a Western politician. It is safe to say that the Palestinian street was not entirely sold on him.

8

The Rise of Hamas

IN NOVEMBER 2005, WITH ABBAS SEEMINGLY WELL ENTRENCHED IN HIS
new position, Salam Fayyad announced his resignation as finance
minister. The economist had scored some modest successes with
his program of transparency and good governance. And now,
with elections approaching in January 2006, Fayyad sought to
throw his hat into the ring.

A byproduct of the Bush Doctrine, a policy of democracy promotion forwarded by the US president, Palestinian elections were
to be the first real test of democracy in the Middle East after the
United States toppled Saddam Hussein's Iraq. It was an opportunity for Palestinians of all political stripes to celebrate.

Longtime PLO official Hanan Ashrawi joined forces with
Fayyad in December 2005 to launch a party called Third Way (*al-
Tariq al-Thalith*). The party platform was consistent with Fayyad's overall approach to governance: land for peace with Israel,
rejection of violence, rejection of Islamic law (shari'a) in Palestinian society, and an overhaul of the Palestinian security apparatus
under a central command. The name of the party said it all; it was
a response to the poor governance of Fatah and the violence of
Hamas. It was a third alternative.[1]

The elections that followed were, indeed, free and fair. How-ever, Fayyad's down-to-earth approach to governance and trans-parency could not compete with the political forces at work in the PA. Fayyad's party captured just 2 out of the 132 seats in the Palestinian parliament. But Fayyad's was not the only party to underperform. Abbas's Fatah party also failed to gain a majority. Hamas captured the biggest bloc, setting off a crisis in Palestinian society that endures to this day.

"HAMAS SWEEPS PALESTINIAN ELECTIONS, Complicating Peace Ef-forts in Mideast," read the *Washington Post* headline on January 26, 2006.[2] That was an understatement. More than 1 million Pal-estinians voted. In the end, Hamas took 76 of the 132 seats (74 under the Hamas banner, plus independents), granting it the right, by Palestinian law, to forge a government.[3]

Critics immediately lashed out at the Palestinian people for electing terrorists to power. But a legitimate argument can be made that West Bankers and Gazans alike were simply looking for new leaders after suffering for years under an ossified regime. Hamas ran under the banner of "change and reform," and its message resonated for a reason. It was impossible to remove the problem of poor governance from the equation. As Elliott Abrams notes, President George W. Bush came to believe that "Palestin-ians voted for a party that looked clean. It was Hamas against a party that they knew was dirty, Fatah."[4]

Since Hamas's inception in late 1987, Palestinians of all stripes increasingly came to view it not only as a violent organization committed to confronting Israel (which Palestinians increasingly found appealing) but also as a political movement that refused to take part in what was commonly seen as an irredeemable Pal-estinian political system. The widely held perception in the West Bank and Gaza Strip, handcrafted by the movement's leaders, was that Hamas was a pious movement that was impervious to

corruption. Hamas accomplished this by portraying the PLO re-
turnees (*a'idoun*)—the Fatah figures who returned from exile to
the Palestinian territories after entering into the Oslo Accords
with Israel—as tainted by the riches they accumulated while in
exile in Jordan, then in Lebanon, and then in Tunisia.[5]

Concurrently, Hamas worked hard to portray itself as the political opponent of the PLO. Hamas was unequivocal in its rejection of the PLO-led peace process with Israel. And while the
PLO continued to fend off allegations that its leaders were growing rich off international donor funds, Hamas continued to cultivate a wide social network, built with money that came from
the Muslim world, to provide much-needed services to the Palestinian people. Through a preexisting social network cultivated
by Hamas founder Sheikh Ahmed Yassin, Hamas controlled as
much as 40 percent of the mosque network in Gaza.[6] So, as the
PLO tried to deflect criticism stemming from the misallocation of
resources, Hamas provided monetary support to the families of
suicide bombers while also providing food to needy families on
holidays.

But the rise of Hamas ran deeper than that. The movement
represented a powerful amalgam of Islamism and nationalism—
both of which appealed to broad swaths of Palestinians. Formed
as a breakaway faction of the Muslim Brotherhood movement in
the early days of the first intifada, Hamas was openly challenging
the political primacy of the PLO, which purported to be the "sole
legitimate representative" of the Palestinian people.

On August 18, 1988, Hamas published its covenant, a document of 36 articles calling for a synthesis of Islamism and Palestinian nationalism. It envisioned Palestine as a state run according to
Islamic law and declared that "*jihad* becomes a duty binding to all
Muslims."[7] Further, it stated that Palestinians should not cede one
inch of land. By simply publishing this document, Hamas broadcast an Islamist vision that openly challenged the PLO charter.

Ties between Hamas and the Fatah-backed PLO deteriorated. Arafat's men rightly viewed Hamas as entering into competition with them. Before long, sporadic conflicts erupted between Hamas and Fatah partisans.[8] Arafat, in fact, described Hamas members as ants that his forces could crush.[9] But the longtime PLO chief was not in a position of strength. Because the PLO leaders were in exile in Tunisia, they were obviously not able to be on the ground, standing shoulder to shoulder with the rock-throwing masses. In all likelihood, this prompted Arafat to seek a means to solidify his position of leadership among the Palestinians.

In December 1988, Arafat tacitly recognized Israel's right to exist. Almost overnight, Arafat was transformed from the leader of a terrorist movement to elder statesman. But Arafat's move was not without its risks. While Arafat set out to demonstrate the viability of the PLO as a government for the Palestinian people, Hamas tapped into the general frustration that was brewing on the Palestinian street. West Bankers and Gazans alike interpreted Arafat's recognition of Israel as a sign of weakness. Some questioned why the PLO had not succeeded in expelling Israel from the territories by force. Hamas portrayed these failures as an outgrowth of the PLO's secular ideology, offering up Islamism as an alternative.

As early as May 1991, analysts observed that the Palestinian political rivalry was intensifying.[10] One academic report noted that sporadic clashes portended "a dangerous stage in the relations between the two groups, and instilled fear among Palestinians that such violence was a prelude to a Palestinian civil war."[11]

AFTER THE PLO AND ISRAEL inked the Oslo Accords in 1993, Hamas entered into a new phase of "resistance." In April 1994, Hamas launched its first successful suicide car bombing in the Israeli town of Afula, killing eight and wounding dozens.[12] After the bombing, both the United States and Israel called on the newly formed PA to crack down on Hamas. Arafat obliged, only too happy to curb the growth of his political rivals. But as one journalist from the Israeli newspaper *Haaretz* noted, "A delicate balance between the two forces was upset, setting in motion a chain of events that verged on all-out civil war."[13]

While Hamas attacks against Israel intensified, so did the internecine fighting. In the fall of 1994, one firefight between Hamas and PA forces left at least 13 people dead and 200 wounded in Gaza. According to hospital officials, more than 20 of the wounded victims had been shot with Soviet-model automatic rifles—the kind carried by Palestinian police. Eight people had apparently been shot point-blank in the head.[14] After the altercation, the PA distributed leaflets charging that Hamas was attempting to establish "a government within a government."[15]

As Hamas opposition to the Oslo peace process intensified, the PA continued to crack down. PA forces illegally detained and even tortured Hamas members.[16] The PA also raided Hamas mosques and charities to weaken the Islamist group's base of support.[17] However, it became clear that Hamas was resilient and not easily dismantled.

Interestingly, PA documents indicate that Arafat attempted to lure in members of Hamas through the same financial incentives he used to control his own cadres. He had a number of Hamas leaders on his payroll.[18] When Hamas leader Ahmed Yassin was released from an Israeli prison in 1997, Arafat even sought to buy him off with a Land Rover and a Palestinian diplomatic passport.[19]

The perception of an ossified and corrupt PA, however, was one of Hamas's greatest strengths. The Islamist group went so far as to drop leaflets throughout the territories, exposing alleged business ventures between PLO figures and Israel. This was a damning allegation, implying that business interests might trump the interests of the Palestinian people.[20]

In the end, the most effective weapon the PA had against Hamas was force. In March 1996, after four Hamas suicide bombings killed 57 Israelis and threatened to destroy the peace process, Arafat's strongman in Gaza, Mohammed Dahlan, made "frequent raids on homes" of Hamas members.[21] As one Hamas leader described, it was a campaign that involved "pursuit, arrests, assassinations, dismantling of institutions, and so on."[22] The PA security services, with the aid of Israeli and US intelligence, rounded up and jailed hundreds of Hamas operatives.[23] One journalist reported that some Palestinians "were held for two, three, four months or more, without seeing a lawyer, without being tried, without charges being brought against them."[24] This gave rise to the popular notion that Arafat's government was collaborating with Israel against Hamas and others as a means to ensure that the international donor funds continued to flow.[25]

THIS DYNAMIC CAME TO AN ABRUPT HALT in September 2000, when Arafat launched the second intifada. After rejecting an American-brokered peace plan, he released hundreds of Hamas operatives whom PA security services had previously held in PA jails.[26] Once they were back out on the streets, Arafat's forces carried out joint operations with them.[27] The PLO's "Radio Palestine" called on Palestinians to take to the streets, while Hamas dropped leaflets with the same message.[28] It appeared that the two factions had finally found common ground: violence against Israel.

But this was not an alliance. As Hamas saw it, the intifada had created more favorable conditions for its continued growth. As one Palestinian journalist noted, "Hamas had no intention of recognizing the PLO, and what was really going on was that it was trying to blaze its own trail to power."[29] As the violence raged, even in the fog of war, one Israeli journalist warned that the "strength of the radical Islamic organization Hamas seems to be growing."[30] Another journalist reported "concerns among senior PA officials over the possibility that Hamas [was] trying to reap political capital among traditionally-minded Palestinians."[31]

Against the backdrop of the intifada, internal tensions continued, with regular reports of internecine violence on the Palestinian streets. In October 2001, clashes between PLO loyalists and Hamas led to the deaths of five Palestinians.[32] PA security forces continued to conduct raids against Hamas assets in Gaza. Arafat placed Yassin under house arrest, prompting even more street violence.[33]

According to documents seized in the Gaza Strip by the Israel Defense Forces (IDF), Hamas appeared to welcome these developments. Leaders noted that the PA had "collapsed, its infrastructure has been destroyed, and it suffers rifts and divisions . . . in short, the PA has been dismantled and must be reassembled according to new conditions."[34] Hamas also appeared to have realized that every time it attacked an Israeli target, the violence elicited an Israeli military response. To be sure, the attacks often weakened Hamas. But, just as often, Israel retaliated against Arafat and the PA infrastructure, such as police stations and government buildings. In other words, Israel's military responses weakened the PA more than it weakened Hamas.

It is also important to note that the PA lost control of parts of the government. Notably, Hamas had an iron grip on the charity committees in the Religious Endowments Ministry.[35] Reports also indicated that Hamas had penetrated the PA's education ministry and even the PA's security services. Hamas was even able to gain critical intelligence about the PA's counterterrorism operations by bribing several officials, helping Hamas operatives escape arrest. According to one PA intelligence document, Hamas had "begun to constitute a real threat to the PA's political vision, its interests, presence, and influence."[36]

With the PA in crisis, Arafat's decision to reject peace with Israel had clearly backfired. Realizing this, he attempted to seize on the proposal by the Middle East Quartet that was to jump-start the peace process with the goal of establishing a Palestinian state in 2005. The key to putting the roadmap in play, however, was a cessation of violence. As Palestinian legislator Ziad Abu Amr noted, Hamas soon realized it could "play the role of the spoiler."[37] In November 2002, Hamas carried out a suicide bombing on a Jerusalem bus, killing 11 Israelis and wounding 50 others. The roadmap was immediately derailed.

In Gaza, tensions reached new heights as clashes continued between the two factions.[38] Arafat issued warnings to Hamas in the form of leaflets, but Hamas appeared unconcerned.[39] By 2003, Hamas politburo chief Khaled Meshal gloated, "The PLO met Hamas in the beginning with total disregard, then cast doubt on its authenticity, then it endeavored to belittle it and refuse to recognize it, then it went into a state of open confrontation followed by an attempt to contain it."[40] Senior Hamas official Mahmoud al-Zahar went a step further, boasting that his faction was poised to take over leadership of the Palestinians, "politically, financially, [and] socially."[41]

WHATEVER GAINS HAMAS THOUGHT it might have made were short-lived, however. Israel soon embarked on a systematic campaign designed to weaken Hamas. Sheikh Ahmed Yassin, the wheelchair-bound founder and spiritual guide for Hamas, was killed on March 22, 2004, when an Israeli helicopter launched an air strike while he was leaving a Gaza City mosque.[42] The attack came as no surprise. Israeli prime minister Ariel Sharon called Yassin the "mastermind of Palestinian terror" and a "mass murderer who is among Israel's greatest enemies."[43]

The Israelis then assassinated Yassin's successor, Abdel Aziz al-Rantisi. In December 1992, Israel had deported Rantisi to southern Lebanon, along with some 400 other Hamas members. After his return the following year, PA security forces regularly detained him for his outspoken criticism of the ongoing peace process with Israel. Rantisi went into hiding after Yassin's demise, fearing his own assassination, but on April 17, 2004, about four weeks after he had been named the leader of Hamas, an Israeli helicopter killed Rantisi with missiles shot at his car.[44] Other Hamas leaders were forced underground, fearing for their lives.[45]

The *New York Times* speculated in 2004 that "each Israeli killing only seems to enhance the popularity of Hamas on the street."[46] But what would buoy Hamas even more was a plan, hatched by Ariel Sharon in December 2003, for a unilateral "disengagement" process that would extricate Israel from the hostile Gaza Strip. The former IDF general believed that Israel stood to gain little by protecting some 9,000 Jews living in the coastal enclave. Sharon was also certain that Israel would face a demographic threat, particularly if the Jewish state one day included the densely populated Gaza Strip, then home to some 1.5 million people.[47]

In a public speech, Sharon announced, "The purpose of the Disengagement Plan is to reduce terror as much as possible, and grant Israeli citizens the maximum level of security. The process of disengagement will lead to an improvement in the quality of life, and will help strengthen the Israeli economy."[48] Nearly two years later, in August and September 2005, Israeli troops evacuated the Gaza Strip.

In retrospect, unilateral separation was a strategic mistake for the Israelis. It only made Hamas stronger. The group could manufacture explosives and procure weapons more easily without needing to worry about possible raids by Israeli troops. Moreover, as then Israeli Likud party figure Benjamin Netanyahu noted, the withdrawal amounted to a defeat for Israel and an overall victory for Hamas because "it could claim that terror works."[49]

Hamas leaders also realized that their fighters could easily continue to kill Israeli civilians and damage property by launching

rockets and mortars into Israeli territory. As such, Palestinian terrorists in Gaza indiscriminately launched some 3,400 Qassam
rockets into Israel between 2005 and 2007. Many hit the Israeli
town of Sderot, killing a few people, wounding many others, and
causing millions of dollars in damage.[50]

Finally, disengagement strengthened Hamas vis-à-vis its secular PLO rivals. With the Israeli security barrier surrounding Gaza,
and with the Palestinian territories separated from one another,
it's possible that the Israeli withdrawal planted the seed among
Hamas leaders that the Islamist group had the potential to govern
Gaza on its own. After all, Hamas's social infrastructure had already helped the organization establish dominance there.

ANOTHER MAJOR BOOST for Hamas was the death of Yasser Arafat
in November 2004. He had been the unquestioned leader of the
Palestinian people since 1967, if not before. Mahmoud Abbas, by
contrast, was not a born leader. He failed to capture the hearts
and minds of the Palestinian people. He attempted to assert himself but was instead weakened by "incitement waged against him
by Hamas and several other groups."[51]

More to the point, Abbas had a mess to clean up. The Palestinian territories were in disarray after five years of low-level
conflict and a decade of financial mismanagement. The PA, under
his leadership, was officially responsible for the well-being of its
inhabitants. And all was not well in the Palestinian territories.
Thus, as Abbas struggled to gain a grip on the apparatus that
Arafat had craftily controlled, Hamas took the opportunity to re-
bound from its losses, stock up on its weapons, and train its ranks
for future battles. This dynamic undoubtedly benefited Hamas for
the challenges ahead.

Hamas also appeared to have recognized that despite the
military defeats it had suffered at the hands of the Israelis—
or perhaps because of them—its popularity was still strong.

Thanks to an impressive welfare system of mosques, charitable associations, sports clubs, and other services, Hamas was in an advantageous position to take part in the Palestinian elections planned for early 2006. And while Hamas had refused to enter into the political process in the past—citing a rejection of the Oslo process that had created the PA—it appeared that Hamas had decided to jump in.[52]

There are many theories as to how Hamas positioned itself for the electoral victory that followed. According to Palestinian journalist Zaki Chehab, after Hamas announced its intention to compete in the election, the group instructed voters to trick pollsters by not revealing their electoral choices.[53] According to this strategy, if Hamas were not forecast as the winner of the elections, Fatah would not work as hard to compete, feeling safe in the belief that another electoral victory was at hand.

Hamas also sought to influence the Palestinian people through its media network. In addition to its print and Internet publications, Hamas broadcast its message through its Gaza-based terrestrial channel, al-Aqsa Television. Programming on this channel included messages from Hamas leaders calling for jihad, songs of incitement to murder, glorification of "martyrdom," videos of Hamas gunmen, and even promises of Israel's destruction.[54]

But the most obvious explanation for Hamas's success at the polls was the economic mismanagement that the PLO and Fatah had presided over for years. As journalist Khaled Abu Toameh noted,

> For many years the foreign media did not pay enough attention to stories about corruption in the Palestinian areas or about abuse of human rights or indeed to what was really happening under the Palestinian Authority. They ignored the growing frustration on the Palestinian street as a result of mismanagement and abuse by the PLO of its monopoly on power.[55]

Similarly, Bassem Eid, head of the Palestinian Human Rights Monitoring Group, noted that "everybody knows that Hamas is just climbing on such corruption of the Palestinian Authority. . . . I think that Hamas is getting more and more supporters, while the Palestinians start in the street talking about the Palestinian corruption."[56] Rashid Khalidi also noted that "the PA itself, thoroughly dominated by Fatah, was widely accused of corruption, featherbedding, and nepotism, accusations that have much substance in fact."[57]

In the lead-up to the January elections, Hamas hammered home that it was the clean governance ticket. It was a matter of message repetition. The movement ran ads that accused Fatah of corruption, nepotism, bribery, chaos, and stealing.[58] Leaders of the movement held dinners during which they promised their constituents that they would battle corruption.[59] In December, when Hamas announced its list for the West Bank town of Tulkarem, one of the candidates explicitly vowed to fight corruption.[60] At an event in Gaza, Hamas leader Ismail Haniyeh said his organization had three primary intentions in the election, one of which was fighting corruption.[61] Another Hamas leader, Sheikh Said Siyam, said that Hamas "will enter the PA process in order to make decisions, fight corruption and fix PA institutions."[62] A statement released by Hamas in late December 2005 said that "lawlessness, illegal operations, and corruption do not represent the Palestinians, but they are an exterior phenomenon that aims to benefit Israel."[63]

In January, down the final stretch, one Hamas candidate said that the movement was seeking to "develop civil society institutions and combat corruption, government favoritism, and unemployment."[64] Similarly, a spokesperson for the Popular Resistance Committees called on Palestinians to vote for Hamas because it would change the "ten years of corruption and bring honest and good people to the PLC."[65]

According to the Congressional Research Service, "Hamas' anti-corruption message during the parliamentary election was apparently successful and many reports and exit polls cited anti-corruption as a motivation to vote for Hamas."[66] Polling conducted by the Palestinian Center for Policy and Survey Research (PCPSR) on the second day of elections found that "71 percent of those who considered corruption the most important consideration in voting voted for Hamas and only 19 percent for Fatah and 11 percent for the other lists." According to the PCPSR, 25 percent of voters made corruption the number one issue.[67]

One Fatah activist, Nasser Abdel Hakim, railed against Fatah's old-guard leadership, as he said that the "people punished us because of mismanagement and the corruption by the mafia that came from Tunis."[68] Interestingly, just weeks before the elections, Abbas ordered the suppression of an internal report which revealed that the PA had possibly lost billions of dollars as a result of financial mismanagement.[69]

The lack of proper management and transparency had caught up with the PA. More to the point, it had caught up with the leaders of the PLO and Fatah, marking a decline in power and leaving a leadership vacuum that would not easily be filled.

9

Civil War

"I HAVE MADE IT VERY CLEAR," GEORGE W. BUSH STATED SOLEMNLY ON January 26, 2006, "that a political party that articulates the destruction of Israel as part of its platform is a party with which we will not deal." He added, "I don't see how you can be a partner in peace if you advocate the destruction of a country as part of your platform."[1]

The American president's position was not a surprise. The Hamas victory in the 2006 Palestinian elections was an embarrassing black eye to US democratization efforts in the region. The election results were also a black eye for the Bush Doctrine, which was designed to promote democracy throughout the Arab world. The US president viewed free elections and transparent governance as a means to combat the ideology of Islamism, which continued to spread unabated and inspire violence against the United States and the West. Obviously, this was not the outcome the administration had been hoping for or expecting.

The US decision to back the Palestinian elections was a calculated one. It was due, in no small part, to polling data that essentially guaranteed a Fatah victory. The data were gathered primarily by pollster Khalil Shiqaqi's Palestinian Center for Policy and Survey Research (PCPSR), which conducted studies of Palestinian opinion in June, September, and December 2005. The data indicated that Fatah's support among Palestinians ranged from 44 percent to 50 percent, while Hamas support was said to range from 32 to 33 percent.[2] "With each new Shiqaqi poll," wrote analyst Martin Kramer, "U.S. policymakers grew more lax when it came to setting conditions for Hamas participation."[3]

In retrospect, US reliance on these polls was a grave error. The notion that Palestinian voters would simply ignore the mounting governance problems that had been dogging the Fatah leadership was simply not realistic. There had simply been too many scandals. The PA was in bad shape. In even worse shape was the Fatah faction that ruled it.

Another grave error was to ignore the implications of the elections. Elliott Abrams recalls that the elections made it abundantly clear to Washington of the "need to clean up Fatah or they're doomed. But we didn't. We didn't get out the broom and have a big, organized program to force, to lead, to persuade Fatah to clean itself up. . . . It's really striking that we did not adopt that as a significant policy goal."[4]

FATAH MANAGED TO WIN just 45 seats out of a possible 132. These dismal results were a clear sign that without Yasser Arafat, the party had little appeal to the Palestinians of the West Bank and Gaza Strip. To be sure, Hamas's unwavering "resistance" ideology was appealing to some, but there could be no doubt that many Palestinians simply wanted change.

One thing did not change, however. Hamas and Fatah continued to challenge each other. Indeed, the contest did not end with the elections. In late January 2006, Fatah and Hamas members clashed in front of the Palestinian parliament building in Ramallah.[5] Tensions between the two factions soon spread, continuing regularly in the weeks and months that followed. According to a 104-page report issued by the Palestinian Center for Human Rights (PCHR), immediately after the elections, there were reports of "attacks on public institutions; armed personal and clan disputes; attacks on international organizations . . . armed conflicts between security services and armed groups; and attacks on officials." Over 15 months, according to the PCHR, 350 Palestinians were killed, including 20 children and 18 women, while 1,900 were wounded. The nongovernmental organization also estimated that 248 Palestinians were killed "by an escalation in the state of lawlessness."[6]

The first serious clashes, which foretold the real possibility of a civil war, were reported in mid-April 2006, when hundreds of Fatah activists marched to Gaza's parliament compound, throwing stones and shattering windows in a government building. Elsewhere in the territories, tens of thousands of Fatah members marched through the streets, denouncing Hamas, setting tires ablaze, and waving the Fatah party's flag.[7]

Tensions escalated on April 22, 2006, when hundreds of students representing the Hamas and Fatah factions at Gaza's al-Azhar University and the Islamic University threw stones and homemade grenades at one another. Fifteen people were wounded, two seriously.[8] Two weeks later, at least nine Palestinians were wounded in two days of fighting between the two rival factions in the Gaza Strip. At least four children were wounded.[9] In another incident, Hamas fighters launched a shoulder-fired missile at a Fatah vehicle, killing two.[10]

The violence grew worse after the creation of the "Executive Force" (EF), a Hamas military unit under the leadership of Hamas interior minister Said Sayyam. For weeks, Sayyam had complained that forces loyal to Fatah and the PA were not following Hamas directives, despite the fact that Hamas was now the faction that had been tapped by the Palestinians to govern the PA. Abbas, it was reported, had ordered Gaza's police officers to stay home in exchange for receiving their salaries as a means to deny Hamas the power that it had earned at the ballot box.[11] Replacing the PA forces, the EF became an authoritarian tool that Hamas used to extend its influence beyond that of its trained terrorist fighting squad, the Izz al-Din al-Qassam Brigades. As one new recruit noted, "I'm not Qassam, but I'm in the police force. It's considered *jihad*."[12]

When Hamas deployed the EF, Fatah viewed the move as a direct challenge to Abbas's PA forces. This again raised the specter of an all-out civil war. Fierce clashes erupted for nearly an hour between the two sides on May 22, including a firefight in front of the Palestinian Legislative Council building in Gaza.[13]

The following month, more brutal fighting was reported between Hamas fighters (including the Al-Qassam Brigades) and Fatah fighters (including the Al-Aqsa Martyrs Brigades). Assaults launched by the two opposing factions against each other continued throughout the month, with reports of abductions, grenade explosions, and rocket fire.[14]

To be sure, Fatah scored some victories in these street battles, but the impact was fleeting. There was no denying the fact that Fatah had lost the election, and now it was being openly challenged in the streets by Hamas.

ARMED CLASHES CONTINUED between Hamas and Fatah throughout the summer and fall of 2006. By October, the violence had spread throughout the West Bank towns of Ramallah, Nablus, Jericho, and Hebron.[15]

In December 2006, Hamas accused Fatah of attempting to assassinate Hamas's Ismail Haniyeh in an attack at the Rafah crossing in Gaza that killed one of his bodyguards. In the war of words that followed, Hamas claimed that Mohammed Dahlan, a senior Fatah strongman in Gaza, was behind the attack. Violence again erupted between the two factions, leading to 20 injuries.[16]

Seeking to regain control, Abbas called for an early election to bring down the Hamas government. Fatah activists in Gaza and the West Bank celebrated this political maneuver, taking to the streets and firing celebratory machine-gun bursts into the air. In response, Hamas accused Abbas of launching a coup against its democratically elected government.[17]

Throughout this period, Hamas complained that the Fatah-backed PA had refused to engage with it on issues of governance.[18] There had also been reports of tensions between the Hamas appointees and Fatah functionaries in various ministries, as well as fragmentation within the security services. Indeed, each faction had developed its own militias.[19] In retrospect, Abbas's call for a new government was probably justifiable. The political tensions that characterized the Hamas–Fatah power struggle had paralyzed the Palestinian legislature.

Meanwhile, violence worsened between the two groups in January and February 2007, leading to the perception that the West Bank and Gaza had become more lawless than ever. Specifically, Hamas carried out a string of abductions of Fatah and PA figures. Those who were kidnapped were often beaten. In some cases, "limbs were fired at to cause permanent physical disabilities." According to the PCHR, the Hamas EF stormed private homes and executed their Fatah enemies by shooting them, point blank, in the head. Reportedly, Hamas also hijacked a convoy of PA trucks, marking a turning point in the conflict. The EF was not simply trying to kill Fatah members; it was attempting to cut off their supply lines as well.[20]

In an effort to halt the fighting, King Abdullah of Saudi Arabia intervened and invited the leaders of Fatah and Hamas to Mecca to engage in a dialogue designed to end the conflict.[21] The top leaders of Hamas and Fatah represented their factions at the Saudi talks. Fatah's representatives included Abbas and Dahlan, while Ismail Haniyeh and Khaled Meshal represented

Hamas. After three days, the two high-level delegations reportedly reached an understanding, leading to the February 8, 2007, Mecca Agreement.[22]

A little more than one month later, on March 17, 2007, the two sides agreed to form a national unity government. But the brokered calm did not last long. There was virtually no way to sweep aside the pain and animosity that lingered; the bloodshed between Fatah and Hamas had resulted in hundreds of deaths and injuries in 2006 and 2007.

JOURNALISTS COVERING the Palestinian–Israeli conflict had been slow to cover the intra-Palestinian conflict. It was a story that many simply did not understand. After all, the conflict was supposed to be one between Israel and the Palestinians. This internecine conflict did not add up. But for those who did seek to write about the factional violence, both Hamas and Fatah made it difficult. The story was an embarrassing moment in the history of Palestinian nationalism, and one that both factions wished to obscure. As a result, relative to the Palestinian–Israeli conflict, which often receives exaggerated coverage, the Hamas–Fatah conflict received very little.

Moreover, with all eyes on the global war on terror, with Iraq and Afghanistan grabbing headlines daily, much of this conflict took place out of the view of the public eye. But the violence was bloody. Multiple kidnappings took place, as well as machine-gun clashes, peppered with explosions caused by homemade bombs and other projectiles. Both sides suffered many casualties. Hamas was particularly devastated by the killing of Ibrahim Suleiman Maniya, the 45-year-old leader of the al-Qassam Brigades, who was shot in the chest during a fierce clash between Hamas and Fatah on May 15, 2007. Fighting that week between Hamas and Fatah resulted in the deaths of 47 Palestinians and many more wounded.[23]

Sensing that the violence could get even worse and perhaps threaten regional security, the government of Egypt stepped in to attempt to broker a cease-fire on May 19. As was the case with previous Hamas–Fatah cease-fires, this calm lasted only for a few weeks. Another round of fighting soon erupted, which quickly came to be known as the Palestinian civil war.

ON JUNE 7, 2007, AFTER MORE than a year of political stalemate and sporadic internecine conflict, Hamas launched a military offensive to wrest the Gaza Strip from the PA. The battle did not take long. By June 13, Hamas forces controlled the streets and government buildings, including Abbas's presidential compound and security compound. By the following day, all of Gaza was under Hamas's control.

The defeat was crushing for Abbas. The forces trained by the West that were purportedly loyal to him had performed poorly. Some even switched sides and joined Hamas. Many of Abbas's top lieutenants fled for Cairo or other locales, where they maintained second homes.

With no recourse, Abbas dismissed the Hamas-led unity government that the Saudis had helped create in March. He soon appointed outgoing finance minister Salam Fayyad to serve as prime minister in an emergency government based only in the West Bank.

Hamas, by contrast, had dominated the battlefield. For one, Hamas had the benefit of surprise; the PA's forces had no idea what hit them. The PA fighters were overwhelmed by a brutal and zealous enemy. According to the PCHR, much of the Hamas violence was indiscriminate, demonstrating a willful disregard for the conventions of war.

The mid-June violence in Gaza, according to the PCHR, was characterized by "extra-judicial and willful killing," including incidents where Hamas fighters pushed Fatah faction members from the roofs of tall buildings. Hamas also abducted and executed some political enemies. Reportedly, Hamas even killed PA supporters who were already injured[24] or shot Fatah fighters at point-blank range to ensure permanent wounds.[25] The PCHR further reported attacks against private homes and apartment buildings, hospitals, ambulances, and medical crews associated with the PA. All told, the June civil war claimed the lives of at least 161 Palestinians, including 7 children and 11 women. At least 700 Palestinians were wounded.[26]

Although history will almost certainly cast Hamas as the aggressor in the battle for Gaza, reports issued by two human rights groups (Amnesty International and the PCHR) blamed both Fatah and Hamas. The two reports issued pleas to both sides to end the violence, protect the civilian population, and return to negotiations.[27]

WHEN THE GUNS FELL SILENT, Sami Abu Zuhri, a senior Hamas spokesman who appeared regularly on Arab television networks, gloated that the war had been a defensive one. Zuhri added insult to the injuries of the Fatah faction when he claimed that Hamas had gone to war to defend Palestine from a Fatah cadre that was collaborating with Washington and Israel. "There is no political goal behind this but to defend our movement and force these security groups to behave," Zuhri said. He also stated that his organization sought to unify the various armed Palestinian factions under its command, insisting that it still sat atop a unity government.[28]

According to the *Wall Street Journal*, US intelligence agencies were concerned over the loss of the Fatah security complex, which housed the PA's intelligence and military infrastructure that Washington had helped to create. Hamas claimed to have "thousands of paper files, computer records, videos, photographs, and audio recordings containing valuable and potentially embarrassing in-telligence information gathered by Fatah."[29]

The message was a powerful one that was not lost on the Palestinian people. The ossified, old-guard Palestinian leadership may have had the backing of the world's only superpower, but had been trounced by a relatively small Islamist faction—first electorally in the West Bank and Gaza, now militarily in Gaza.

10

Backslide

IN THE AFTERMATH OF THE PALESTINIAN ELECTIONS, AND THEN A YEAR and a half later after Hamas's violent takeover of Gaza, the Palestinians were split in two. The West Bank and Gaza were effectively two separate states. As former peace negotiator Aaron David Miller cynically observed, it was a "Palestinian Noah's Ark, where there is two of everything."[1]

With the Palestinian Authority (PA) in disarray, there were expectations that the leadership would engage in soul-searching. The elections were a clear indication that the Palestinian people were tired of the autocratic style of governance that had for too long characterized the PA—first under Arafat and then under Abbas. The Hamas military victory in Gaza was an indication that the PA was more brittle than most observers had previously imagined. The resulting status quo—the emergence of two disparate Palestinian governments in the Gaza Strip and West Bank—was a constant reminder of the failure of the old guard in nearly every way.

However, rather than prompting change and reform, the West Bank government reverted to its old form. The reports of financial mismanagement and poor governance continued to pile up. Indeed, after several years of promise stemming from Fayyadism, it appeared that the Palestinian leadership was backsliding into Arafatism.

IN 2006, THE PA UNDER ABBAS was little different than the PA under Arafat. In January, for example, a former Palestinian oil executive was detained in connection with corruption and embezzlement charges.[2] He was subsequently found guilty. In February 2006, PA attorney general Ahmed al-Mughani noted, "There are underground files of corruption and also corruption cases well known to the public. . . . The Palestinian law and courts would run after anyone who is involved in these cases of corruption."[3] Al-Mughani alleged that "at least $700 million in Palestinian public funds had been stolen in recent years, though the actual total may be much higher." Indeed, al-Mughani went so far as to say that the total "might [actually] be billions of dollars."[4]

In April 2006, PA officials revealed, according to the *Jerusalem Post,* that "many of [their] embassies had gone bankrupt because of mismanagement and corruption and the refusal of Arab and EU governments to provide the PA with financial aid. . . . Most of the Palestinian diplomats and ambassadors are affiliated with Fatah and some have been serving in their jobs for over three decades."[5] Three months later, Ma'an News Agency reported that the Palestinian ambassador to Romania was under investigation by Fatah for alleging that donor money given to the PA had disappeared.[6] It was unclear whether this case was resolved.

The Palestinian leadership was keenly aware of its reputation and took efforts to silence its critics. In May 2006, Abbas reportedly lodged a libel suit against Abdel Bari Atwan, the editor in chief of the London-based *Al-Quds Al-Arabi.* Atwan had suggested that Abbas was a mafia leader and had engaged in financial corruption.[7] The status of this case is unknown.

THE PERCEPTION THAT FATAH was slipping backward was not lost on the party's leadership. In June 2006, Fatah announced that it was planning to reform "their corruption-riddled party especially by getting rid of many representatives of the old guard who were responsible for the defeat."[8] However, in August, when Fatah's Central Committee held discussions on how to reform the party, members of the young guard were not invited. A Fatah member from Ramallah publicly lamented the decision; he told the *Jerusalem Post* that "[i]nstead of learning from the mistakes of the past and searching for ways to reform Fatah after its defeat in the election, they are working to advance their private interests."[9] Former Fatah strongman Mohammed Dahlan was even blunter about it. The toppled Gaza security chief proclaimed that it was "time for the committee members to retire because they are all old. Fatah needs young leaders to fill the vacuum."[10] When the Fatah Central Committee failed to come to a decision on when to hold a general conference to elect new leaders, some members threatened rebellion. Senior Fatah official Azzam al-Ahmed admitted that the Central Committee's failure was an "indication that we are moving backward not forward."[11]

Squabbling within Fatah continued into the following year. In April 2007, 33 Fatah members called on the group's leadership to investigate all cases of corruption within Fatah.[12] A member of the Al-Aqsa Martyrs Brigades said that Fatah "military groups" need "to stand firm together and support each other in the face of corruption in order for reform to prevail."[13] Another Fatah military leader, Abu al-Walid al-Jabari, further proclaimed that "we don't want to be fragmented and we don't want to secede from the movement, but we will not accept the corruption and we tell the Fatah leadership that they have to keep their differences out of the movement."[14]

AFTER THE HAMAS OFFENSIVE that conquered Gaza in the summer of 2007, Fatah was reeling. The faction had lost control of the Gaza Strip completely, and fears lingered that a similar fate could befall the West Bank. The West, led by the United States, rushed to support Abbas, supplying him with arms, cash, and intelligence. The message to the Palestinian leader was a simple one: Do not lose power in the West Bank.

It was at this point that Abbas apparently realized that there was little that would prompt the West to challenge his rule in the West Bank. Hamas, thanks to its record of suicide bombings and rocket attacks, was the bogeyman. Next to that, whatever problems associated with Abbas's Fatah faction didn't seem like much of a problem in the grand scheme of things. As Michael Singh, a Bush administration official, recalled, there was a sense that "focusing on Palestinian politics is actually harmful . . . maybe you shouldn't rock the boat."[15]

The international community did not seem terribly alarmed when the deputy chairman of the Palestinian power authority, in August 2007, revealed "[d]etails of financial and administrative corruption in the Palestinian power company in Gaza."[16] Nor was there an outcry when it became clear that the West Bank Palestinian leadership was employing autocratic tactics not seen since the Arafat days. For example, in November 2007, PA security forces arrested the owner of the private Al-Amal TV station in Hebron after the station broadcasted a press conference of Hamas leader Ismail Haniyeh. In the same month, two other journalists were arrested for simply reporting "positively on Hamas."[17]

The allegations of corruption also continued to mount. In March 2008, the *Jerusalem Post* reported that a Palestinian official deposited $3 million of PLO funds into one of his private bank accounts. The official, in his defense, insisted that the money ended up in a PLO bank account.[18]

FRUSTRATED, SOME FATAH STAKEHOLDERS openly hammered the party for the seemingly endless stream of scandals. In September 2008, Husam Khader, a young-guard Fatah leader who had been imprisoned by Israel, called for substantial reforms within the faction. According to Khader, longtime Fatah faction loyalists were leaving the party "because of the corruption and the traditional mentality of the Fatah leaders and because they ignore democratic aspects and democratic needs to heal Fatah as we wish." In addition, he lamented, "Our traditional leaders still don't accept the young generation. . . . They have blocked all the ways in front of us and they have even broken the ladders to prevent us from rising."[19]

This did not stop the West Bank government's abuse of power. In October 2008, employees in the PA Endowments Ministry admitted to taking bribes from Palestinians participating in the Muslim pilgrimage to Mecca known as *hajj*.[20] Two months later, the Ramattan News Agency was reportedly forced to cease operations after "relentless and heightened persecution" by the PA in response to the agency's coverage of Hamas events.[21]

As Ma'an News Agency reported, the PA "carried out an unprecedented campaign of censorship and intimidation against West Bank and Gaza Strip journalists" in 2008. One of the primary targets was the Gaza-based Donia al-Watan News Agency. Users in the West Bank were blocked from accessing the agency's website. According to the editor in chief of Donia al-Watan, Abdulla Issa, "The block was aimed at pressuring us to stop publishing articles on corruption, which we were forced to do, following further threats at taking us to court, accusing us of 'defaming the (Palestinian) Authority.'" Issa further charged that the office of Abbas was "fighting any independent nonpartisan media outlets. The case is it's either you are affiliated (with them) and enjoy the protection and funds, in one way or another, or you are engaged in an increasingly dangerous and escalating media war." Issa lamented, "Abbas doesn't want to fight corruption or bring the corrupt into account."[22]

SALAM FAYYAD, MEANWHILE, was lured back into government service following the 2007 Hamas coup in Gaza. Fayyad was appointed as prime minister of the emergency government of the

West Bank PA, but no longer held the finance portfolio. In this new role, he no longer served in a position to oversee the Palestine Investment Fund (PIF).

In the aftermath of Hamas's election victory, in an effort to avoid sanctions against PA assets, Abbas issued a presidential decree that gave the PIF a new board. A State Department cable, released by Wikileaks, observed that the move ensured that the PIF was "now more securely in the hands of President Abbas with a board that is of his choosing."[23]

According to the PIF, Abbas undertook this measure "to ensure that Hamas would not gain control of PIF's investments, to insulate PIF from political influence, and to secure PIF's independence."[24]

Jim Prince, one of the original accountants who helped create the PIF, contests this. He counters that, even if the intentions were pure, the move violated the primary purpose of the PIF, which was to establish a firewall between the president's office and commercial investments of the PA.[25]

Under the new regime, Mohammad Mustafa, now chairman and CEO of the PIF, was also Abbas's economic adviser. This raised additional questions about the firewall.

A PIF representative asserts that the "practice of the PIF CEO acting as an economic advisor to the President of the PA has a long history. Mohammed Rachid, who was the CEO of PIF under Salam Fayyad, served as an economic advisor to then President Arafat." PIF further "disputes that Dr. Mustafa's role as an economic advisor to the president compromises the independence of PIF or Dr. Mustafa."[26]

Prince challenges this assertion. "When the PIF was established and Mohammed Rachid was named the original CEO, he resigned his position as economic adviser to Arafat," he says, adding that when the fund was created, "this was deemed by [Pricewaterhouse Coopers] as a clear conflict of interest."[27] PIF had no record of Rachid's resignation.

Reuters reported in 2009 that the PIF board was "dominated by prominent businessmen, some of whose companies have taken part in ventures in which the fund has important asset stakes."[28] The PIF noted it "maintains an independent board of advisors comprised of members of the Palestinian business community, academia, the civil sector, and regulatory officials."[29] But again, Prince contests the assertions of the sovereign wealth fund, noting "an independent board cannot be chosen by someone. If they are chosen, not elected, they cannot be independent."[30]

Other issues surrounding the PIF surfaced over the years. In 2009, the full breakdown of the PIF's assets was not publicly published.[31] According to Reuters, the PIF reportedly withheld these data "to limit the risk of holdings being seized in suits against the PA."[32] To its credit, the PIF released its financial statements after the suits were settled.

Regardless of the specific questions raised, the concern with the PIF among Palestinians was that the fund had made it harder, not easier, to grow small- and medium-size businesses in the PA.[33]

THE ISSUE OF MOST CONCERN to the West was that the Palestinian security program put in place by Fayyad began to wobble. Reports emerged that the PA used Dayton's forces to suppress dissent.[34] As the head of one Palestinian human rights group noted, the PA had emerged from "a state of lawlessness [and] shifted to a sort of a security state, a police state."[35] There were even questions about whether the security forces were receiving funds from the single treasury account that Fayyad had helped to establish.

Washington, however, continued to push for peace with Israel over reform. With no reason to alter his course, Abbas embarked on a bold, new policy that included the crushing of political challengers and the systematic repression of dissent.

11

Crushing Political Challengers

IN THE SPRING OF 2013, THE PALESTINIAN MEDIA WAS ABUZZ OVER A new reality TV show. *The President*, launched by two non-profits, allowed young Palestinians to "campaign" for the position of the presidency.[1] The very existence of the show was controversial. One might say that it was an outlet for Palestinians who felt stifled by the current political climate. The political reality in the West Bank was such that nobody could run for president. While Abbas had been advocating for Palestinian independence on the world stage, he took steps domestically to neutralize his political adversaries and potential challengers. Increasingly, the Palestinian president dispatched those who dared to disagree with him publicly in a ruthless manner.

YOUNG AND CHARISMATIC, former Fatah strongman Mohammed Dahlan likely had the most promise as a potential challenger to Abbas. It was undoubtedly for this reason that Abbas moved against him.

The feud between Dahlan and the Palestinian leader dates back to the mid-1990s, when Dahlan, a young PLO member, was named the head of preventive security in Gaza, making him one of the more powerful figures in Arafat's PA. Abbas, whose loyalty to the cause dated back to the origins of the Fatah faction in Kuwait in the 1950s, reportedly felt that someone of higher pedigree would have been better for the position.

Of course, under Arafat's "divide and rule" neopatriarchy, such spats were par for the course. As was common during the Arafat era, the two men ultimately reached a modus vivendi that endured until Arafat's death in November 2004.

After becoming president in 2005, Abbas reportedly viewed Dahlan as a political threat but kept him on as national security adviser. Like many other senior officials, Dahlan knew too many of the PA's secrets, so it was safer to keep him on the inside. Dahlan gave his own political survival a boost when he was elected to the Palestinian Legislative Council (PLC) in 2006.[2]

After the Hamas electoral victory in 2006, Dahlan was instrumental in the PA's attempts to mitigate the power of the Islamist faction in Gaza. Unsurprisingly, Hamas reviled Dahlan for speaking out against the faction[3] and for his oversight of the Fatah raids on businesses and charities.[4] Hamas official Yehya Mussa went as far as to identify Dahlan as one of three people "responsible for the continued tensions between Fatah and Hamas."[5]

Dahlan, however, took more heat in the summer of 2007, when Hamas overran the Gaza Strip. With the West Bank and Gaza now divided and the Palestinian cause in crisis, Dahlan was the fall guy. Although he had been abroad at the time for medical treatment, Fatah officials began calling for Dahlan's removal as national security adviser.[6] Dahlan tried to defend himself, stating that his apparatus was "never prepared for internal fighting," and he attempted to point the finger at Iran and Qatar for their sponsorship of Hamas.[7] In the end, his pleas fell on deaf ears. The Gaza strongman resigned but affirmed to Abbas, "I will always remain a loyal soldier behind you."[8]

At the time, amid fears of a similar Hamas takeover in the West Bank, the PA was in panic mode. Bush administration officials moved quickly to stabilize the West Bank and sought out people they could trust in Ramallah. By October, Washington was actively pushing Dahlan, who maintained strong ties with US intelligence and the Israeli defense establishment, to serve as Abbas's deputy in the newly formed emergency government. Abbas rejected this suggestion, and the feud went public.[9]

By 2008, Dahlan was effectively in exile, spending most of his time in Cairo.[10] However, his popularity had apparently not waned within the Fatah party. In 2009, the party named him to its Central Committee, a group responsible for many key Palestinian decisions.[11] Emboldened, Dahlan began brazenly challenging Abbas over the Palestinian leader's lack of transparency and increasingly tight grip on power.

Dahlan created an anti-Abbas TV station, Falastin al-Ghad (Palestine Tomorrow), in the West Bank in 2010. Abbas quickly shut it down.[12] Amid reports that Dahlan was maneuvering to succeed him, Abbas ordered a probe into allegations that Dahlan had embezzled public funds.[13] PA security forces also questioned Fatah members over reports that Dahlan was forming a militia.[14] In addition, Abbas accused Dahlan of speaking badly of his sons.[15] By December 2010, Abbas had Dahlan's membership in Fatah's Central Committee permanently revoked.[16]

In January 2011, Dahlan bravely traveled to Ramallah to answer the charges against him of embezzlement and planning a coup. Predictably, Dahlan denied all the claims against him. But as one Abbas aide observed, the spat could be distilled down to "a personal or business dispute . . . many of the reports that talked about a coup are exaggerated."[17]

But the probe did not end. In April 2011, Fatah announced a new investigation alleging that Dahlan had provided Libyan leader Muammar Qaddafi with weapons to repel the uprising that soon spiraled into the Libyan civil war.[18] By June 2011, Abbas had shuttered a number of Dahlan's political websites that were critical of him[19] and officially expelled Dahlan from Fatah.[20] In response, Dahlan boldly stated on al-Hayat TV, "Abu Mazen [Mahmoud Abbas] can shove it."[21]

The following month, Palestinian security forces arrested 15 of Dahlan's supporters[22] and raided Dahlan's villa in Ramallah, arresting more than 20 security guards and confiscating two cars and more than a dozen weapons.[23] This raid was widely viewed as illegal because it ignored Dahlan's immunity as a member of the PLC. Irate, Dahlan fired back, alleging that Abbas had stolen more than $1 billion from the Palestine Investment Fund (PIF).[24] The Abbas camp upped the ante with a 118-page report alleging that Dahlan had stolen $300 million in aid from the United States and poisoned Arafat.[25] None of these charges or countercharges have been substantiated.

Samir Mashharawi, a Fatah member and Dahlan ally, confirmed what was already known: The dispute between Dahlan and Abbas was "personal." Mashharawi went further, adding, "Abbas wants to run away from five years of failure in running the Palestinian Authority and the political portfolio."[26] But while Dahlan retained the sympathies of Mashharawi and other Fatah members, it was clear that Abbas had gained the upper hand. In August 2011, an official proclaimed that Dahlan's expulsion from Fatah "is now final. It can't be appealed or canceled."[27]

But Abbas was not done. In early 2012, he issued a presidential decree to lift Dahlan's parliamentary immunity.[28] In response, Dahlan quipped, "If the war being fought by Abu Mazen against me was against the occupation, Palestine would have been liberated twice and all the prisoners would have been released and the refugees would have returned."[29]

On January 9, 2012, acting on Abbas's direct orders, Jordan's Central Bank reportedly seized Dahlan's assets. The report came just days after PA anticorruption commission head Rafiq al-Natsheh announced he would pursue corruption suspects living abroad.[30] Reports suggested that Dahlan's assets in Jordan amounted to 10 million Jordanian dinars ($14.1 million) or even more.[31]

DAHLAN, HOWEVER, WAS NOT ALONE. Abbas also began to pursue Arafat's former economic adviser, Mohammed Rachid. In fact, on January 9, 2012, the day that Jordanian authorities seized Dahlan's assets, they were also looking for Rachid's.

Rachid, also known as Khaled Salaam, is an Iraqi Kurd who was the subject of considerable controversy. A former journalist,[32] Rachid became an integral part of the PLO as a trusted confidant of Arafat's. He began working for Arafat in Beirut in the 1970s.[33]

Rachid's role was an enduring one. When the Israelis forced the PLO out of Lebanon, Rachid accompanied Arafat to Tunis, where he acted as the PLO chief's media adviser.[34] In the mid- to late 1980s, he was believed to have assumed the role of financial adviser. In 1994, after the signing of the Oslo Accords, Rachid returned to Gaza with Arafat.[35] For the decade of problematic state building and poor governance that followed in the West Bank and Gaza, Rachid remained Arafat's right-hand man on financial matters. Some observers have suggested that his non-Palestinian background made it easier for Arafat to trust him on a number of issues, as he was less of a political threat.

But not all of the PLO appreciated Rachid's presence. Abbas, in particular, reportedly resented Rachid because he was an Iraqi Kurd—not even a Palestinian—who had gained Arafat's trust and was part of his inner circle, whereas Abbas was often on the outside looking in. "There was a huge amount of jealousy,"[36] a former adviser said. Nevertheless, under Arafat's neopatriarchy, there was little recourse for Abbas. The two men learned to get along.

Perhaps the point of sharpest disagreement between Rachid and Abbas during the Arafat era came during the Camp David negotiations of 2000. Both men attended the talks, but they found themselves to be in opposite camps. During that intense period, Rachid was an advocate of working with Israel to find a solution. As the *New York Times* noted, Rachid was "the most pragmatic and least ideological of the delegation," and he repeatedly tried to "steer Mr. Arafat toward the practical if he could."[37] Meanwhile, Abbas called diplomacy a "trap that was laid for us."[38] One former Palestinian negotiator even suggested that Abbas staked out this position because it was the opposite of what Rachid wanted. The rivalry between the two men was that great.[39]

In the end, Arafat rejected President Clinton's offers at the 2000 peace summit, plunging the Palestinians and their nascent protostate into chaos. Although the PLO leader had rejected his counsel, Rachid remained loyal to Arafat as he struggled to maintain control of the West Bank and Gaza Strip. But his role as the gatekeeper of Arafat's secret finances and other political dealings reportedly became a liability as the violence raged.

As journalist Daoud Kuttab noted, "The escalation of the violence in Palestine and the key role that community activists had in it caused a major setback to war rich individuals like Mr. Rachid. Not only were they affected by the collapse of the Palestinian economy, but direct calls against Rachid and others like him became louder and louder, at times repeated publicly in official forums like the Palestinian Legislative Council."[40]

Rachid was at the center of controversy when new information about the PLO's finances was revealed as an unintended result of the creation of the PIF, an endeavor he actually endorsed. But Kuttab observed that the calls for Rachid's departure became particularly strong after he worked behind the scenes with the

Israelis to help resolve the crisis surrounding the Israeli siege of the Church of Nativity in April 2002: "As a result of the agreement brokered by Rachid, 13 Palestinians who were inside the church were forcibly deported to a host of European countries. Another group of Palestinians who were under siege in the church were forcibly deported to the Gaza Strip. Many Palestinians felt this was a bad deal, which legitimized deportation, even though international treaties make it a war crime." Kuttab observed that "no one was hurt but the message was clear, Palestinians had seen enough . . . after consultation with Arafat, Rachid left Palestine for Cairo where he [was] reported to be carrying out odd jobs for the Palestinian leadership."[41]

Rachid's departure from the scene was rapid. Although he was instrumental in the creation of the PIF and the concurrent effort to bring all of Arafat's accounts into the light of day, his alleged role in the creation of those assets was clearly a liability. Rachid still had the ear of Arafat, however. During the long standoff with the Israeli military that kept Arafat holed up in his Ramallah Muqata compound, Rachid reportedly took care of Arafat's finances from afar. When the longtime leader of the Palestinians was rushed to Paris for treatment, Rachid made preparations for him.[42] Rachid was also reportedly on hand when Arafat died.

With Abbas's rise to the presidency in 2005, Rachid was instantly marginalized. The new president reportedly "stopped dealing" with Rachid entirely.[43] There was a brief moment when rapprochement between the two men seemed possible. In January 2007, amid the Hamas–Fatah standoff stemming from the 2006 elections, Abbas sent Rachid to engage in a secret dialogue with Hamas's Khaled Meshal.[44] Rachid returned to Ramallah after that and began to officially advise Abbas on the ongoing reconciliation process with Hamas.[45]

But this cooperation was short-lived. Abbas continued to marginalize the former adviser, who was now vulnerable without the protection of Arafat. In March 2008, the PA's attorney general began an investigation into Rachid's finances.[46] In February 2011, one official called on "the PA [to] seek Interpol's help in locating Mohammad Rachid . . . and seize his assets."[47] These calls intensified in April 2011, when Fatah announced plans to investigate allegations that Dahlan and Rachid were supplying Libyan strongman Muammar Qaddafi with Israeli weapons originally given to the PA.[48]

In May 2012, Palestinian authorities officially announced they were targeting Rachid in a corruption and embezzlement case. According to Rafiq al-Natsheh, head of the Palestinian anticorruption commission, Rachid had business interests in Jordan, Egypt, Montenegro, Iraq, and the United Arab Emirates (UAE). The corruption czar further said that the PA had requested that those countries freeze Rachid's assets.[49]

Here again, the PA was stalking a figure that had long left the PA and arguably posed little threat to the financial well-being of the PA. Azmi Shuaibi, a leading anticorruption campaigner in the West Bank, observed that the "priorities (for investigations) are being set on a personal basis . . . we have concerns that the issue is being handled in a way of settling personal scores." The Associated Press further observed that "the probe . . . appeared to be tinged with political intrigue."[50]

Before long, Rachid went on the offensive, unleashing a torrent of allegations against Abbas and his associates. Meanwhile, the PA requested Interpol's help in arresting Rachid, but because Palestine was not an officially recognized state, the international law-enforcement agency declined to get involved.[51] This did not stop the PA from its campaign against Arafat's former adviser. On May 25, Mahmoud Habash, the Palestinian Religious Endowments minister and a close ally of Abbas, asserted that Rachid was a thief and traitor who deserved to be imprisoned.[52] On June 7, a Palestinian court conducted a lightning trial of Rachid in absentia. According to the *Jerusalem Post*'s Khaled Abu Toameh, "Rachid [was] the most senior PA official to be sentenced for corruption by a PA court."[53] Rachid and two of his associates, Abdul Rahman al-Rachid Najab and Khalid Abdul Ghani Farra, were "convicted of taking a total of $33.5 million from the foreign donor-financed Palestinian Investment Fund." The punishment for Rachid was a 15-year jail term, a $15 million fine, and calls for his properties to be confiscated.[54]

Rachid insisted on his innocence. He contended that Abbas was corrupt. Through the Arabic language InLight Press website (www.InLightPress.com), the former Arafat adviser leveled a barrage of charges, mostly of corruption, at Abbas, his family, and his inner circle.

DAHLAN AND RACHID WERE ABBAS'S main targets, but other political figures who disagreed with the Palestinian leader or maintained strong ties to Dahlan and Rachid also incurred his wrath.

In December 2011, Palestinian media outlets reported that Abbas was actively looking for someone to replace Yasser Abed Rabbo as the secretary-general of the PLO.[55] The relationship between the two reportedly soured following Abbas's attempt to declare a Palestinian state at the United Nations a few months earlier in New York. Abed Rabbo had been publicly against the move but denied that there was a feud, dismissing the reports as "lies."[56]

Over the years, Abed Rabbo learned how to play the game. He became a member of the PLO Executive Committee in 1971[57] and ascended as secretary-general in 2006.[58] But he apparently stepped over the line when he challenged Abbas openly over the controversial UN strategy that defined Abbas's diplomacy in recent years.

In April 2012, the London-based *Al-Quds Al-Arabi* reported that Abbas was gunning for Abed Rabbo because the latter refused to be part of a delegation that handed a rather undiplomatic letter from Abbas to Netanyahu. The paper further reported that Abed Rabbo convinced Fayyad to also refuse to be part of the delegation,[59] which led to Abbas and Fayyad cutting off contact with each other for a period of time.[60] A few days after that report, the Chinese news agency Xinhua reported that Abbas had removed Abed Rabbo as the PA's media supervisor.[61]

According to a senior Fatah official, Abed Rabbo's decision not to be part of the delegation that delivered Abbas's letter to Netanyahu "was the straw that broke the camel's back."[62] Interestingly, the *Times of Israel* later reported that Abed Rabbo had been involved in secret talks with a high-level Israeli official. It was unclear whether this colored his decision.[63] Nevertheless, Abbas was reportedly so upset with Abed Rabbo in the lead-up to the UN maneuver of 2011 that he had banned Abed Rabbo from coming on tours to garner support.

SAMIR MASHHARAWI, A SENIOR FATAH OFFICIAL in Gaza with strong ties to Dahlan, was also at odds with Abbas during this period. Over the course of a decade, if not longer, there had been a general conflict between Fatah's old and young guard. Mashharawi was decidedly in the young-guard camp, led by such figures as Dahlan and the imprisoned Marwan Barghouti.

In December 2005, Mashharawi ran in the Palestinian parliamentary elections, but he ran on a Fatah list separate from Abbas.[64] Following the January 2006 elections (in which Fatah was handed a crushing electoral defeat), Mashharawi said that "Fatah paid the price because of its corrupt administration and . . . leaders."[65] Admittedly, this was mild compared to the words of Dahlan, who, following the elections, said, "We have to reform this piece of shit called Fatah."[66] However, Mashharawi then called for the resignation of Fatah's Central Committee and the insertion of a leadership that "can restore dignity and deliver a message that Fatah is a national project and not just a ruling project."[67] To say the least, this put him on the outs with the West Bank government. This rift was cemented further when the spat between Abbas and Dahlan became ugly, and Mashharawi sided with Dahlan.[68]

In late January 2012, Mashharawi was expelled from Fatah and the Revolutionary Council.[69] According to the Fatah-aligned *Palestine Press*, he slammed Fatah in an interview on *Al-Arabiya*, in which he said that the movement "lacked leadership."[70] According to Mashharawi, "Since President Mahmoud Abbas took the reins in Fatah and the [PA], one defeat after another has been inflicted on us. We have lost the municipalities, the [PLC], and Gaza; the political process has been deadlocked; Fatah has lost the spirit of struggle and resistance."[71]

In response to the expulsion of Mashharawi, Dahlan said, "The decision to dismiss the brother Samir Mashharawi is only what is expected of people who have lost their loyalty and affiliation to the movement."[72]

SOME MIGHT ARGUE that the punishments Abbas meted out to Dahlan and Rachid were deserved. And with the cases of Mashharawi and Abed Rabbo, some could argue that they were lesser figures whom the Palestinian president had every right to cast aside. In other words, they served at the pleasure of Abbas.

But perhaps the greatest casualty in Abbas's campaign against political challengers has been Fayyad. "Fayyadism" was once hailed in Washington's corridors of power—and by *New York Times* columnist Tom Friedman—as a refreshing alternative to the governing philosophy of other Middle Eastern regimes. As Friedman wrote in 2009, "Fayyadism is based on the simple but all-too-rare notion that an Arab leader's legitimacy should be based

not on slogans or rejectionism or personality cults or security services, but on delivering transparent, accountable administration
and services."[73]

Abbas, however, appeared to have other ideas for the PA. Al-
ternatively, he may simply not have appreciated a potential political challenger being so openly adored by governments in the
West. Either way, in a move that can best be described as political
cannibalization, the Palestinian president went out of his way to
marginalize his own prime minister.

The tensions between the two men were first apparent in
2005, when Fayyad resigned from his cabinet post as finance minister to run in the 2006 elections. Ma'an News Agency suggested
that Fayyad resigned because "of hiring issues with President Abbas."[74] The *Jerusalem Post* suggested that differences between
Fayyad and Abbas over how to handle the economy also led to
the resignation.[75]

Of course, Abbas brought Fayyad back into government after the Hamas coup in Gaza. But the tensions quietly continued
between the two men, although whatever differences they had
were often kept out of the public eye. That changed in 2011,
however, when Abbas began to orchestrate a series of trials
against his prime minister's top officials. On November 29, the
Palestinian prosecutor-general charged economy minister Has-
san Abu Libdeh with corruption, paving the way for him to
stand trial. The charges—breach of trust, fraud, insider trading,
and embezzlement of public funds—dated back to Abu Libdeh's
tenure as director of the Palestinian Capital Market Authority in
2008. In other words, Abbas was not trying Abu Libdeh for anything he did while serving in his current role in the PA.[76] On top
of this, the newly formed Palestinian anticorruption commission
had charged agriculture minister Ismail Daiq with corruption.[77]
The charges against Daiq were tax evasion and money launder-
ing.[78] Both cases are pending.

In Abbas's PA, corruption probes aren't usually launched unless the president wants them launched. From all appearances,
Abbas chose to pursue these cases to discredit Fayyad and cast
doubt on the prime minister's ability to deliver on his celebrated
mandate of countering corruption. After all, the corruption
reached the highest levels, and Fayyad had appointed the officials
who were under fire.

In other words, these probes were not designed to rid the PA
of corruption. Rather, by ousting ministers and hobbling Fayyad,
Abbas created a possible window to replace them with figures
more to his liking.

Meanwhile, from his sprawling Muqata compound in Ramallah, Abbas made the major foreign policy decisions affecting
Palestinians while Fayyad worked with a skeleton crew in a modest office nearby. Abbas traveled around the world to generate
support for the Palestine 194 campaign while Fayyad labored
to bring in international donor funds. In fact, Abbas's initiative
at the United Nations endangered those sources of funding. The
leadership styles of the two men were very different, to say the
least. In 2011, according to officials who worked with them, the
two figureheads of the Palestinians were barely on speaking terms.

In 2011, when Abbas began openly angling for international
recognition of Palestinian statehood at the United Nations—a finger in Washington's eye—Fayyad went on record opposing him.[79]
Although Fayyad had created the plan announced in 2009 to prepare the Palestinians for statehood,[80] and as it became clear the
approach was infuriating Washington and prompting Congress
to mull a cutoff in aid, he openly questioned the wisdom of the
endeavor. As he stated in December 2011, "This is not the state
we are looking for."[81]

Fayyad was marginalized further when Abbas entered into
negotiations to form a unity government with the terrorist group
Hamas—a deal that would undoubtedly prompt a full cut in US

funding. He claimed that he was prepared to step aside in the name of "national unity,"[82] but Fayyad later went on record as refusing to serve the future Hamas–Fatah coalition government in any capacity.[83]

Meanwhile, the West failed to provide him with the support he needed to ensure political survival. The Obama administration, not to mention the State Department, was fully aware of the power struggle in Ramallah and the toll it took on Fayyad. However, Washington feared that weakening Abbas—even if the end result would empower Fayyad—would lead to a power vacuum from which only Hamas would benefit.

For his part, Abbas knew that Washington valued his ability to fend off Hamas more than it valued Fayyad's ability to govern. This explains why he felt unencumbered to test Washington's patience, both when it came to political reform in Ramallah and the statehood bid at the United Nations. It also explains why Washington stood by silently as Fayyad struggled.

INTERESTINGLY, WHILE FAYYAD STRUGGLED SILENTLY, Dahlan re-emerged as a player in the Palestinian arena, challenging Abbas's primacy. In early January 2013, after Abbas successfully upgraded the PLO's UN mission with overwhelming international support, Abbas began to flirt openly with the question of political reconciliation with Hamas. The West Bank government had allowed several Hamas rallies to take place on its turf in December 2012, marking the twenty-fifth anniversary of Hamas's founding in 1987. In response, Hamas allowed Fatah to hold anniversary celebrations of its own in Gaza, marking the forty-eighth anniversary of the first Fatah attacks against Israel.

But Dahlan, the former strongman of Gaza under Arafat, was not prepared to allow Abbas to have his day in the sun. As Agence France-Presse reported, hundreds of thousands poured into the streets on January 4, 2013, for a mass rally marking the anniversary of Fatah's armed struggle—the first since 2007 in fact. But they soon were disrupted by Dahlan loyalists who "brandished portraits and chanted slogans."[84] Palestinian media outlets reported that there were thousands of Dahlan backers, and they were chanting, "Dahlan is the president."[85] This challenge to Abbas quickly led to clashes, which were documented by several news outlets. As the Associated Press reported, some of the Dahlan supporters jumped onto the stage, prompting the rally to end prematurely, marring what would have otherwise been a triumphant day for Abbas.[86]

That Dahlan would rain on his parade likely came as no surprise for Abbas. After all, the Palestinian president had been pursuing him for years. The *Jerusalem Post* even cited a Hamas official as being concerned that Dahlan loyalists were planning to disrupt the festivities in the days leading up to the event.[87]

Some reports even suggested that Dahlan was planning a comeback. *Al-Quds Al-Arabi* ran a piece in September 2012 pointing to Dahlan's influence over the renegade Fatah candidates in the municipal elections, citing his furnishing of "big money" to gain influence.[88]

Dahlan did not limit himself to an on-the-ground political campaign. He continued to maintain a network of websites critical of the Palestinian president[89] and occasionally launched into Abbas on other sites, too.[90]

Interestingly, the impact of Dahlan's attacks against Abbas paled in comparison with the problems that arose between Abbas and the UAE as the result of this ongoing spat. As the *Economist* noted, "Cash from the Gulf has dwindled, partly because the United Arab Emirates, which used to send $200m a year, seems to have sided with Mr. Dahlan."[91] The Associated Press similarly noted that the UAE "cut aid from $174 million in 2009 to $42.5 million since the beginning of 2011—according to Palestinian officials in an attempt to pressure Abbas to reinstate a disgraced former aide, Mohammed Dahlan."[92]

In March 2013, the Lebanese newspaper *Al-Safir* reported on the "possibility of reconciliation between Abbas and Dahlan."[93] The Ma'an News Agency also reported that the Palestinian courts were considering an appeal by Dahlan to have his immunity reinstated.[94] But in the end, Dahlan's appeal was rejected.[95] The two men remained political foes. Dahlan threatened to sue Abbas in July 2013.

THE TENSION BETWEEN ABBAS AND FAYYAD, meanwhile, was a constant. For months, it was rumored that Fayyad might be on his way out. Then, somewhat suddenly, in April 2013, Reuters reported that he had tendered his resignation.[96] Fayyad's office declined to comment, but American officials offered reassurances that Fayyad was "sticking around."[97] The timing of the reports was decidedly awkward. President Obama, during his visit to the Middle East the month before, publicly lauded Fayyad as a partner for peace.[98]

Abbas's Fatah faction was apparently not terribly concerned with the optics. The faction was among the more strident voices calling for Fayyad to go. "Fatah has been left with no authority at all. All claims that Fatah had been in control of the West Bank are baseless and wrong," said Najat Abu Baker, a Fatah leader in the West Bank, in an interview with the UAE-based Gulf News. "Fayyad who is not a Fatah cadre has been in total control of the entire West Bank."[99]

On April 13, with rumors swirling, international news outlets confirmed that Abbas had finally accepted Fayyad's resignation.[100] The news was a blow to US diplomacy efforts, recently rekindled by new Secretary of State John Kerry. But the prime minister's departure also raised troubling questions about the future of the PA's leadership.

With Fayyad on his way out, Abbas appeared to have overcome any institutional restraints on his power. He sat atop the

PLO, the Fatah faction, and the PA, where he was four years past the end of his legal term with no new elections in sight. Abbas had no political challengers. He had no heir apparent. And he would not allow for a healthy exchange of political ideas in the public space. With Fayyad's resignation, his domination of Palestinian politics in the West Bank appeared complete.

12

Quashing Critical Media and Protesters

WHILE THE PA WAS NEVER A FULL-FLEDGED DEMOCRACY, ONE COULD argue that the Palestinians enjoyed more freedoms under the PA than the majority of their neighbors in the Middle East. These freedoms are enshrined in Palestinian law. Article 19 of the Palestinian Basic Law, amended in 2003, states, "Every person shall have the right to freedom of thought, conscience and expression, and shall have the right to publish his opinion orally, in writing, or in any form of art, or through any other form of expression, provided that it does not contradict with the provisions of law." Additionally, Article 27 states, "Censorship on media shall be prohibited."[1]

Palestinian journalists are quick to note that Israel obstructs Palestinian press freedoms. From blocking access to certain locales to detentions, George Hale, an editor for Ma'an News Agency, notes that "Israeli restrictions" are common. "The restrictions I face as an American passport holder are negligible compared to what Palestinian journalists put up with, but they are prohibitive," he notes.[2]

But under the leadership of Mahmoud Abbas, Palestinian press freedom has suffered further. Specifically, the West Bank government has reportedly carried out a campaign against websites and journalists who have dared to challenge Abbas and his old-guard order.

According to the Palestinian human rights group Al-Haq, "It is difficult to know exactly how many people have been detained in violation of the right to freedom of expression because victims, in many cases, are charged with or accused of penal offenses to mask the political motivation behind their arrest."[3] Since 2007, in particular, incidents have skyrocketed in which PA security forces have violated the rights of journalists in the West Bank.

IN THE SUMMER OF 2007, after the Gaza war between Hamas and Fatah, the West Bank became a highly inhospitable environment for Hamas members. It was common to see Fatah and PLO loyalists attack Hamas members. But these attacks were not limited to militants or even political figures. Those loyal to Abbas attacked Hamas media outlets, much as Hamas attacked Fatah and PLO outlets in Gaza.[4]

Early on, many Hamas media outlets were simply shut down. In 2007, Hamas press conferences,[5] TV, and even journalists who were not critical of Hamas were all targets of the PA security forces.[6] The following year, Palestinian forces arrested two Palestinian journalists, charging them with being Hamas members.[7] The PA also banned a number of journalists from entering the presidential compound in Ramallah, including those from Al-Jazeera, reportedly due to the Qatar-based satellite station's decision to air a speech by Hamas leader Khaled Meshaal in Damascus, rather than remarks by Abbas to the PLO in Ramallah.[8]

Around the same time, the pro-Hamas Ramattan News Agency was forced to stop operations after "relentless and heightened persecution" by the PA following positive coverage of Hamas events.[9] And in January 2009, Mohammed Suleiman Abu Shtayyeh, a journalist who reported on a pro-Hamas rally in Ramallah, was attacked by PA loyalists and sustained a broken nose.[10] The crackdown continued the following month, when the PA refused to release six journalists who had been detained for allegedly being Hamas supporters.[11]

The campaign against Hamas media outlets continued as the internecine conflict remained unresolved. However, it was increasingly unclear whether the media outlets were aligned with Hamas or simply reporting in a way that was not critical enough of Abbas's rival faction. In January 2012, Palestinian security forces arrested *Al-Ahram* reporter Khaled Amayreh for criticizing Abbas and referring to Hamas strongman Ismail Haniyeh as the "legitimate Palestinian prime minister."[12] As the United Nation's rapporteur on the Palestinian–Israeli conflict noted, the PA also banned many newspapers from circulation in the West Bank because they were "perceived to be sympathetic" to Hamas. As of June 2012, that list included *Al-Risala, Falastin,* and *Minbar al-Islah.*[13]

As Hale notes, "At this point, there is no denying that the Palestinian Authority is actively involved in repressing not only Hamas and Islamic Jihad in an official capacity . . . but also individuals who happen to share those views. [The PA is] rarely, if ever, called out for routine arrests of Hamas members or attacks on Hamas media, and I think this is because the PA's supporters in Washington and Brussels support this."[14]

VIOLATIONS OF FREE SPEECH increasingly extended to include attacks on nonaligned journalists and even bloggers who challenged the authority of Abbas or the government over which he presides.

In July 2009, the PA banned Al-Jazeera from operating in the West Bank[15] for a few days after the news channel reported on allegations that Abbas and Mohammad Dahlan were accomplices in Yasser Arafat's death.[16] The move had a chilling effect. As one former Palestinian intelligence official noted, "Al-Jazeera and other Arab media outlets told me that they are afraid to publish anything that angers the Palestinian Authority."[17] Al-Jazeera felt the wrath of the PA again in January 2011, following the channel's publication of the "Palestine Papers,"[18] which revealed some 1,700 confidential documents, maps, emails, and conversations detailing some of the Palestinian leadership's secret negotiation sessions with Israel. After they were leaked, Palestinian security officers attempted to storm Al-Jazeera's Ramallah offices.[19]

But the Qatari TV juggernaut was not the only target. In December 2010, for example, a journalist in Bethlehem was arrested for his reporting on the bitter dispute between Abbas and Dahlan.[20] The following month, a correspondent for the Al-Quds TV station was arrested for merely posting a Facebook missive that was critical of Abbas.[21]

Amid such reports, rights groups and nongovernmental organizations (NGOs) began to sound alarms. Groups such as the Independent Commission for Human Rights castigated the PA for its repression. Ironically, the PA banned journalists from reporting on the NGO's findings.[22]

All of this led to a general climate of fear. The PA continued to threaten or punish writers who criticized the government, and the journalists appeared to have little recourse. In August 2011, a Palestinian journalist was forced into hiding due to her coverage of a number of sit-in strikes.[23] In September 2011, PA forces arrested Christian journalist George Canawati of Bethlehem 2000 Radio over a Facebook post.[24] The *Jerusalem Post* later reported that he was set to face trial due to his critical comments on the city's medical services.[25]

In February 2012, PA forces arrested an editor at the official PA news agency WAFA for his comments on social media sites. Rami Samara later recounted that plainclothes security agents escorted him from his office and held him for four hours. "They showed me about 100 pages of comments I made on Facebook, mostly criticizing the Palestinian Authority and the PLO," he said.[26]

The PA then went a step too far as it detained a Palestinian journalist who wrote an article that was critical of the Palestinian mission in France, detailing how diplomats allegedly hired Arab students to spy on Islamic groups in France.[27] The journalist, Yousef al-Shayeb of the Jordanian newspaper *Al-Ghad,* was arrested after a complaint by several Palestinian diplomats who were impacted by the story.[28]

The PA subsequently extended Shayeb's detention and demanded that the journalist pay $6 million in restitution, even though he was not charged with a crime. The Palestinian Journalists Syndicate organized a sit-in to protest.[29] The International Federation of Journalists—the world's largest journalist union—also condemned the move.[30] In late March 2012, al-Shayeb began a hunger strike to protest his detention.[31] He was eventually released.

The PA continued to arrest bloggers, however. Among them was Jamal Abu Rihan, who ran the Facebook page "The people want an end to corruption."[32] The PA also arrested journalist Ismat Abdel Khaleq over a comment she posted on Facebook criticizing the PA leadership and calling for the dismantlement of the PA. "Yes to bringing down the traitor Mahmoud Abbas," "Abbas is the fascist," and "Abbas has held a party of immorality and shame at the blood of martyrs" were reportedly some of the comments she posted.[33] According to the *Jerusalem Post,* she was held in solitary confinement by the West Bank government.[34]

The PA, for its part, continued to deny wrongdoing. As the Ma'an News Agency reported, a spokesman said at a Ramallah press conference that criticisms against the government concerning its suppression of freedom of speech and journalists were exaggerated, emphasizing the need to differentiate between censorship and defamation or slander.[35] The PA's attorney general defended Khaleq's arrest, adding that he had "no problem" with his government detaining journalists, adding that "lawyers and judges" had recently been detained, too.[36]

THE PA, HOWEVER, COULD NOT QUASH all dissent. Indeed, what could the Abbas government do when criticism came from outside its jurisdiction? In April 2012, a scandal erupted when the Ma'an News Agency reported that Palestinian officials had "quietly instructed Internet providers to block access to news websites whose reporting is critical of President Mahmoud Abbas."[37]

This tactic was not a new one. In 2008, the PA had targeted the Gaza-based Donia al-Watan news agency, which had been reporting on political corruption in the PA. Users in the West Bank were blocked from accessing a website that published a scathing piece about Abbas's government called "Ramallah's Banana Republic." According to the site's editor, Abdulla Issa, "The block was aimed at pressuring us to stop publishing articles on corruption." Issa added, "The attorney general did not call us and we were not given the chance to defend ourselves." Reportedly, the order stemmed directly from a complaint filed by Abbas's office.[38]

By 2011, the spats with Mohammad Rachid, Dahlan, and other exiled political rivals prompted an unprecedented wave of anti-Abbas invective online from websites outside the West Bank. With mounting allegations of corruption and wrongdoing, Abbas responded by blocking them in the territories where he had control.

On January 28, 2012, hackers took down InLight Press, a stridently anti-Abbas website believed to be linked to Rachid,[39] after the site alleged that Abbas had ordered his security forces to tap his political opponents' phones.[40] When InLight Press returned online, its editors claimed that the cyber-attack, which it called "treacherous barbarism," originated from "the Palestinian Authority with the approval of President Abbas." InLight Press also alleged that Abbas had created a "crisis cell," headed by Sabri Saidam, former head of the PA Ministry of Telecommunications and Information Technology, to coordinate the attack.[41]

A week later, on February 3, InLight Press was hacked again,[42] but it continued to publish scathing criticisms of Abbas and the PA when it came back online. In response, the Palestinian leadership again reportedly blocked access to InLight Press in the territories.[43] Days later, the Gaza-based website Amad, which was also critical of Abbas, reported that Palestinian users could not access its website because the Palestinian government had blocked it.[44]

Reporters soon began to sniff around. As the Ma'an News Agency reported, the PA attorney general personally delivered the order to block these sites and was reportedly "acting on instructions from higher up in the government—either from the president's office or an intelligence director."[45]

InLight Press quoted a Telecommunications and Information Technology Ministry official who claimed that the site was spreading "sedition and lies to break up the structure of Palestinian society." As a result, the official claimed, the PA had the "right to defend . . . against this malicious and suspicious campaign."[46]

The West Bank erupted in scandal when the extent of the censorship was revealed.[47] On April 25, the Palestinian Telecommunications Company (Paltel) issued a statement admitting it had "no choice except to abide by" orders from Palestinian officials to block websites.[48] The following day, the Palestinian minister of communication and information technology, Mashour Abu Daka, resigned, citing "personal reasons" for his departure.[49]

Abbas has since reversed the censorship order.[50] However, there appears to be no law criminalizing what the PA has done.

FOR PALESTINIANS, THE LACK OF FREEDOM of the press and the accompanying repression on the Internet led to frustration. Few knew how it might manifest. But on June 30, 2012, Palestinian protests erupted. It started when young Palestinians in Ramallah protested a scheduled meeting between Abbas and then Israeli vice premier Shaul Mofaz.[51]

In many ways, protesting against Israel—the lowest common denominator among Palestinians—was a safe and acceptable way to protest the PA. It was not a particularly large demonstration, but according to the Ma'an News Agency, the protesters "were blocked by riot police and some plain clothes agents." Palestinian forces subsequently attacked protesters and journalists; at least six people were injured, and six others were detained.[52]

The following day, as protesters organized with the help of social media, Palestinians took to the streets again, calling on the PA to "end negotiations with Israel" and for "the police to respect free speech."[53] Again, the protesters appeared to merge the two disparate issues in an attempt to create a more palatable political package. According to Ma'an, "Police attacked protesters with batons, beating and injuring at least seven people. Another seven protesters were taken to a police station along with at least two journalists."[54]

The Palestinian Center for Human Rights (PCHR) further reported that "police officers and members of the security services in civilian clothes used clubs to beat demonstrators and media professionals."[55] One journalist was quoted as saying, "It was more crazy than yesterday, you can't imagine—they hit girls and were laughing like they don't care about Palestinians."[56] Eyewitnesses told the PCHR "that the Chief of Police in Ramallah . . . Colonel Abdul Latif Qaddoumi and his assistant, Mohammed Abu Bakr, were present and participated in the use of force against the demonstrators."[57]

Activists began calling for the dismissal of Ramallah's police chief.[58] The PCHR,[59] the Palestinian Center for Development and Media Freedoms (MADA),[60] the Palestinian Journalists Syndicate,[61] and the Committee to Protect Journalists[62] issued statements condemning the crackdown, too. Senior Palestinian official Hanan Ashrawi joined in condemning the violence,[63] while the PA minister of interior Said Abu Ali called for a committee to investigate the incidents.[64]

On July 3, 2012, protesters once again took to the streets of Ramallah, calling on the Palestinian leadership to end negotiations with Israel but also to respect freedom of speech. After gathering in Ramallah's central Manara Square, the protesters headed for the presidential Muqata compound. Outside Abbas's offices, protesters chanted, "The people want to bring down Oslo" but also "Down with military rule."[65]

This protest and other subsequent smaller protests passed without incident. However, Palestinians remained irate over the West Bank government's heavy-handed tactics. Abbas ordered one inquiry into the Ramallah police officials who mismanaged the protests. But that was insufficient to many Palestinians, who called for additional oversight.

In August, the Council of Palestinian Human Rights Organizations announced the results of its own inquiry and formally acknowledged that "high-ranking" PA officials ordered the suppression of the Ramallah protests. As the Ma'an News Agency noted, "Officials in the president's office ordered security forces to prevent demonstrators from reaching the presidential compound, the rights groups found."[66] Human Rights Watch, for its part, urged Palestinian officials to hold the perpetrators accountable.[67] The PA rejected the report. Adnan Dmeiri, a spokesman for the Palestinian security forces, said the report was a "clear attack on the presidency."[68]

ABBAS, FOR HIS PART, CALLED ON official media outlets to stop focusing so much of their efforts on his activities.[69] But his government continued to attract negative attention. On July 22, 2012, Palestinian security forces reportedly threatened to kill Mahmoud

Mattar, a journalism student who had written a critical article about "the political situation" in the West Bank. According to Mattar, Palestinian authorities threatened him, saying, "We will hang you and say that you committed suicide."[70]

In early September, PA TV censored the audio of audience members who expressed views that were critical of Abbas and the PA.[71] Later that month, Palestinian forces arrested the director of the West Bank office of the *Falastin* newspaper, Walid Khalid. Mohammad Muna of Quds Press Agency was arrested the following day.[72] Both were released on bail in late October.[73]

In October 2012, Jihad Harb, a Palestinian columnist, was summoned for interrogation by PA security forces over an article he had written in August.[74] The article had raised troubling questions as to the hiring and promotion process within the PA.[75]

In February 2013, a man from the Nablus area was sentenced to one year in prison for criticizing the PA leadership and "fomenting sedition and sectarian strife." Anas Awwad was sentenced by the PA Magistrate's Court in Nablus, which based its verdict on a 50-year-old Jordanian law banning "extending one's tongue" against the monarch. Awwad had been arrested four times in the past by Abbas's security apparatus.[76] In March 2013, a Palestinian court sentenced Mamdouh Hamamreh of Al-Quds TV in Bethlehem to a year in jail for a picture on Facebook that was deemed insulting to Abbas.[77] Abbas issued a presidential pardon on the same day that the court upheld his one-year sentence.[78]

As Hale notes, "For Palestinian journalists in the West Bank, I think the biggest obstacle is the legal system and the selective enforcement of libel and slander laws to go after journalists. . . . A Palestinian official can file a 'complaint' accusing a journalist of libel that results in his arrest . . . and they can hold people for 15 days for 'investigation.' The legal system also favors the rich and powerful because, to sue someone, you have to put up something like 10 percent of the amount you're suing him for. So, if you're a powerful minister, for example, suing a newspaper reporter, the odds are stacked against the reporter."[79]

IN APRIL 2013, THE PCHR REPORTED that Palestinian security officers broke up two peaceful sit-ins organized by the Islamist group Hizbut-Tahrir. In one confrontation, officers reportedly "started beating the participants with sticks and clubs." More than 30 protesters were arrested.[80]

There is nothing to indicate that these abuses will cease. Indeed, the self-censorship has shown no signs of ceasing, either. This atmosphere of fear has only inhibited the Palestinians from engaging in critical political discussion about their future government and ultimately has made it more difficult for the Palestinian people to make the choices necessary to effect real change. As outgoing prime minister Salam Fayyad told a group of Palestinian photojournalists in May 2013, freedom of the press must be an essential component of the Palestinian state.[81]

13

Unilateralism

"IN OUR ENDEAVOR TODAY TO ACQUIRE NON-MEMBER STATE STATUS FOR Palestine in the United Nations," said Mahmoud Abbas at the United Nations on November 29, 2012, "we reaffirm that Palestine will always adhere to and respect the charter and resolutions of the United Nations and international humanitarian law, uphold equality, guarantee civil liberties, uphold the rule of law, promote democracy and pluralism, and uphold and protect the rights of women."[1]

The Palestinian president made this plea for nonmember observer state status for Palestine against the stated wishes of US president Barack Obama. He also did so against the wishes of Canadian premier Stephen Harper. And it goes without saying that he did so against the wishes of Israeli prime minister Benjamin Netanyahu. Nevertheless, the Palestinian leader won the support of the UN General Assembly by a vote of 138 to 9.

Rather than seeking ways to deprive the Palestinian leader of the power that he had been abusing since coming to office seven years earlier, the international community was looking for new ways to prop him up. Diplomats quietly conceded that the UN vote was just as much about countering the growing influence of

Hamas, particularly after the Gaza-based group claimed victory in a rocket war with Israel earlier in the month, as it was about the Palestinian national project.

THE UN INITIATIVE had been in the works since 2005. That year, Abbas reportedly traveled to Brazil for a summit of South American and Arab states and met privately with Brazil's leftist president, Luiz Inácio Lula da Silva. There, Lula told Abbas that by the end of his second term (which expired on January 1, 2011), he would help build a Latin American consensus for a unilateral Palestinian statehood declaration at the UN.

Latin America proved fertile ground for the initiative, especially with the rise of other left-wing governments in South America's most important countries—not only Brazil, but also Chile, Argentina, and, especially, Venezuela. In early February 2009, Costa Rica officially recognized a Palestinian state,[2] and just two months later, Palestinian and Venezuelan officials established diplomatic relations and inaugurated a Palestinian embassy in Caracas.[3] In November 2009, Abbas toured the region, visiting Brazil, Argentina, Chile, Paraguay, and Venezuela.[4] That month, Venezuela formally announced support for Palestinian statehood.

The following year, Lula continued to advocate for Abbas. In March 2010, he visited Israel and the Palestinian territories, expressing support for the Palestinians and criticizing the construction of Jewish settlements in the West Bank.[5] In December, as promised, just before his term in office was to expire, Lula announced that Brazil recognized an independent Palestinian state.[6] With that, the Latin American floodgates opened. Shortly after Lula's announcement, Argentina, Bolivia, and Ecuador expressed support for a Palestinian state.[7] In addition, Uruguay announced its intention to offer recognition in 2011 and further indicated that it would establish diplomatic representation, most likely in Ramallah.[8]

On New Year's Eve 2010, Abbas attended a ceremony in Brasilia, where he laid the cornerstone for a new Palestinian embassy.[9] Over the coming weeks, additional Latin American states joined the diplomatic parade. Chile, home to a Palestinian population of about 300,000, offered its unsurprising support.[10] Guyana, Peru, and Paraguay followed.[11] In February 2011, Suriname joined in.[12] Uruguay's official recognition followed in March.[13]

Latin America was not the only region to support the initiative. In June 2010, France announced it would upgrade the Palestinian delegation in Paris to a mission led by an ambassador.[14] Spain, Portugal, and Norway did the same later in the year.[15]

Remarkably, the Palestinians leveraged the sympathy within the international bureaucracy and exploited the pervasive frustration over the continued failure of the peace process. It was an unquestionably successful campaign. The effort to garner widespread international support was a new and decidedly evolved approach to their campaign against Israel, where the government was flummoxed by the speed and cleverness of the Palestinian maneuverings. The Israelis couldn't keep up.

IN THE FALL OF 2010, the Palestinian leadership first began making it clear that statehood was their agenda. The October issue of the *Monocle,* a London-based magazine, revealed that the PA in the West Bank was planning to roll out a currency—the Palestinian pound. In a one-on-one interview, Palestine Monetary Authority Chairman Jihad al-Wazir, son of Fatah founder and PLO terrorist Khalil al-Wazir, insisted that the step was "not necessarily immediate." However, based on the interview with the Marquette University graduate, it was also clear that a great deal of planning had already gone into the currency. For example, the *Monocle* reported that a photo of the late Yasser Arafat "is almost certain" to appear on the currency and that the design of the currency would likely be decided by competition. Reserves of the currency would also be held in the Palestinian Central Bank, which was under construction in Ramallah.[16]

The currency has deep historical meaning. In short, because the Palestinians have never had an independent nation, they've never had their own currency. The pound was the currency of the British Mandate of Palestine from 1927 until the creation of Israel in 1948. From 1948 until 1967, when the West Bank was under Jordanian occupation, citizens were forced to do business in Jordanian dinars. Similarly, thanks to the Egyptian occupation of the Gaza Strip, citizens there had little choice but to trade in Egyptian pounds. Since 1967, the Palestinians in both territories have primarily done business in Israeli currency—the lira until 1980, and the shekel since.

Meanwhile, Abbas continued to enlist the assistance of foreign leaders to recognize a Palestinian state without Israel's agreement. On December 5, he visited Turkish prime minister Recep Tayyip Erdoğan in Ankara. Shortly thereafter, the Palestinian envoy to Turkey announced that Erdoğan would recognize a Palestinian state (within the 1967 borders) at an unspecified time.[17] Erdoğan also reportedly promised to go to bat for the initiative with other heads of state.

By the end of 2010, almost 100 countries had already recognized an independent Palestine, and it was unclear how many others Abbas had asked to sign on to his plan. Palestinian negotiator Saeb Erekat approached UN and European officials, demanding that they force Israel to stop imposing "facts on the ground" in the West Bank through the construction of settlements.[18] Abbas adviser Nimer Hammad added that the Palestinians were considering a plan whereby the United Nations would approve of a Palestinian state in the West Bank, Gaza Strip, and East Jerusalem.[19]

IN THE FIRST MONTHS OF 2011, Cyprus, Greece, and Ireland upgraded their Palestinian diplomatic missions. In March, the

United Kingdom and Denmark did the same.[20] By the spring of 2011, Slovenia and Spain had announced their recognition of a Palestinian state.[21] They were then followed by the Dominican Republic and Peru.[22] In July, Bulgaria, Belgium, and Norway announced their support.[23] The Palestinians clearly had the upper hand, despite protests from the United States, Israel, Canada, and a handful of other countries.

Europe was a particularly interesting battleground. The Palestinian drive for recognition at the United Nations exposed deep fault lines among the 27 member states of the European Union.[24] German chancellor Angela Merkel observed, "It is not certain that unilateral recognition will contribute to promoting peace."[25] Italian foreign minister Franco Frattini echoed her concerns: "Peace is made through negotiation, not through imposition."[26]

By contrast, French president Nicolas Sarkozy stated in May 2011, "If the peace process is still dead in September, France will face up to its responsibilities on the central question of the recognition of a Palestinian state."[27] Spain's foreign minister, Trinidad Jimenez, similarly opined, "There's the feeling that now is the time to do something, to give the Palestinians the hope that a state could become reality."[28] Spain had upgraded its mission, too.[29]

Many of the European countries did not heed Israel's warnings over how the unilateral Palestinian initiative might create challenges for a two-state solution. Instead, many insisted that such a move would help prod the two sides toward peace. The logic: a stronger Palestinian hand would force the Israelis to respect the Palestinian side's positions.

As the Palestinians openly mulled their options, the international community failed to make any demands on the Palestinians. There was no discussion about conditioning international aid based on good governance. There was no discussion about improving upon the state-building program.

Some states may have felt that such a move might undercut the Palestinians. But amending the UN resolution would not have rejected the premise of taking steps toward a Palestinian state. Rather, it would have placed realistic conditions on Abbas in exchange for recognizing his maneuver. This, however, was the road not taken.

Another road not taken was congressional oversight. The Palestinian leadership was traveling to dozens of countries to drum up support for the statehood bid.[30] Accordingly, the Palestinians were spending huge sums of money to pursue this diplomatic initiative, and it was entirely unclear where those funds were coming from. Were they being drawn from the PA's coffers? If so, this subject fell squarely in the wheelhouse of Congress, which controls the purse strings for the estimated $600 million in aid furnished yearly by the United States to the PA.

The Palestinians were traveling frenetically across the globe. From Mahmoud Abbas to Hanan Ashrawi to Nabil Sha'ath, the Palestinians were spending untold sums of cash to press their case in international capitals. All of that travel could not have been cheap. And it was all happening while the PA was suffering from a cash crunch. Indeed, Prime Minister Salam Fayyad openly complained that the PA was facing a financial crisis because donor nations were delaying or withholding funds.[31]

US lawmakers, for their part, registered their disapproval of the Palestinian UN gambit and were threatening to withhold aid. The maneuver, after all, was an outright rejection of the Oslo Accords, the legal framework for US–Palestinian relations. In many ways, it was also a rejection of the US role as the primary broker for continued diplomacy. And whether intended or not, the move also had the effect of isolating the United States from the Arab world. Indeed, how could the United States deny the yearning of the Palestinian people, particularly as it supported other Middle

Eastern people's struggles for independence during the "Arab Spring"?

A potential full cut-off by Congress threatened the Palestinians with a complete financial collapse. The Israelis, who collect some $100 million in value-added taxes (VAT) on behalf of the Palestinians each month, also threatened to withhold funds. At the time, US aid and Israeli VAT amounted to more than $1.5 billion per year.[32] This sum was roughly three-quarters of the PA's annual budget.

With the maneuver at the United Nations slated for the September 2011 UN General Assembly, Palestinian newspapers reported plans for a mass rally the day of the vote, which leaders called "Palestine 194," marking their desire to become the United Nation's 194th member state.[33]

Al-Jazeera quoted PLO official Yasser Abed Rabbo calling for "millions to pour into the streets" in support of the bid.[34] Marwan Barghouti, a popular Palestinian figure now serving five life sentences in Israel for terrorism, also expressed support for mass demonstrations.[35] Abbas, the architect of the statehood drive, embraced the protests as well.[36]

Amid these calls for peaceful rallies, analysts began to question whether they would remain peaceful. With the United States poised to block a Palestinian request for full statehood, Palestinian columnist Daoud Kuttab warned, "If this path is blocked, there is no telling which route the Palestinians will take."[37]

Kuttab was not simply hypothesizing. A poll conducted by the Palestinian Center for Public Opinion in May showed that more than 70 percent of Palestinians thought a new uprising was around the corner.[38] Facebook pages had popped up calling for orchestrated Palestinian uprisings against Israel. There was even a "Third Palestinian Intifada" iPhone app, which Apple later removed at Israel's urging.[39]

Bracing for the worst, former Israeli defense minister Shaul Mofaz announced that the country would call up military reservists in advance of the UN vote.[40] To the relief of the Israelis, violence never erupted.

"LADIES AND GENTLEMEN," Mahmoud Abbas told the UN General Assembly on September 23, 2011, "I would like to inform you that, before delivering this statement, I submitted, in my capacity as the President of the State of Palestine and Chairman of the Executive Committee of the Palestine Liberation Organization, to His Excellency Mr. Ban Ki-moon, Secretary-General of the United Nations, an application for the admission of Palestine on the basis of the 4 June 1967 borders, with Al-Quds Al-Sharif [Holy Jerusalem] as its capital, as a full member of the United Nations."

He continued, "I call upon Mr. Secretary-General to expedite transmittal of our request to the Security Council, and I call upon the distinguished members of the Security Council to vote in favor of our full membership. I also call upon the States that did not recognize the State of Palestine as yet to do so."[41]

With that, Abbas made history. He appealed to the United Nations for statehood. And while it can certainly be argued that Arafat had already done this in 1988, the Palestine 194 campaign felt distinctly different. The Palestinians had put in the effort to rally the international community, and they had done so successfully. The only hitch: The United States, as a permanent member of the Security Council, was poised to veto their efforts. The Palestinian bid was, therefore, symbolic at best.

Nevertheless, Abbas was roundly rewarded at home. As Al-Jazeera reported, "A welcome party was planned at the Muqata, the presidential headquarters [in Ramallah], and a stage was set up next to the grave of the former president, Yasser Arafat, inside the compound."[42]

Not surprisingly, Abbas's own loyalists sponsored the celebrations. The Palestinian workers' union called on its members to join the celebration, and government offices closed to enable employees to attend. The teachers' union also announced that schools would close early to allow students and teachers to join the party. Both state TV and the state-run news agency WAFA called on the public to rally at the Muqata. Palestinians across the West Bank received text messages advertising "the official mass reception." Palestine TV devoted its broadcast to Abbas, showing photographs of the leader throughout the years as well as footage of him meeting ordinary Palestinians and international figures.[43]

As expected, Abbas's reception was considerably cooler in Washington. The House of Representatives, led by then Foreign Affairs Committee chairman Ileana Ros-Lehtinen (R-FL), sought to punish Abbas and his West Bank government for snubbing American-led diplomacy. Some legislators wanted to reduce US aid to the PA, whereas others wanted to slash it entirely. The White House, for its part, wanted to keep aid flowing so that Washington retained leverage to bring the Palestinians back to the negotiating table.

In the end, the compromise in Washington was to withhold $200 million in financial assistance as a warning to the Palestinians not to return to the United Nations. There was considerable disagreement between the executive and legislative branches of the US government, but the end result was a victory for Congress.[44]

HOWEVER, THE PALESTINIANS were not prepared to accept defeat. With more than 100 countries in support of the "State of Palestine," the Palestinians had earned support that they could leverage. Abbas and his advisers made a play for membership at the UN Educational, Scientific, and Cultural Organization (UNESCO) in 2011. As soon as the discussion of the broader UN bid had subsided, the UNESCO debate began to heat up.

As had been the case with the broader UN maneuver, the United States, Israel, Canada, and a handful of other countries were opposed. Among the more vocal supporters was France's Sarkozy. But this position soon appeared to backfire on the French leader.

According to a little-known American law passed during the Clinton administration in the 1990s, the United States is prohibited from giving funds to any part of the UN system that grants the PLO the same standing as member states.[45] So, as the Palestinians pushed for full membership, they were effectively pushing for a $70 million per year (America's 22 percent) slashing of the UNESCO budget, which operated on a $325 million per annum budget.[46]

Apparently, the Quai d'Orsay began to have second thoughts. French diplomats noted that despite their earlier backing of the Palestinian unilateral bid, it was "not the right time or the right place" to wrestle with the question of Palestine. These statements came only a few months after Sarkozy had signaled support for the broader initiative.[47] The reason: UNESCO is headquartered in Paris, and the French did not wish to see its funding cut.

France retreated, but the UNESCO train had effectively left the building. In October 2011, UNESCO's 58-nation executive board approved a draft resolution for Palestinian membership, sponsored by several Arab states, by a 40-to-4 vote.[48] The four countries opposed were the United States, Germany, Latvia, and Romania. France was among the 14 countries abstaining.[49]

Around the same time, senior UNESCO officials made the rounds in Washington, meeting with Obama administration officials, legislators, and other influential Beltway types, trying to convince them that UNESCO's activities were in America's interest. They were also desperately hoping to find a loophole that could help circumvent the aforementioned law that would leave the organization without US taxpayer funds as a result of Palestinian admission.

UNESCO voted in October 2011, with 107 of 173 countries voting in favor, 14 opposing, and 52 abstaining. Immediately thereafter, US funds were slashed.[50] The UNESCO victory for the Palestinians was a Pyrrhic one at best.

IN JANUARY 2012, ISRAELI ENVOY Isaac Molho met Palestinian negotiator Saeb Erekat for a series of diplomatic exchanges.[51] The talks, widely praised across the international community, were billed as a much-needed impetus for negotiations between the two sides. But, in retrospect, they were a distraction from Palestinian attempts to jump-start its stalled bid at the United Nations.

On January 1, 2012, several countries that would have voted against the Palestinian bid rotated off the Security Council, making way for Guatemala, Pakistan, Azerbaijan, Morocco, and Togo.[52] Although the exact intentions were not clear, Abbas's advisers were again telegraphing their intentions to return for another round at Turtle Bay. Even as the talks between Molho and Erekat were taking place, Nabil Sha'ath said that 2012 "will be the start of an unprecedented diplomatic campaign on the part of the Palestinian leadership, and it will be a year of pressure on Israel that will put it under a real international siege. The campaign will be similar to the one waged against apartheid in South Africa."[53]

By the end of January, the Palestinian Ma'an News Agency reported that Abbas "refused and will continue to refuse" more meetings with Israel,[54] and the Palestinian leadership was planning to revive the bid at the United Nations.[55] PLO spokeswoman Hanan Ashrawi declared, "We will persist in our efforts to pursue membership in the United Nations Security Council, the United Nations General Assembly, and other multinational agencies and organizations."[56]

In mid-February, Abbas told the Arab League that if Israel did not accept his preconditions for negotiations, including a full settlement freeze, he would "go to the Security Council and the General Assembly."[57] Abbas received the full support of the Arab League.[58] A month later, Saeb Erekat, the lead Palestinian negotiator, said that an agreement had been reached between the Palestinian leadership and Qatar to return to the United Nations.[59] In April, during a visit to Tunisia, Abbas reiterated, "If you do not see any progress with the peace process, we will go to the United Nations."[60]

By mid-May, a Palestinian official admitted that the Palestinians were preparing another bid at the United Nations.[61] Shortly thereafter, Abbas again threatened that "we will go to the UN to extract a seat for Palestine as a non-member state"[62] if no diplomatic progress was made.

Meanwhile, reports in the Israeli media suggested that the Palestinians were planning to launch a campaign, along the lines of the UNESCO bid, to be recognized as an "observer state" at Rio+20, the UN Conference on Sustainable Development in Brazil. Israel, the United States, and Canada were reportedly working against the initiative.[63] A few days before the beginning of the conference, Palestinian ambassador Ibrahim Alzeben said, "We expect full-status participation because we already have it in UNESCO and we have ties with Brazil (the host country which recognizes the Palestinian state) and with more than 130 countries."[64]

AS IT BECAME INCREASINGLY APPARENT that the PLO was poised for another run at the United Nations, Washington reportedly began to push back against the leadership in Ramallah. In an interview with the Saudi *Okaz* newspaper, Saeb Erekat said the United States was threatening to suspend aid and close down the PLO mission in Washington, DC, if the Palestinians returned to the United Nations.[65] The PLO representative to Washington, Maen Rashid Areikat, later denied reports that the United States was threatening to cease aid or close the PLO mission in response to the UN bid, but it was clear that US pressure was taking its toll.[66] On July 23, *Al-Hayat* reported that Abbas preferred to postpone the UN bid until after the US elections in early November.[67]

On August 2, the Associated Press reported, "The possibility of repercussions abroad has sparked a growing debate in [Abbas's] inner circle over the timing of such a call, and whether it should be delayed until after the U.S. presidential election."[68] According to PLO official Hanan Ashrawi, "There are some who might want to wait until after November because of American pressure, but the Americans have done nothing but put pressure on the Palestinians, without delivering anything. . . . What we need is to move fast."[69]

On August 5, the *Times of Israel* reported that Israel was "offering incentives to the PA to drop the unilateral statehood gambit."[70] *Maariv* reported that "Israeli Prime Minister Benjamin Netanyahu has offered to release 50 prisoners detained before the Oslo Accords if the Palestinian Authority cancels its proposed UN bid."[71] Mahmoud Abbas, however, stated that the Palestinians would continue toward the UN "even if this step conflicts with other parties' interests."[72]

In mid-August, *Ynet News* reported that the Arab League was considering submitting the Palestinian bid on behalf of the leadership in Ramallah in an attempt to draw the fire from the Western states that sought to cut aid to the PA. Around this time, November 29 was floated as the date the Palestinians would return to New York. On that date in 1947, the United Nations first accepted an Arab and a Jewish state in the British Mandate of Palestine. That symbolic date has also since been marked by the United Nations as the International Day of Solidarity with the Palestinian People.[73]

But the Palestinian leadership continued to waver. Reports differed from day to day. Abbas and his inner circle remained in limbo about their maneuver, weighing whether it was worth angering the United States and potentially putting relations with Israel on a collision course. The Associated Press reported in late August that "the Palestinians are putting their quest for international recognition at the U.N. on hold for now." The report also said that Abbas would "not apply at the General Assembly session next month, although he will informally appeal for recognition in a speech."[74] According to the *Jerusalem Post,* "threats and extortion" by the United States pressured the Palestinians to make the decision.[75]

On September 5, in an about-face, Mahmoud Abbas said that the Palestinian leadership would proceed with the statehood bid at the end of the month. "I am going this month to the UN General Assembly in light of the latest decision in Doha, the Islamic summit and the Non-Aligned Movement summit,"[76] Abbas said. The same day, however, Palestinian foreign minister Riyad al-Maliki said that no date had been set and that Arab states would lobby on behalf of the PLO throughout the fall.[77]

The driving force behind the bid was the Fatah Central Committee. This powerful group "reiterated its support for President Mahmoud Abbas to seek upgraded status for Palestine at the United Nations this month,"[78] according to Ma'an News Agency, in mid-September. By September 20, the *New York Times* reported that the Palestinians were pursuing a "subdued campaign" to gain nonmember state status. According to the report, "The delegation heading to New York this weekend is half the size of last year's. And there are no concerts or street parties planned this time around President Mahmoud Abbas's September 27 speech to the General Assembly." Nonetheless, Saeb Erekat said that the Palestinians were expecting to garner between 150 and 170 votes for their resolution.[79]

On September 24, the *Washington Post* reported that "it is far from clear that his [Abbas's] words will be followed anytime soon with a draft resolution to change the Palestinians' status at the U.N. from an 'observer entity' to a non-member 'observer state.'" The report further noted that "Palestinian officials acknowledge that any such resolution is unlikely to be presented in the weeks leading up to the U.S. election [in November], so as not to antagonize President Obama at a politically sensitive moment."[80]

In his UN speech on September 27, Mahmoud Abbas stated, "We have begun intensive consultations with various regional organizations and Member States aimed at having the General Assembly adopt a resolution considering the State of Palestine as a non-Member State of the United Nations during this session."[81]

In the days and weeks that followed, the Palestinian issue was given relatively short shrift, thanks to the election cycle in the United States and the civil war in Syria. But it was increasingly clear that the November 29 date was the target. On October 1, Saeb Erekat revealed that the Palestinians had "started consultations with Arab countries and other geopolitical groups over phrasing a draft resolution to the UN General Assembly requesting acceptance of Palestine as a non-member state."[82] Erekat was similarly quoted as saying that "the Palestinian train toward membership in the UN has started to move and it will not be stopped by threats."[83]

While it openly did not issue threats, the United States remained adamantly opposed. On October 15, US ambassador to the United Nations Susan Rice said that the Palestinian bid "would only jeopardize the peace process and complicate efforts to return the parties to direct negotiations."[84] The following day, Abbas sent a letter to President Obama stating that the Palestinians would return to negotiations "after obtaining international recognition."[85] Days later he told reporters, "We're ready to go back to negotiations straightaway. Going to the U.N. is not a substitute for negotiations. We are in need of negotiations to solve the final status of issues that face us both."[86]

WITH A MONTH TO GO before the November 29 bid, Reuters reported that the "Palestinians have launched a diplomatic blitz aimed at garnering a strong majority for a vote granting the non-member statehood at the United Nations slated for next month." A PLO official said, "From the E.U. we will have a minimum of 12 votes and maybe up to 15, as some are not yet decided."[87] On October 31, Palestinian official Mohammad Shtayyeh left for Denmark, Sweden, and Finland to garner additional support for the upcoming bid.[88] Additionally, "envoys were dispatched to Germany, Austria, [and] the United Kingdom," according to the Associated Press.[89] Writing in the *Telegraph*, Nabil Sha'ath said it would be "reprehensible" for British diplomats to discourage the Palestinian UN bid.[90]

The Israelis, meanwhile, were apparently looking to launch a counter-offensive. On November 6, *Haaretz* reported that nine senior Israeli ministers prepared to meet to discuss the Palestinian UN bid and potential retaliatory measures.[91] However, there was no discernible Israeli strategy.

WITH THE US ELECTIONS OVER on November 7 and a second Obama presidential term secured, Abbas congratulated the US president on his victory and "expressed hope that Obama will stand by the Palestinian decision to gain a non-member state status in the United Nations."[92] Reuters quoted Erekat as saying, "We did him [Obama] a favor [delaying the UN bid until after US elections] and we hope he will remember that."[93]

On November 8, the Palestinians began circulating a draft resolution calling for an upgrade in their status.[94] The following day, an Arab League official revealed that 51 states were still undecided how they would vote.[95] Over the three weeks that followed, the numbers fluctuated, but the prevarication had ended. The Palestinians were set to return to the United Nations. Only this time, they would not make the mistake of asking for full membership and risk a US veto at the Security Council. Instead, they planned to go directly to the General Assembly, where they had the numbers advantage and where the United States and Israel were only 2 of 193.

While the lead-up to the vote on November 29, 2012, was filled with international intrigue and drama, the vote itself was rather uneventful. Everyone assembled in Turtle Bay that day knew the vote would redound overwhelmingly in Abbas's favor. And it did; 138 countries voted in favor of the initiative. Only nine voted against—eight, not including Israel.

France, expectedly, voted in favor of the bid. The surprises, though, were the abstentions by Germany and Great Britain because they had been among the countries initially opposed. Both countries viewed their vote as a means to contest Israeli settlement construction. Other countries that voted in favor indicated that they saw the bid as an important step to advance the Palestinian national project. However, prior to the vote, Western diplomats from around Europe also quietly conceded that they believed their vote would help the PLO counter Hamas's growing influence, particularly after the Gaza-based terrorist group claimed victory in its mini war with Israel in November.[96]

But supporting a bureaucratic maneuver at the United Nations, which merely granted Abbas a temporary boost in approval, was not a viable strategy for developing a functioning democratic state in the West Bank. The move, in fact, only exacerbated the challenges in the West Bank. It bolstered the current leadership without pushing for much-needed reform.

14

Righting the Ship

IN JANUARY 2013, JUST MONTHS AFTER MAHMOUD ABBAS HAD SUCCESS-
fully upgraded the PLO to nonmember observer status at the
United Nations, the PA was in dire straits. The government was
strapped for cash, and the United States, its largest donor, was
withholding aid. Even Arab states were slow to provide the West
Bank government with the funds it needed to function. The PA
sought assurances of a safety net from the Arab League,[1] but using the past as a guide, there were few signs that the Arab states
intended to do more than merely pledge funds that would likely
never be transferred to a PA account.[2]

At the time, some Palestinian officials suggested that US pressure, as an expression of displeasure with the UN upgrade, was
preventing Arab states from aiding the PA.[3] True or not, the Palestinian leadership was forced to look for alternative financing. One
of the solutions to the financial crisis presented to the Palestinian
leadership was to take out loans from the Palestine Investment
Fund (PIF). As Palestinian finance minister Nabil Qassis said,
"We don't like to do it, but our options are very limited."[4] The
PIF stated that no such loans were made.[5]

In the meantime, the PA government was not doing itself any favors. Reports suggested that poor administration continued to eat into the government's coffers. The Ma'an News Agency reported that between January 2008 and January 2012 alone, the government had lost $43 million in border fees.[6] Meanwhile, according to the Associated Press, one Palestinian watchdog group was investigating 20 claims that senior PA officials "stole public funds."[7]

Financial mismanagement was only part of the story. In February 2013, within a span of just a few days, a series of articles published in surprising places hammered the PA for its continued campaign to restrict press freedom. Left-leaning media watchdog commentator Jillian C. York lambasted the PA on the Al-Jazeera website.[8] George Hale, an editor at the Ma'an News Agency, penned an academic survey for Global Information Society Watch.[9] And the *New York Times* ran an op-ed slamming the PA's authoritarian practices.[10]

The very fact that the *New York Times* ran a piece on the topic was notable. Just weeks before in an uncharacteristic editorial, the newspaper made a plea to save the flailing government. The *Times*' primary goal, it seemed, was to fundraise for the government as a means to save the remaining shreds of the Oslo Accords.[11] After all, the PA was designed to be the caretaker government according to the agreement. Without that caretaker government, there would not be much left of the accords.

But the *Times* may have already been too late. Within days of his UN victory, Abbas had requested that the United Nations begin referring to the PA government as the "State of Palestine."[12] In other words, the PLO had already potentially scuttled the PA, the interim government put in place by the Oslo Accords and the cornerstone of Palestinian–Israeli negotiations since 1994.

Perhaps for these reasons, Shawan Jabarin, director of Al-Haq, a human rights organization in Ramallah, expressed concern about potential "legal and political complications" and a "lack of clarity that needs to be sorted out."[13]

And the complications didn't end there. Abbas also issued a decree that all stamps, signs, and letterheads would be changed to reflect the new name.[14] The move, according to one Palestinian official, was aimed at enhancing Palestinian "sovereignty on the ground" and was a step toward "real independence."[15]

The Palestinian Economic Council for Development and Reconstruction, an aid institution more commonly known as PECDAR, was reportedly the first Palestinian institution to comply with Abbas's decree.[16] The Palestinian Ministry of Information followed suit,[17] and other ministries followed after.

But Abbas was not done making moves. The PLO's official mouthpiece, Palestine News and Information Agency (WAFA), ran a piece on January 5, 2012, stating that "an earlier decision has been reached [by the PLO] to delegate to the [PLO] Central Council the duties of the Palestinian Authority's government and parliament."[18]

In other words, Abbas appeared to be taking steps that would enable him to consolidate power by facilitating the transfer of key components of the PA into the hands of the PLO, which has never been subject to public scrutiny in the way that the PA has been since its inception in 1994. It was entirely unclear at the time whether Abbas was testing to see whether such a move was feasible or whether he was truly softening the ground for a big move.

Abbas never framed it this way, of course. Instead, he declared that he was prepared to shut down the PA in the face of continued Israeli settlement construction. In fact, more than 25 times since assuming leadership in 2005, according to journalist Khaled Abu Toameh, Abbas has threatened to quit as the PA's president or simply dismantle the PA.[19] Partisans of the Palestinian cause have roundly supported him. They say that the Palestinians should not have to ask permission to do anything, not least from their occupiers. They support the notion that collapsing the PA would saddle the Israelis again with the full administrative burden of the West Bank. (Gaza, under the control of Hamas, is another kettle of fish.)

But what Abbas's supporters—both domestic and international—didn't seem to realize was that by shutting the doors of the PA, the PLO could leverage its newfound status at the United Nations (not Abbas's elected presidential authority, which expired in 2009) to consolidate power.

And, as this book has explained, the last thing anyone needs is a more muscular PLO. The PA was created, in part, to curb the bloated PLO, which has earned a reputation over the years as being ossified and less than transparent.

This was lost on the *New York Times* editorial writers. But they did get one thing right: "If there is ever to be a peace agreement between Israel and the Palestinians, there has to be a competent government to run a Palestinian state and leaders with whom to make a deal."[20]

IN MARCH 2013, PRESIDENT BARACK OBAMA traveled to the Middle East to jump-start the peace process and nudge the Palestinians and Israelis back toward President Bush's roadmap. In July 2013, diplomacy resumed under Secretary of State John Kerry. But there is an inherent problem. One cannot talk about a roadmap when there is no clear road to take.

For peace to be achieved, it would be great for the Palestinians and Israelis to see eye-to-eye on a host of issues. It would be wonderful for both sides to renounce their hatred. But, more basically, both sides need to be able to have functioning governments and viable economies. The Israelis have both. The Palestinians do not.

Both sides need to have a legitimate public administration and an active civil society. The Israelis have both. The Palestinians do not.

Salam Fayyad, in the wake of his resignation, made this abundantly clear when he slammed the Palestinian leadership in the pages of the *New York Times*. "Our story is a story of failed leadership," he told columnist Roger Cohen, adding, "it is incredible that the fate of the Palestinian people has been in the hands of leaders so entirely casual, guided by spur-of-the-moment decisions, without seriousness."[21] Fayyad's office later denied that the outgoing reformer had made these comments,[22] but Cohen insisted that Fayyad's quotes were genuine. "It happened. He spoke out,"[23] he wrote via Twitter.

Fayyad's apparent frustration is understandable. Despite his best efforts, the Palestinians do not have the kinds of durable government institutions that will allow them to subsist side-by-side with Israel. In all likelihood, with the current infrastructure, Palestinian independence could actually mean collapse.

So, what can be done in the future? Quite a lot. In the spirit of President Woodrow Wilson, the Palestinians and supporters of Palestinian independence should consider the following 14 points:

1. The West should begin to make Palestinian aid conditional on meeting objectives of state building, transparency, and good governance. Aid should not be based solely as a reward for the Palestinians engaging in the peace process, as it has been until now. Funding the peace-based process makes international donors feel good, but what has it accomplished? Aid needs to be conditional and performance-based. This is not to say that international donors should tolerate the presence of incitement or jihadism in the public discourse. That is a serious problem that should be constantly monitored. But that should not be the yardstick for aid. Good governance must be the top priority.

2. The West must keep expectations high. Too often the West is guilty of what US president George W. Bush termed "the soft bigotry of low expectations." The right

approach is not to simply cheerlead for the Palestinians when they start to do things right. The goal is to push them harder. A good example of this was a critical essay penned by George Washington University professor Nathan Brown, who challenged openly the notion that Fayyadism was winning the day.[24] Fayyad supporters roundly booed Brown's "glass is half empty" approach. But, in the end, Brown was right. Despite Fayyad's thoughtful and productive approach, not enough progress had been made. And it should be reasonable to make these criticisms when they are deserved. If the Palestinians are serious about their statehood project, such criticisms should be viewed as challenges that need to be met.

3. The West must insist that, if further aid is to be furnished, Palestinian economic development must be based on sustainable practices, not on political patronage. As Dennis Ross notes, "People need to get contracts based upon a legitimate process, not based on favoritism."[25] The process needs to be a completely objective one in which the best and most transparent companies are awarded contracts. This cannot be tainted by political objectives. Nepotism, waste, and corruption have already eroded Palestinian growth.

4. To accomplish points 1 through 3, we must take the "peace processors" away from the economic process. Economic development must be left to the economists. Too many sweetheart deals were cut during the heyday of the peace process. The prevailing thinking appeared to be that if the most important Palestinians were sated by lucrative business deals, then they would not have the stomach to engage again in hostilities. That thinking was wrong. When the peace process unraveled, so did the Palestinian economy.

5. Conversely, it will also be imperative to leave the economists out of the peace process. In fact, along the lines of
point 4, diplomats should now know the importance of
leaving all economics out of the peace process. This is
what led to corruption—on both the Palestinian and Israeli sides—during the Oslo years. To paraphrase Israel's
first prime minister, David Ben-Gurion, the Palestinians
must pursue peace as if there were no state-building process and pursue state-building as if there were no peace
process.

6. The international community must cease placing its trust
in former or recovering terrorist organizations to create
viable economic and political systems. As Aaron David
Miller asks, "Can a national liberation organization
make the jump from terrorist organization, or violent
organization, to a bureaucracy, and a functioning one at
that?"[26] While there may be exceptions, public administration has never been the strong suit of subnational
guerrilla groups. It is not their core competency and likely
never will be. It was a huge mistake to expect the PLO to
turn into a government overnight. The Palestinians must
seek out trained public administrators to help build their
state. Failure to do so will invite further failure.

7. The Palestinians must consolidate all of their armed and
security forces. The West must demand this for two reasons. First, it is imperative for peace with Israel. Second,
it is critical to do this if a future Palestinian state is to be
viewed as stable by the donor community. All investors
seek stability and predictability. Conversely, no outside
investor will truly trust Palestine as an investment as long
as Hamas, Al-Aqsa Martyrs Brigades, Palestinian Islamic
Jihad, Popular Resistance Committees, and other jihadi
groups roam the streets.

8. Foreign aid should not be the primary source of income for a Palestinian state. That's not to say that foreign aid is wrong. It just means that the Palestinians need to develop private enterprise. The Israelis need to allow for it, too. On this score, the Israelis will need to think long and hard about a good number of their restrictive policies—particularly those not directly tied to security—in the West Bank (and maybe even the Gaza Strip). Israeli cooperation is critical for allowing the Palestinian economy to thrive.

9. Foreign aid, if and when it flows, must flow through a single treasury account. That account must be governed by legitimate accounting practices, ensuring that the funds go to public administration, not special interests. This is a central tenet of Fayyadism. It remains as necessary today as it was when Fayyad began his project.

10. The Palestinians must have a free press. A free press is crucial to maintaining a free society. But in the case of the Palestinians, a free press can also serve as a much-needed corruption watchdog. Until now, the Palestinian leadership has largely frowned upon such reporting, both domestically and internationally. This must end.

    Similarly, there must be freedom to protest, which is currently lacking in Palestinian society. This lack of freedom is a symptom of larger problems created by a government that does not provide its people with other fundamental rights.

11. To address these problems, the Palestinians must maintain an independent judiciary. As Ross notes, "This is the most fundamental thing . . . if that was done, a lot of other things would fall into place."[27] Real checks and balances would ensure that Palestinian governance is clean and functioning. An independent judiciary should

also be able to prevent the PA security forces from abuses of power, which continue unabated. For example, a report in March 2013 indicated that the documented cases of torture in the West Bank rose from 112 to 116.[28]

12. In keeping with some of these fundamental issues, the Palestinians also need to allow for new parties and leaders to emerge. As former George W. Bush administration official Michael Singh notes, "We've got to cultivate relationships with a broader swath of the Palestinian polity . . . who are one way or the other going to represent the future of a Palestinian state. . . . We have to know who they are. We have to have relationships with them."[29] The Palestinians need a clash of ideas to take place for the right kind of governance to emerge. Right now, political challengers are crushed. This portends poorly for the future of the system.

13. The PLO needs to go. As Syracuse University's Osamah Khalil notes, "The PLO's institutions were designed for a national liberation movement in the context of the Cold War and were deliberately constructed to limit broad-based representation until victory was achieved. In the absence of victory, the same institutional structures have been used to hinder potential reforms and distance the Palestinian leadership from the population it purports to represent."[30] The PLO has also made it difficult for the international community to hold the Palestinian leadership accountable. For example, Mahmoud Abbas is the president of the PA and also the head of the PLO. When he undertakes decisions, it is not always clear which hat he is wearing. Additionally, the PLO has no oversight. One US Treasury official notes, "The PLO is not the business of the Treasury."[31] But then, whose business is it? The PLO finances are a black box, as is much of its

decision making. This is a huge impediment to Palestinian transparency.

14. The Palestinians need to bring back their best people. Many Palestinians have been trained to help implement these 14 points. They have studied at the top schools and worked at the top companies in the diaspora. They know how to implement good governance and good business practices. But they have fled. Some of them came back with the promise of the Oslo Accords in the mid-1990s, but many of them took flight again. There has been a brain drain. Not only that, there has been a cash drain, too. The economic mismanagement, political suppression, and overall dysfunction have pushed some of the best, wealthiest, and brightest away. But even a glimmer of hope can bring many of them back to take part in their national project.

The good news is that the Palestinian leadership can still make these changes and right the ship. But this will not happen in a vacuum. World leaders must begin to make their demands heard. The United States and Europe will need to lead the charge. And when they do so, they should make it clear that these demands are not punishment for past transgressions. Rather, they are heightened expectations that can help the Palestinians actualize their dream.

NOTES

CHAPTER 1   COLLAPSE OR STATEHOOD?

1. "The Elders Welcome UN Recognition of Palestine as an Observer State," *The Elders,* November 29, 2012, www.theelders.org/article/elders-welcome-un-recognition-palestine-observer-state.
2. Ibid.
3. Bernard Avishai, "EXCLUSIVE: Former Israeli PM Olmert Supports Palestine U.N. Bid," *Daily Beast,* November 28, 2012, www.thedailybeast.com/articles/2012/11/28/exclusive-former-israeli-pm-olmert-supports-palestine-u-n-bid.html.
4. "Statement by Mr. Ahmet Davutoğlu, Minister of Foreign Affairs of the Republic of Turkey at the UN General Assembly," Republic of Turkey, Ministry of Foreign Affairs, November 29, 2012, www.mfa.gov.tr/statement-by-mr_-ahmet-davutoglu_-minister-of-foreign-affairs-of-the-republic-of-turkey-at-the-un-general-assembly_-29-nov-2012.en.mfa.
5. "China Reaffirms Support for Palestinian UN Bid," Reuters, November 13, 2012, www.haaretz.com/news/middle-east/china-reaffirms-support-for-palestinian-un-bid-1.477441.
6. "Statement by Egypt on Palestine's Obtaining the Status of an Observer State to the United Nations," Arab Republic of Egypt, Ministry of Foreign Affairs, December 2, 2012, www.mfa.gov.eg/English/Minister/Articles/Pages/ArticleInterviewDetails.aspx?Source=6781921f-3993-444a-859e-ee26ce851de8&articleID=ac518ad8-0895-40e6-a457-24fbc7eeb432.
7. "Roger Waters' Speech at the UN General Assembly," The Russell Tribunal on Palestine, November 29, 2012, www.russelltribunalonpalestine.com/en/sessions/future-sessions/videos/roger-waters-speech-at-the-united-nations-on-29-november.
8. Jonathan Schanzer, "Gaza Prepares to Declare Independence (From Palestine)," *New Republic,* September 10, 2012, www.newrepublic.com/blog/plank/107081/gaza-prepares-declare-independence-palestine.
9. Email correspondence with Hussein Ibish, May 2, 2013.
10. See Virgil Hawkins, *Stealth Conflicts: How the World's Worst Violence Is Ignored* (Burlington, VT: Ashgate, 2008).

CHAPTER 2   THE UNITED STATES AND THE QUESTION OF PALESTINE

1. John J. Mearsheimer and Stephen M. Walt, *The Israel Lobby and U.S. Foreign Policy* (New York: Farrar, Straus and Giroux, 2008).
2. Rashid Khalidi, *Palestinian Identity: The Construction of Modern National Consciousness* (New York: Columbia University Press, 1997), p. 11.

3.   "President Woodrow Wilson's Fourteen Points," The Avalon Project, January 8, 1918, http://avalon.law.yale.edu/20th_century/wilson14.asp.

4.   "The King-Crane Commission Report," Israel-Palestine Center for Research and Information, December 21, 2012, www.ipcri.org/files/kingcrane.html.

5.   Kathleen Christison, *Perceptions of Palestine: Their Influence on U.S. Middle East Policy* (Berkeley: University of California Press, 2001), pp. 27–33.

6.   Ibid., p. 28.

7.   "U.S. Congress Endorses the Balfour Declaration," Jewish Virtual Library, December 21, 2012, www.jewishvirtuallibrary.org/jsource/History/Congress_Endorses _the_Balfour_Declaration.html.

8.   "Remembering the Hebron Riots, 1929," *Forward,* August 20, 2004, http:// forward.com/articles/5186/remembering-the-hebron-riots-/.

9.   "The Neutrality Acts, 1930s," US Department of State—Office of the Historian, December 21, 2012, http://history.state.gov/milestones/1921-1936/Neutrality_acts.

10. Rachel Bronson, *Thicker Than Oil: America's Uneasy Partnership with Saudi Arabia* (New York: Oxford University Press, 2006), p. 17.

11. Baruch Kimmerling and Joel S. Migdal, *Palestinians: The Making of a People* (New York: Free Press, 1993), p. 123.

12. Ann Mosely Lesch, "The Palestine Arab Nationalist Movement Under the Mandate," in *The Politics of Palestinian Nationalism,* ed. William B. Quandt, Fuad Jabber, and Ann Moseley Lesch (Berkeley: University of California Press, 1973), pp. 36–39.

13. David G. Dalin and John F. Rothman, *Icon of Evil: Hitler's Mufti and the Rise of Radical Islam* (New York: Random House, 2008), p. 43.

14. Ibid., pp. 50–57.

15. Christison, *Perceptions of Palestine,* pp. 47, 53.

16. Ibid., p. 55.

17. Charles D. Smith, *Palestine and the Arab-Israeli Conflict* (New York: St. Martin's Press, 1992), p. 129.

18. Sheldon L. Richman, "U.S. Conduct in the Middle East Since World War II and the Folly of Intervention," CATO Institute, August 16, 1991, www.cato.org/pubs/pas /pa159.pdf.

19. Christison, *Perceptions of Palestine,* p. 78.

20. Richard Holbrooke, "Washington's Battle over Israel's Birth," *Washington Post,* May 7, 2008, www.washingtonpost.com/wp-dyn/content/article/2008/05/06/AR20 08050602447.html.

21. Christison, *Perceptions of Palestine,* p. 90.

22. Khalidi, *Palestinian Identity,* p. 178.

23. "Highlights of Main Events 1947–1974," Israeli Ministry of Foreign Affairs, December 21, 2012, www.mfa.gov.il/MFA/Foreign+Relations/Israels+Foreign+Relati ons+since+1947/1947-1974/HIGHLIGHTS+OF+MAIN+EVENTS-+1947-1974. htm.

24. Khalidi, *Palestinian Identity,* pp. 181–182.

25. "Special Message to Congress on the Situation in the Middle East," The American Presidency Project, January 5, 1957, www.presidency.ucsb.edu/ws/index.php ?pid=11007.

26. Christison, *Perceptions of Palestine,* p. 105.

27. Abraham Ben-Zvi, *John F. Kennedy and the Politics of Arms Sales to Israel* (London: Frank Cass, 2002).

28. Christison, *Perceptions of Palestine,* p. 114.

29. Michael B. Oren, *Six Days of War: June 1967 and the Making of the Modern Middle East* (Oxford: Oxford University Press, 2002), p. 52.

30. "Resolution Adopted at the Arab Summit Conference in Khartoum," Israeli Ministry of Foreign Affairs, December 21, 2012, www.mfa.gov.il/MFA/Foreign+Relations /Israels+Foreign+Relations+since+1947/1947-1974/31+Resolution+Adopted+at +the+Arab+Summit+Conferenc.htm.

31. Caroline Taillandier, "Middle East Connected Attacks on Americans," *Middle East Review of International Affairs* 5, no. 4 (December 2001), www.gloria-center .org/2001/12/taillandier-htm-2001-12-05/.

32. "Jordan and PLO Turn Page on 'Black September,'" *Al-Arabiya,* September 16, 2010, www.alarabiya.net/articles/2010/09/16/119411.html.

33. Tzvi Ben Gedalyahu, "Abbas Eulogizes Munich Massacre Mastermind," *Arutz Sheva,* July 4, 2010, www.israelnationalnews.com/News/News.aspx/138398.

34. Scott W. Johnson, "How Arafat Got Away with Murder," *Weekly Standard,* January 29, 2007, www.weeklystandard.com/Content/Public/Articles/000/000/013/192 ioiwy.asp.

35. "The Seizure of the Saudi Arabian Embassy in Khartoum," US Department of State—Office of the Historian, December 21, 2012, http://history.state.gov /historicaldocuments/frus1969-76ve06/d217.

36. "US Agency Helped Uncover 1973 NYC Plot to Kill Golda Meir," Associated Press, February 3, 2009, www.ynetnews.com/articles/0,7340,L-3665848,00.html.

37. "The President's News Conference," The American Presidency Project, March 2, 1973, www.presidency.ucsb.edu/ws/index.php?pid=4123.

38. See Abraham Rabinovich, *The Yom Kippur War: The Epic Encounter That Transformed the Middle East* (New York: Random House, 2004).

39. William B. Quandt, *Decade of Decisions* (Berkeley: University of California Press, 1977), pp. 233–257.

40. Mark Tessler, *A History of the Israeli-Palestinian Conflict* (Bloomington: Indiana University Press, 1994), p. 485.

41. "A/PV.2282 and Corr.1," *United Nations,* November 13, 1974, http://unispal .un.org/unispal.nsf/9a798adbf322aff38525617b006d88d7/a238ec7a3e13eed1852 5624a007697ec?OpenDocument.

42. Christison, *Perceptions of Palestine,* p. 142.

43. Ibid., pp. 142–146.

44. Tessler, *A History of the Israeli-Palestinian Conflict,* p. 481.

45. Taillandier, "Middle East Connected Attacks on Americans," www.gloria-center .org/2001/12/taillandier-htm-2001-12-05/.

46. Tessler, *A History of the Israeli-Palestinian Conflict,* p. 488.

47. Mohamed Heikal, *Secret Channels: The Inside Story of Arab-Israeli Peace Negotiations* (London: Harper Collins, 1996), p. 248.

48. Smith, *Palestine and the Arab-Israeli Conflict,* p. 252.

49. Tessler, *A History of the Israeli-Palestinian Conflict,* p. 508.

50. "Highlights of Main Events 1977–79," Israeli Ministry of Foreign Affairs, December 21, 2012, www.mfa.gov.il/MFA/Foreign%20Relations/Israels%20Foreign%20 Relations%20since%201947/1977-1979/HIGHLIGHTS%20OF%20MAIN%20 EVENTS%201977-1979.

51. Smith, *Palestine and the Arab-Israeli Conflict,* pp. 252–253.

52. Noam Chomsky, *Fateful Triangle: The United States, Israel & the Palestinians* (Cambridge, MA: South End Press, 1999), p. 55.

53. Christison, *Perceptions of Palestine,* p. 177.

54. "Highlights of Main Events 1977–79," Israeli Ministry of Foreign Affairs, December 21, 2012, www.mfa.gov.il/MFA/Foreign%20Relations/Israels%20Foreign%20 Relations%20since%201947/1977-1979/HIGHLIGHTS%20OF%20MAIN%20 EVENTS%201977-1979.

55. "A Sabbath of Terror," *Time,* March 20, 1978, www.time.com/time/magazine /article/0,9171,919454,00.html.

56. "Camp David Accords," Israeli Ministry of Foreign Affairs, December 21, 2012, www.mfa.gov.il/MFA/Peace+Process/Guide+to+the+Peace+Process/Camp+David +Accords.htm.

57. Christison, *Perceptions of Palestine,* p. 205.

58. Tessler, *A History of the Israeli-Palestinian Conflict,* p. 587.

59. Ronald Reagan, *An American Life* (New York: Pocket Books, 1990), p. 423.

60. Betty Glad, "The United States' Ronald Reagan," in *Leadership and Negotiation in the Middle East*, ed. Barbara Kellerman and Jeffrey Z. Rubin (New York: Praeger, 1988), pp. 217–218.
61. Tessler, *A History of the Israeli-Palestinian Conflict*, p. 589.
62. Chomsky, *Fateful Triangle*, p. 213.
63. Tessler, *A History of the Israeli-Palestinian Conflict*, pp. 600–616.
64. Robert Schulzinger, *U.S. Diplomacy since 1900* (Oxford University Press, 2007), p. 343.
65. Chomsky, *Fateful Triangle*, pp. 107–108.
66. William E. Smith, "Terror Aboard Flight 847," *Time*, June 24, 2001, www.time.com/time/magazine/article/0,9171,142099,00.html.
67. Stanley Meiselt and Dan Fisher, "Israeli Jets Attack PLO's HQ in Tunis," *Los Angeles Times*, October 2, 1985, http://articles.latimes.com/1985-10-02/news/mn-16021_1.
68. King Hussein, "The Jordanian-Palestinian Peace Initiative: Mutual Recognition and Territory for Peace," *Journal of Palestine Studies* 14, no. 4 (Summer 1985): 15–22.
69. Tessler, *A History of the Israeli-Palestinian Conflict*, p. 666.
70. Taillandier, "Middle East Connected Attacks on Americans," www.gloria-center.org/2001/12/taillandier-htm-2001-12-05/.
71. Taillandier, "Middle East Connected Attacks on Americans," www.gloria-center.org/2001/12/taillandier-htm-2001-12-05/.
72. Tessler, *A History of the Israeli-Palestinian Conflict*, p. 682.
73. David Lea, *A Survey of Arab Israeli Relations 1947–2001* (Routledge, 2002), p. 17.
74. Tessler, *A History of the Israeli-Palestinian Conflict*, pp. 712–713.
75. "Palestinian Declaration of Independence (1988)," Al-Zaytouna Centre for Studies & Consultations, December 21, 2012, www.alzaytouna.net/en/resources/documents/palestinian-documents/97756-palestinian-declaration-of-independence-1988.html#.UNT5fOQSeN4.
76. "US Decision on PLO Hailed Worldwide," *Los Angeles Times*, December 15, 1988, http://articles.latimes.com/1988-12-15/news/mn-527_1_u-s-congressional-leaders.
77. Tessler, *A History of the Israeli-Palestinian Conflict*, p. 714.
78. The Arab League was founded in 1945 as a regional body for the countries of the Middle East and North Africa to coordinate on political, economic, and security matters.
79. Smith, *Palestine and the Arab-Israeli Conflict*, p. 291.
80. Ahmed Janabi, "Arafat's Costly Gulf War Choice," *Al Jazeera*, August 22, 2009, http://english.aljazeera.net/programmes/plohistoryofrevolution/2009/2009/08/200981294137853350.html.
81. Tricia McDermott, "Arafat's Billions: One Man's Quest to Track down Unaccounted-For Public Funds," *CBS News*, November 9, 2003, www.cbsnews.com/stories/2003/11/07/60minutes/main582487.shtml.
82. "In Jordan, Arafat Refutes Rumor of Saddam Hussein's Demise," *New York Times*, February 17, 1991, www.nytimes.com/1991/02/17/world/war-in-the-gulf-in-jordan-arafat-refutes-rumor-of-saddam-hussein-s-demise.html.
83. Tessler, *A History of the Israeli-Palestinian Conflict*, p. 737.
84. Lea, *A Survey of Arab Israeli Relations 1947–2001*, p. 19.
85. James Baker, "Letter of Assurance to the Palestinians," United States Institute for Peace, December 21, 2012, www.usip.org/files/file/resources/collections/peace_agreements/letter_of_assurance.pdf.
86. Schulzinger, *U.S. Diplomacy Since 1900*, p. 366.
87. "Chronology of Events June 1992– December 1994,"Israeli Ministry of Foreign Affairs," December 21, 2012, www.mfa.gov.il/MFA/Foreign%20Relations/Israels%20Foreign%20Relations%20since%201947/1992-1994/CHRONOLOGY%20OF%20EVENTS-%20JUNE%201992-DECEMBER%201994.
88. Bill Clinton, *My Life* (New York: Knopf, 2002), p. 546.
89. "Communiqué Following the Meeting of the Foreign Ministers of Israel-Egypt-Jordan–the US Secretary of State and a PA Representative," Israeli Ministry of

Foreign Affairs, December 21, 2012, www.mfa.gov.il/MFA/Foreign%20Relations
/Israels%20Foreign%20Relations%20since%201947/1995-1996/Communique
%20following%20the%20meeting%20of%20the%20foreign%20mi.

90. Taillandier, "Middle East Connected Attacks on Americans," www.gloria-center
.org/2001/12/taillandier-htm-2001-12-05/.

91. "Words of Warning," PBS, December 18, 1996, www.pbs.org/newshour/bb/middle
_east/december96/letter_12-18a.html.

92. "Chronology of Events 1998_1999," Israeli Ministry of Foreign Affairs, December 21, 2012, www.mfa.gov.il/MFA/Foreign%20Relations/Israels%20Foreign%20
Relations%20since%201947/1998-1999/CHRONOLOGY%20OF%20EVENTS
-%201998-1999.

93. John M. Broder, "White House Is Quietly Pro-Barak," *New York Times,* May
17, 1999, www.nytimes.com/1999/05/17/world/white-house-is-quietly-pro-barak
.html.

94. "Remarks by President Clinton to the Palestinian National Council and Other Palestinian Organizations," Israeli Ministry of Foreign Affairs, December 21, 2012,
www.mfa.gov.il/MFA/Foreign%20Relations/Israels%20Foreign%20Relations
%20since%201947/1998-1999/119%20Remarks%20by%20President%20
Clinton%20to%20the%20Palestinia.

95. Benny Morris, "Camp David and After Part 1," *New York Review of Books,* June
2002, www.nybooks.com/articles/archives/2002/jun/13/camp-david-and-after-an
-exchange-1-an-interview-wi/.

96. "The Clinton Parameters," Israel Palestine Center for Research and Information,
December 21, 2012, www.ipcri.org/files/clinton-parameters.html.

97. "President Bush Condemns Terrorist Attack in Israel," US Department of State,
June 1, 2001, http://2001-2009.state.gov/p/nea/rt/3244.htm.

98. "Arafat Condemns Bombing, Calls for Ceasefire," CNN, June 2, 2001, http://
edition.cnn.com/2001/WORLD/meast/06/02/israel.explosion.03/index.html.

99. "Reuters Statement on False Claim it Used Old Video," CNN, September 20, 2001,
http://archives.cnn.com/2001/US/09/20/reuters.statement/index.html.

100. "President Bush Condemns Assassination of Rehavem Zeevi," US Department of
State, October 17, 2001, http://2001-2009.state.gov/p/nea/rt/5428.htm.

101. "United States Position on Terrorists and Peace in the Middle East," US Department of State, November 19, 2001, http://2001-2009.state.gov/secretary/former
/powell/remarks/2001/6219.htm.

102. "President Discusses Middle East," The White House, January 25, 2002, http://
georgewbush-whitehouse.archives.gov/news/releases/2002/01/20020125-4.html.

103. "President Bush Calls for New Palestinian Leadership," US Department of State,
June 24, 2002, http://2001-2009.state.gov/p/nea/rls/rm/11408.htm.

104. "'Quartet' Joint Statement," US Department of State, July 16, 2002, http://2001
-2009.state.gov/r/pa/prs/ps/2002/11882.htm.

105. "August 12th Press Briefing," US Department of State, August 12, 2002, http://
2001-2009.state.gov/p/nea/rls/rm/12731.htm.

106. "Bush Outlines Middle East Peace Plan," CNN, June 24, 2002, http://articles.cnn
.com/2002-06-24/politics/bush.mideast.speech_1_palestinian-state-borders-and
-certain-aspects-palestinian-parliament?_s=PM:ALLPOLITICS.

107. "Hopeful Moment for Progress towards Middle East Peace," US Department of
State, March 24, 2003, http://2001-2009.state.gov/p/nea/rls/rm/18717.htm.

108. "Roadmap for Peace in the Middle East: Israeli/Palestinian Reciprocal Action,
Quartet Support," US Department of State, July 16, 2003, http://2001-2009.state
.gov/r/pa/ei/rls/22520.htm.

109. "President Bush Presses for Peace in the Middle East," US Department of State,
May 9, 2003, http://2001-2009.state.gov/p/nea/rls/rm/20497.htm.

110. "Remarks at the American-Arab Anti-Discrimination Committee's National Convention," US Department of State, June 14, 2003, http://2001-2009.state.gov
/secretary/former/powell/remarks/2003/21573.htm; "Joint Press Conference with

Palestinian Prime Minister Abbas," US Department of State, June 20, 2003, http://2001-2009.state.gov/secretary/former/powell/remarks/2003/21807.htm.

111. "Prime Minister Abbas' Resignation," US Department of State, September 6, 2003, http://2001-2009.state.gov/p/nea/rls/24106.htm.

112. "Assistant Secretary of State William J. Burns' Opening Remarks at the Ad Hoc Liaison Committee Meeting," US Department of State, December 8, 2004, http://2001-2009.state.gov/r/pa/prs/ps/2004/39555.htm.

113. "Palestinian Elections," US Department of State, January 9, 2005, http://2001-2009.state.gov/p/nea/rls/rm/40775.htm.

114. "President Bush Meets with Palestinian President Abbas," US Department of State, May 26, 2005, http://2001-2009.state.gov/p/nea/rls/rm/46824.htm.

115. "President Welcomes Palestinian President Abbas to the White House," The White House, October 20, 2005, http://georgewbush-whitehouse.archives.gov/news/releases/2005/10/20051020.html.

116. "Israel Completes Gaza Withdrawal," BBC, September 12, 2005, http://news.bbc.co.uk/2/hi/4235768.stm.

117. "Security and the Palestinian Elections," US Department of State, January 11, 2006, http://2001-2009.state.gov/secretary/rm/2006/58926.htm.

118. Scott Wilson, "Hamas Sweeps Palestinian Elections, Complicating Peace Efforts in Mideast," Washington Post, January 27, 2006, www.washingtonpost.com/wp-dyn/content/article/2006/01/26/AR2006012600372.html.

119. "Statement on Palestinian Elections," US Department of State, January 26, 2006, http://2001-2009.state.gov/secretary/rm/2006/59870.htm.

120. "US-Palestinian Relations," House International Relations Committee, March 2, 2006, www.c-spanvideo.org/program/191430-1.

121. "Statement on Palestinian Assistance," US Department of State, April 7, 2006, http://2001-2009.state.gov/secretary/rm/2006/64237.htm.

122. Email correspondence with James Prince, March 27, 2013.

123. "President's Statement on S.2370 the Palestinian Anti-Terrorism Act of 2006," The White House, December 21, 2006, http://georgewbush-whitehouse.archives.gov/news/releases/2006/12/20061221-4.html.

124. "Statement with Palestinian President Mahmoud Abbas and Israeli Prime Minister Ehud Olmert After Their Meeting," US Department of State, February 19, 2007, http://2001-2009.state.gov/secretary/rm/2007/feb/80659.htm.

125. "Memorandum for the Secretary of State," The White House, June 1, 2007, http://georgewbush-whitehouse.archives.gov/news/releases/2007/06/20070601-16.html.

126. "Hamas Takes Control of Gaza Strip," USA Today, June 15, 2007, www.usatoday.com/news/world/2007-06-14-gaza_N.htm.

127. "President Bush Discusses the Middle East," The White House, July 16, 2007, http://georgewbush-whitehouse.archives.gov/news/releases/2007/07/20070716-7.html.

128. "Announcement of Annapolis Conference," US Department of State, November 20, 2007, http://2001-2009.state.gov/r/pa/prs/ps/2007/nov/95458.htm.

129. "President Bush Attends Annapolis Conference," US Department of State, November 27, 2007, http://2001-2009.state.gov/p/nea/rls/rm/2007/95695.htm; "The Annapolis Conference," Israeli Ministry of Foreign Affairs, December 21, 2012, www.mfa.gov.il/MFA/History/Modern+History/Historic+Events/The+Annapolis+Conference+27-Nov-2007.htm.

130. "Remarks at the United Nations Security Council," US Department of State, December 16, 2008, http://2001-2009.state.gov/secretary/rm/2008/12/113242.htm.

131. "Remarks at the U.S.-Palestinian Public-Private Partnership Promoting Economic and Educational Opportunities for the Palestinian People," US Department of State, December 3, 2007, http://2001-2009.state.gov/secretary/rm/2007/12/96142.htm.

132. "Transcripts of Bush, Abbas Remarks," Wall Street Journal, April 24, 2008, http://blogs.wsj.com/washwire/2008/04/24/transcript-of-bush-abbas-remarks/.

133. "Remarks at a Conference in Support of Palestinian Civil Security and Rule of Law," US Department of State, June 24, 2008, http://2001-2009.state.gov/secretary/rm/2008/06/106196.htm.

134. "The President's News Conference," The American Presidency Project, February 9, 2009, www.presidency.ucsb.edu/ws/index.php?pid=85728.

135. Gwen Ackerman and Viola Gienger, "Clinton Says Two-State Answer to Mideast Conflict 'Inescapable,'" Bloomberg, March 3, 2009, www.bloomberg.com/apps/news?pid=newsarchive&sid=aVcCyrU_g5wc&refer=home.

136. "Remarks by the President at Cairo University," The White House, June 4, 2009, www.whitehouse.gov/the_press_office/Remarks-by-the-President-at-Cairo-University-6-04-09/.

137. "Remarks at the US-Islamic World Forum," US Department of State, February 14, 2010, www.state.gov/secretary/rm/2010/02/136678.htm.

138. "Remarks by Vice President Biden and Palestinian Authority President Mahmoud Abbas," The White House, March 10, 2010, www.whitehouse.gov/the-press-office/remarks-vice-president-biden-and-palestinian-authority-president-mahmoud-abbas.

139. Adrian Bloomfield, "Obama Snubbed Netanyahu for Dinner with Michelle and the Girls, Israelis Claim," Telegraph, March 25, 2010, www.telegraph.co.uk/news/worldnews/barackobama/7521220/Obama-snubbed-Netanyahu-for-dinner-with-Michelle-and-the-girls-Israelis-claim.html

140. "Report: Obama Promised Abbas a Palestinian State within Two Years," Haaretz, April 29, 2010, www.haaretz.com/news/diplomacy-defense/report-obama-promised-abbas-a-palestinian-state-within-two-years-1.287415.

141. Dan Ephron, "The Wrath of Mahmoud Abbas," Newsweek, April 24, 2011, www.thedailybeast.com/articles/2011/04/25/mahmoud-abbas-interview-palestinian-leaders-frustration-with-obama.html.

142. Interview with Aaron David Miller, Washington, DC, March 11, 2013.

CHAPTER 3   GUERRILLA GOVERNANCE

1. Hans Wehr, A Dictionary of Modern Written Arabic (London: MacDonald & Evans, 1980), p. 693.

2. Martin Kramer, "Khalidi of the PLO," Sandbox, October 30, 2008, www.martinkramer.org/sandbox/2008/10/khalidi-of-the-plo/.

3. Rashid Khalidi, Palestinian Identity: The Construction of Modern National Consciousness (New York: Columbia University Press, 1997), p. 178.

4. Said K. Aburish, Arafat: From Defender to Dictator (London: Bloomsbury, 1998), pp. 40–41.

5. Yasser Arafat interview with Playboy, September 1988; Andrew Gowers and Tony Walker, Behind the Myth: Yasser Arafat and the Palestinian Revolution (New York: Olive Branch Press, 1992), pp. 28–29.

6. Aburish, Arafat, p. 51.

7. Gowers and Walker, Behind the Myth, p. 29.

8. Aburish, Arafat, p. 52.

9. Ibid., pp. 49–50.

10. Danny Rubinstein, The Mystery of Arafat (South Royalton, VT: Steerforth Press, 1995), pp. 52–53; Ehud Yaari, Strike Terror: The Story of Fatah (New York: Sabra Books, 1970), pp. 67–86.

11. Yaari, Strike Terror, pp. 98–111.

12. Charles D. Smith, Palestine and the Arab-Israeli Conflict (New York: St. Martin's Press, 1992), p. 196.

13. J. Paul De B. Taillon, Hijacking and Hostages: Government Responses to Terrorism (Westport, CT: Praeger, 2002), p. 15.

14. Raphael Israeli, PLO in Lebanon: Selected Documents (London: Weidenfeld and Nicolson, 1983).

15. Rashid Khalidi, *The Iron Cage: The Story of the Palestinian Struggle for Statehood* (Boston, MA: Beacon Press, 2006), p.176.
16. "British Bank of the Middle East, 1976," *Time*, March 11, 2010, www.time.com /time/specials/packages/article/0,28804,1865132_1865133_1865218,00.html.
17. Yonah Alexander and Joshua Sinai, *Terrorism: The PLO Connection* (New York: Crane Russak, 1989), pp. 32–33.
18. Herbert Krosney, "Defector Says PLO Is Corrupt," *Globe and Mail*, September 20, 1979 (accessed via LexisNexis).
19. Fouad Moughrabi, "The Palestinians After Lebanon," *Arab Studies Quarterly* 5, no. 3 (Summer 1983): 214.
20. Jillian Becker, *The PLO: The Rise and Fall of the Palestine Liberation Organization* (New York: St. Martin's Press, 1984), p. 268.
21. Neil Livingstone and David Halevy, *Inside the PLO: Covert Units, Secret Funds, and the War Against Israel and the United States* (New York: Morrow, 1990), p. 168.
22. Becker, *The PLO*, p. 275.
23. Ibid.
24. Khalidi, *The Iron Cage*, p. 176.
25. Barbara Rosewicz and Gerald Seib, "Aside From Being a Movement, the PLO Is a Financial Giant," *Wall Street Journal*, July 21, 1986 (accessed via ProQuest).
26. Becker, *The PLO*, p. 148.
27. Adam Zagorin, "Auditing the PLO," in *The International Relations of the Palestine Liberation Organisation*, ed. Augustus Richard Norton and Martin Greenberg (Carbondale & Edwardsville: Southern Illinois University Press, 1989), p. 200.
28. Rosewicz and Seib, "Aside From Being a Movement, the PLO Is a Financial Giant."
29. "Other Chinese Reports; More Chinese Aid to PLO," *Xinhua*, December 5, 1983 (accessed via LexisNexis).
30. "Fatah Delegation to Moscow," *Kuwait News Agency—BBC Summary of World Broadcasts*, June 2, 1983 (accessed via LexisNexis); "PLO Delegations Flies to Moscow to Ask for Military Aid," Associated Press, June 1, 1983 (accessed via LexisNexis).
31. Becker, *The PLO*, p. 144.
32. Livingstone and Halevy, *Inside the PLO*, p. 165.
33. Ibid., p. 167.
34. Robin Wright, "PLO's Pinstripes, Money Behind Fatigues and Guns," *Christian Science Monitor*, October 1, 1981 (accessed via LexisNexis).
35. Alexander and Sinai, *Terrorism*, p. 31.
36. Livingstone and Halevy, *Inside the PLO*, p. 175.
37. Cameron Smith, "PLO War Strands Refugees," *The Globe and Mail*, November 22, 1983 (accessed via LexisNexis).
38. Alexander and Sinai, *Terrorism*, pp. 31–32; Wright, "PLO's Pinstripes, Money Behind Fatigues and Guns."
39. Rosewicz and Seib, "Aside From Being a Movement, the PLO Is a Financial Giant."
40. Mark Tessler, *A History of the Israeli-Palestinian Conflict* (Bloomington & Indianapolis: Indiana University Press, 1994), pp. 678–679.
41. Edward Said, *The Politics of Dispossession: The Struggle for Palestinian Self-Determination, 1969–1994* (New York: Vintage Books, 1994), p. 197.
42. Don Peretz, *Intifada: The Palestinian Uprising* (Boulder, CO: Westview Press, 1990), p. 99.
43. Said, *The Politics of Dispossession*, p. 166.
44. Barry Rubin and Judith Colp Rubin, *Yasir Arafat: A Political Biography* (New York: Oxford University Press, 2003), p. 119.
45. Yizhar Be'er and Saleh 'Abdel-Jawad, "Collaborators in the Occupied Territories: Human Rights Abuses and Violations," B'Tselem, January 1994, www.btselem.org /Download/199401_Collaboration_Suspects_Eng.doc.

46. Bard E. O'Neill, "The Intifada in the Context of Armed Struggle," in *The Intifadah: Its Impact on Israel, the Arab World and the Superpowers,* ed. Robert O. Freedman (Miami: Florida International University Press, 1991), pp. 57–58.

47. Jamie Tarabay, "In Duel of Intelligence Services, Palestinians Hunt Down Informers," Associated Press, August 21, 2001 (accessed via LexisNexis).

48. "December 14 Is a Historical Date in the Palestinian Struggle for Freedom," Ezzedeen Al Qassam Brigades website, December 13, 2007, www.qassam.ps/news -514-December_14_is_a_Historical_Date_in_the_Palestinian_Struggle_for_Free dom.html.

49. Michel Jubran and Laura Drake, "The Islamic Fundamentalist Movement in the West Bank and Gaza Strip," *Middle East Policy* 2, no. 2 (May 1993): 7.

50. Tessler, *A History of the Israeli-Palestinian Conflict,* p. 722.

51. For full text, see www.mfa.gov.il/mfa/peace%20process/guide%20to%20the%20 peace%20process/declaration%20of%20principles.

CHAPTER 4 THE OSLO YEARS

1. Said K. Aburish, *Arafat: From Defender to Dictator* (London: Bloomsbury, 1998), p. 275.

2. Hillel Frisch, "From Palestine Liberation Organization to Palestinian Authority: The Territorialization of 'Neopatriarchy,'" in *The PLO and Israel: From Armed Conflict to Political Solution, 1964–1994,* ed. Avraham Sela and Moshe Ma'oz (New York: St. Martin's Press, 1997), pp. 56–57.

3. Interview with Aaron David Miller, Washington, DC, March 11, 2013.

4. Nathan J. Brown, *Palestinian Politics After the Oslo Accords: Resuming Arab Palestine* (Berkeley: University of California Press, 2003), p. 8.

5. Rashid Khalidi, *The Iron Cage: The Story of the Palestinian Struggle for Statehood* (Boston, MA: Beacon Press, 2006), pp. 159, 174, 176.

6. Janet Wallach and John Wallach, *Arafat: In the Eyes of the Beholder* (New York: Carol Publishing Group, 1990), pp. 23–24.

7. Neil C. Livingstone and David Halevy, *Inside the PLO: Covert Units, Secret Funds, and the War Against Israel and the United States* (New York: Morrow, 1990), p. 169.

8. Brian Duffy, Richard Chesnoff, David Makovsky, Khaled Abu Toameh, Jihan El-Tahri, and Louise Lief, "Who Pays Arafat?" *U.S. News & World Report,* April 26, 1993, www.usnews.com/usnews/culture/articles/930426/archive_015023_print.htm.

9. Amos Perlmutter, "Arafat's Police State," *Foreign Affairs* 73, no. 4 (July–August, 1994): 8.

10. Interview with Dennis Ross, Washington, DC, April 19, 2013.

11. Khalidi, *The Iron Cage,* p. 143.

12. Ibid., pp. 143, 147.

13. Hillel Frisch, "Modern Absolutist or Neopatriarchal State Building? Customary Law, Extended Families and the Palestinian Authority," *International Journal of Middle East Studies* 29, no. 3 (August 1997): 352.

14. Frisch, "From Palestine Liberation Organization to Palestinian Authority," p. 67.

15. Central Elections Commission—Palestine, "The 1996 Presidential and Legislative Elections," August 21, 2012, www.elections.ps/Portals/0/pdf/Resultselection1996 .pdf.

16. Interview with Dennis Ross, Washington, DC, April 19, 2013.

17. Interview with Aaron David Miller, Washington, DC, March 11, 2013.

18. Nathan J. Brown, *The Palestinian Reform Agenda* (Washington, DC: US Institute of Peace, 2002), p. 32; Samar Assad, "Arafat Ordered to Dissolve Cabinet," Associated Press, July 31, 1997 (accessed via LexisNexis).

19. Said Ghazali, "Audit: Quarter Billion Dollars Lost to Corruption, Mismanagement," Associated Press, May 24, 1997 (accessed via LexisNexis).

20. Brown, *Palestinian Politics After the Oslo Accords,* p. 4.
21. Ibid.
22. Stacey Lakind and Yigal Carmon, "The PA Economy (II)," The Middle East Media Research Institute, January 8, 1999, www.memri.org/report/en/0/0/0/0/0/0/256.htm.
23. Matt Rees, "Where's Arafat's Money?" *Time,* November 14, 2004, www.time.com/time/magazine/article/0,9171,782141,00.html.
24. Ronen Bergman and David Ratner, "The Man Who Swallowed Gaza," *Haaretz,* April 4, 1997. Link no longer available. Excerpts here: www.israelbehindthenews.com/bin/content.cgi?ID=573&q=1.
25. Ibid.
26. Ibid.
27. "ConGen Abington Remarks, USAID Grant to Palestinian Council," US Embassy in Israel, February 4, 1997, www.usembassy-israel.org.il/publish/press/state/archive/1997/february/sd20205.htm.
28. Marwan Bishara, "The Undeclared Palestinian Civil War," Middle East Online, November 15, 2007, www.middle-east-online.com/english/?id=23095.
29. "Clinton Should Press Arafat to Abolish State Security Courts," Human Rights Watch, March 22, 1999, www.hrw.org/news/1999/03/21/clinton-should-press-arafat-abolish-state-security-courts.
30. Brown, *Palestinian Politics After the Oslo Accords,* pp. 19, 41.
31. David Hirst, "Shameless in Gaza," *Guardian,* April 21, 1997 (accessed via LexisNexis).
32. Vernon Silver, "Citigroup Banked for Arafat as He Paid Fighters," Bloomberg, November 19, 2004, www.bloomberg.com/apps/news?pid=newsarchive&sid=aKqaG5RWlATQ&refer=us.
33. James Neuger, "EU Ends Probe of Palestinian Funds, Urges Better Safeguards," Bloomberg, March 17, 2005, www.bloomberg.com/apps/news?pid=newsarchive&sid=a7CXuldTOYkg&refer=top_world_news.
34. "Strengthening Palestinian Public Institutions," Council on Foreign Relations, 1999, www.pcpsr.org/domestic/strengtheningpalinstfull.pdf.
35. Brown, *Palestinian Politics After the Oslo Accords,* pp. 1–2.
36. Azmi Shuaibi, "Elements of Corruption in the Middle East and North Africa: The Palestinian Case," paper presented at the 9th International Anti-Corruption Conference, October 1999, http://9iacc.org/papers/day1/ws5/dnld/d1ws5_ashuaibi.pdf.
37. Brown, *Palestinian Politics After the Oslo Accords,* p. 11.
38. David Hirst, "Arafat Hits Out at Dissidents," *Guardian,* November 29, 1999, www.guardian.co.uk/world/1999/nov/30/davidhirst.
39. William A. Orme Jr., "Palestinian Investment Fund, No Longer Secret, Will Close," *New York Times,* July 7, 2000, www.nytimes.com/2000/07/07/world/palestinian-investment-fund-no-longer-secret-will-close.html.
40. Ibid.
41. Ibid.
42. "Camp David Summit, Chances for Reconciliation and Lasting Peace, Violence and Confrontations, Hierarchies of Priorities, and Domestic Politics," Palestinian Center for Policy and Survey Research, July 27–29, 2000, www.pcpsr.org/survey/polls/2000/p1a.html.
43. Brown, *Palestinian Politics After the Oslo Accords,* p. 14.
44. Khalidi, *The Iron Cage,* p. 149.
45. Interview with Dennis Ross, Washington, DC, April 19, 2013.

CHAPTER 5   THE AL-AQSA INTIFADA

1. Isabel Kershner, "One Step Away from Chaos," *Jerusalem Report,* December 18, 2000 (accessed via LexisNexis).

2. "Palestinian Death Toll From Intifada Stands at 2,647: Official," Agence France-Presse, August 13, 2003, www.miftah.org/PrinterF.cfm?DocId=2336.

3. Nathan J. Brown, *Palestinian Politics After the Oslo Accords: Resuming Arab Palestine* (Berkeley: University of California Press, 2003), p. 43.

4. Arieh O'Sullivan, "IDF Warns PA Losing Control of Gaza Strip," *Jerusalem Post,* November 19, 2001 (accessed via LexisNexis).

5. Sandra Cotenta, "Arafat's Regime in Shambles," *Toronto Star,* November 11, 2001.

6. Tom Rose, "Arafat's Naval Adventure," *Weekly Standard,* January 21, 2002, www.weeklystandard.com/Content/Public/Articles/000/000/000/773kvxmi.asp.

7. Daniel Sobleman, "Palestinian Writer Charges That PA Officials Are Leaving the Country," *Haaretz,* September 5, 2001, www.imra.org.il/story.php3?id=8035.

8. "Suicide Bombing in the Beit Yisrael Neighborhood in Jerusalem," Israeli Ministry of Foreign Affairs, August 28, 2012, www.mfa.gov.il/MFA/MFAArchive/2000_2009/2002/3/Suicide+bombing+in+the+Beit+Yisrael+neighborhood+i.htm.

9. Matthew Kalman, "Terrorist Says Orders Come from Arafat," *USA Today,* March 14, 2002, www.usatoday.com/news/world/2002/03/14/usat-brigades.htm.

10. "The Involvement of Arafat, PA Senior Officials and Apparatuses in Terrorism Against Israel: Corruption and Crime," Israeli Ministry of Foreign Affairs, May 6, 2002, www.mfa.gov.il/MFA/MFAArchive/2000_2009/2002/5/The%20Involvement%20of%20Arafat-%20PA%20Senior%20Officials%20and.

11. The Middle East Quartet, which is composed of the United Nations, the United States, the European Union, and Russia, was formed in 2002.

12. "Hamas, Fatah to Resume Ceasefire Talks Within Days: Palestinians," Agence France-Presse, December 8, 2002 (accessed via LexisNexis).

13. "Members Accused by Hamas of Belonging to Fatah," *Asharq al-Awsat,* December 6, 2002.

14. Lamia Lahoud, "Fatah Threatens Hamas in Leaflet," *Jerusalem Post,* December 11, 2002 (accessed via LexisNexis).

15. Ronen Bergman, "Where Does the Money Go?," *Yediot Ahronot,* November 10, 2000, www.israelbehindthenews.com/bin/content.cgi?ID=1043&q=1.

16. Lewis Dolinsky, "Notes From Here and There," *San Francisco Chronicle,* December 20, 2000 (accessed via LexisNexis).

17. "The Mitchell Report, Cease Fire, and Return to Negotiations; Intifada and Armed Confrontations; Chances for Reconciliation; and, Internal Palestinian Conditions," Palestinian Center for Policy and Survey Research, July 5–9, 2001, www.pcpsr.org/survey/polls/2001/p2a.html.

18. "Palestinians Support the Ceasefire, Negotiations, and Reconciliation Between the Two Peoples but a Majority Opposes Arrests and Believe That Armed Confrontations Have Helped Achieve National Rights," Palestinian Center for Policy and Survey Research, December 19–24, 2001, www.pcpsr.org/survey/polls/2001/p3a.html.

19. "Start Spreading the News," *Jerusalem Post,* April 2, 2002 (accessed via LexisNexis).

20. "The Involvement of Arafat, PA Senior Officials and Apparatuses in Terrorism Against Israel: Corruption and Crime," Israeli Ministry of Foreign Affairs, www.mfa.gov.il/MFA/MFAArchive/2000_2009/2002/5/The%20Involvement%20of%20Arafat-%20PA%20Senior%20Officials%20and.

21. Ibid.

22. Ibid.

23. "Diplomats Say EU Knew Palestinians Misappropriated Cash to Finance Terrorism," Independent Media Review Analysis, May 11, 2002, http://imra.org.il/story.php3?id=11955.

24. Brown, *Palestinian Politics After the Oslo Accords,* pp. 115, 250.

25. Ibid., p. 251.

26. "While Sharply Divided Over the Ceasefire and Bombing Attacks Against Civilians, an Overwhelming Majority Supports Political Reform but Have Doubts About the

PA's Intentions to Implement It," Palestinian Center for Policy and Survey Research, August 26, 2002, www.pcpsr.org/survey/polls/2002/p5epressrelease.html.

27. "Former PLO Finance Chief Flees to London: Palestinians," Agence France-Presse, August 17, 2002 (accessed via LexisNexis).

28. Laurie Copans, "Ex-Aide Accuses Arafat of Corruption," Associated Press, August 18, 2002 (accessed via LexisNexis).

29. Brown, *Palestinian Politics After the Oslo Accords,* p. 115.

CHAPTER 6   FAYYADISM

1. Lee Hockstader, "Israeli Troops Move Into West Bank City; Ramallah Incursion Follows Arafat's Announcement of a New, Smaller Cabinet," *Washington Post,* June 10, 2002 (accessed via LexisNexis); James Bennet, "Palestinian Assets 'a Mess,' Official Says," *New York Times,* March 1, 2003, www.nytimes.com/2003/03/01/world/palestinian-assets-a-mess-official-says.html.

2. Email correspondence with James Prince, February 21, 2013.

3. Interview with James Prince, Los Angeles, CA, November 14, 2012.

4. Ibid.

5. Issam Abu Issa, "Arafat's Swiss Bank Account," *Middle East Quarterly* 11, no. 4 (Fall 2004), www.meforum.org/645/arafats-swiss-bank-account.

6. Email correspondence with James Prince, February 21, 2013.

7. Issam Abu Issa, "Arafat's Swiss Bank Account."

8. Email correspondence with James Prince, February 21, 2013.

9. Janine Zacharia, "Bush Touts New PA Finance Minister," *Jerusalem Post,* May 31, 2002 (accessed via LexisNexis).

10. Robert Satloff, "Karine-A: The Strategic Implications of Iranian-Palestinian Collusion," Washington Institute for Near East Policy, Policywatch 593, January 15, 2002, www.washingtoninstitute.org/policy-analysis/view/karine-a-the-strategic-implications-of-iranian-palestinian-collusion.

11. Interview with Elliott Abrams, Washington, DC, March 8, 2013.

12. Interview with Dennis Ross, Washington, DC, April 19, 2013.

13. "Start Spreading the News," *Jerusalem Post,* April 2, 2002 (accessed via LexisNexis).

14. "The Involvement of Arafat, PA Senior Officials and Apparatuses in Terrorism Against Israel: Corruption and Crime," Israel Ministry of Foreign Affairs, May 6, 2002, www.mfa.gov.il/MFA/MFAArchive/2000_2009/2002/5/The%20Involvement%20of%20Arafat-%20PA%20Senior%20Officials%20and.

15. Ben Caspit, "The $300 Million Affair: How a Former Senior General Security Service Official Set Up Arafat's Secret Financial Empire,"*Maariv,* December 2, 2002, www.memri.org/report/en/print783.htm.

16. See Uzrad Lew, *Inside Arafat's Pocket* (Or Yehuda, Israel: Kinneret Zmora-Bitan Divir Publishing House, 2005).

17. Interview with Uzrad Lew, Los Angeles, CA, November 13, 2012.

18. Serge Schmemann, "An Arafat Aide Blames Hamas for Thwarting Efforts to Form a Palestinian Unity Platform," *New York Times,* August 16, 2002, www.nytimes.com/2002/08/16/world/arafat-aide-blames-hamas-for-thwarting-efforts-form-palestinian-unity-platform.html.

19. Khaled Abu Toameh, "Abbas 'Feels He's Above the Law,' Charges Dahlan," *Jerusalem Post,* July 31, 2011, www.jpost.com/MiddleEast/Article.aspx?id=231686.

20. Email correspondence with James Prince, February 21, 2013.

21. Ben Lynfield, "The Palestinians' Fiscal Fighter," *Christian Science Monitor,* August 20, 2002, www.csmonitor.com/2002/0820/p06s01-wome.html.

22. "Letter From PA President Abbas to the Secretary Concerning Legal Action Against the Palestine Investment Fund," Wikileaks, December 7, 2006, http://wikileaks.org/cable/2006/12/06JERUSALEM4915.html.

23. Email correspondence with James Prince, February 21, 2013.
24. Interview with James Prince, Los Angeles, CA, November 14, 2012.
25. Vernon Silver, "Arafat's Investments Included Dotcoms, New York Bowling Alley," Bloomberg, December 21, 2004, www.bloomberg.com/apps/news?pid=news archive&sid=ag2fQ5pMZXc8&refer=uk.
26. "About the Palestine Investment Fund," Palestine Investment Fund, September 9, 2011, www.pif.ps/index.php?lang=en&page=124402202521.
27. Steven Weisman, "U.S. Presses Mideast and Europe to Reduce Ties to Arafat," New York Times, April 26, 2003, www.nytimes.com/2003/04/26/world/us-presses-mideast-and-europe-to-reduce-ties-to-arafat.html.
28. Ibid.
29. "Fayyad and Al-Wazir on PA's Current and Future," Wikileaks, February 24, 2006, http://wikileaks.org/cable/2006/02/06JERUSALEM802.html.
30. Mathew Kalman, "Professor Tackles Cleanup of Palestinian Corruption: Palestinian Authority's Finance Minister Believes in Democracy, Transparency," Vancouver Sun, February 22, 2003 (accessed via LexisNexis).
31. Weisman, "U.S. Presses Mideast and Europe to Reduce Ties to Arafat."
32. Ibid.
33. Stephen Farrell and Robert Tait, "Reformer Rules out Taking Key Job With Arafat," The Times (UK), February 19, 2003 (accessed via LexisNexis).
34. Weisman, "U.S. Presses Mideast and Europe to Reduce Ties to Arafat."
35. Ibid.
36. Ibid.
37. Ibid.
38. Karin Laub, "After Decade, International Donors See Little Result in West Bank and Gaza," Associated Press, December 9, 2003 (accessed via LexisNexis).
39. "Appointment of Prime Minister, Political Reform, Roadmap, War in Iraq, Arafat's Popularity, and Political Affiliation," Palestinian Center for Policy and Survey Research, April 2003, www.pcpsr.org/survey/polls/2003/p7a.html.
40. Weisman, "U.S. Presses Mideast and Europe to Reduce Ties to Arafat."
41. Khaled Abu Toameh, "Revenue Files 'Disappear' From PA Finance Ministry," Jerusalem Post, December 3, 2003, http://web.archive.org/web/20050420062051/http://www.jpost.com/servlet/Satellite?pagename=JPost/JPArticle/ShowFull&cid=1070444894725&p=1008596981749.
42. "Economic Performance and Reforms Under Conflict Conditions," International Monetary Fund, September 15, 2003, www.imf.org/external/pubs/ft/med/2003/eng/wbg/wbg.pdf.
43. Tricia McDermott, "Arafat's Billions," CBS News, November 2003, www.cbsnews.com/2100-18560_162-582487.html.
44. Marc Perelman, "Israeli Says PA Used Swiss Accounts to Fund Terror," The Forward, March 26, 2004, http://forward.com/articles/6577/israeli-says-pa-used-swiss-accounts-to-fund-terror/&reason=0/#ixzz24mvpnoOy.
45. Interview with Uzrad Lew, Los Angeles, November 13, 2012.
46. Matthew Kalman, "Militants Put Arafat's Leadership in Jeopardy; Gaza in Chaos as Palestinian Authority Teeters on the Brink of Collapse," Globe and Mail, July 19, 2004, (accessed via LexisNexis).
47. Steven Erlanger, "Sharon Rebuffed by Party, as Arafat Admits Making Mistakes," New York Times, August 19, 2004, www.nytimes.com/2004/08/19/world/sharon-rebuffed-by-party-as-arafat-admits-making-mistakes.html.
48. "After Four Years Of Intifada, an Overwhelming Sense of Insecurity Prevails Among Palestinians Leading to High Level of Support for Bombing and Rocket Attacks on One Hand and to High Levels of Demand for Mutual Cessation of Violence and Questioning of the Effectiveness of Armed Attacks on the Other," Palestinian Center for Policy and Survey Research, September 23–26, 2004, www.pcpsr.org/survey/polls/2004/p13a.html.

49. Vernon Silver, "Citigroup Banked for Arafat as He Paid Fighters," Bloomberg, November 19, 2004, www.bloomberg.com/apps/news?pid=newsarchive&sid=aKqaG 5RWlATQ&refer=us.
50. Matt Rees, "Where's Arafat's Money?" *Time,* November 14, 2004, www.time.com /time/magazine/article/0,9171,782141-1,00.html.
51. Interview with Elliott Abrams, Washington, DC, March 8, 2013.
52. George Wright, "Mahmoud Abbas Named as Palestinian PM," *Guardian,* April 28, 2003, www.guardian.co.uk/world/2003/apr/29/israel2.
53. "Abbas Achieves Landslide Poll Win," BBC, January 10, 2005, http://news.bbc .co.uk/2/hi/middle_east/4160171.stm.

CHAPTER 7 THE RISE OF ABU MAZEN

1. Mahmoud Abbas, *Through Secret Channels* (Reading, UK: Garnet Publishing, 1995).
2. Website of PA president Mahmoud Abbas, June 1, 2012, http://presidency.ps /general.aspx?id=42&T=m7.
3. Interview with Palestinian activist, Washington, DC, September 13, 2012.
4. Karl Vick, "On the Brink, Palestinian President Mahmoud Abbas Hangs Tough on Statehood," *Time,* September 9, 2011, www.time.com/time/world/article/0,8599 ,2092492,00.html.
5. Website of PA President Mahmoud Abbas, http://presidency.ps/general.aspx?id=42 &T=m7.
6. "Abbas, Mahmoud," The Palestinian Academic Society for the Study of International Affairs, May 29, 2012, www.passia.org/palestine_facts/personalities/alpha _a.htm.
7. Mahmoud Abbas, "The Long Overdue Palestinian State," *New York Times,* May 16, 2011, www.nytimes.com/2011/05/17/opinion/17abbas.html.
8. "PA Chairman Mahmoud Abbas Criticizes Arafat's Approval of Anti-Israeli Terror Attacks in the 1990s and Talks About the Arab Evacuation of Safed in 1948," The Middle East Media Research Institute, July 6, 2009, www.memritv.org/clip _transcript/en/2212.htm.
9. Website of PA President Mahmoud Abbas, http://presidency.ps/general.aspx?id=42 &T=m7.
10. Abbas, "The Long Overdue Palestinian State."
11. Website of PA president Mahmoud Abbas, http://presidency.ps/general.aspx?id=42 &T=m7.
12. Ibid.
13. "Abbas in the Spotlight: Who Is the Palestinian President?" CNN, September 21, 2011, http://news.blogs.cnn.com/2011/09/21/abbas-in-the-spotlight-who-is-the-pale stinian-president/; Website of PA president Mahmoud Abbas, http://presidency.ps /general.aspx?id=42&T=m7.
14. Website of PA president Mahmoud Abbas, http://presidency.ps/general.aspx?id=42 &T=m7.
15. Ibid.
16. Ibid.
17. "Abbas, Mahmoud," www.passia.org/palestine_facts/personalities/alpha_a.htm.
18. Website of PA president Mahmoud Abbas, http://presidency.ps/general.aspx?id=42 &T=m7.
19. Danny Rubinstein, *The Mystery of Arafat* (South Royalton, VT: Steerforth Press, 1995), pp. 52–53.
20. Ibid., pp. 98–111.
21. Ehud Yaari, *Strike Terror: The Story of Fatah* (New York: Sabra Books, 1970), pp. 67–86.
22. Website of PA president Mahmoud Abbas, http://presidency.ps/general.aspx?id=42 &T=m7.

23. "Profile: Mahmoud Abbas," BBC, November 5, 2009, http://news.bbc.co.uk/2/hi/middle_east/1933453.stm.
24. "Jordan, PLO Turn Page on 'Black September,'" Agence France-Presse, September 17, 2010, www.thedailystar.net/newDesign/news-details.php?nid=154695.
25. Website of PA president Mahmoud Abbas, http://presidency.ps/general.aspx?id=42&T=m7.
26. "Profile: Mahmoud Abbas," http://news.bbc.co.uk/2/hi/middle_east/1933453.stm.
27. Alexander Wolff, "The Mastermind," *Sports Illustrated,* August 26, 2002, http://sportsillustrated.cnn.com/si_online/news/2002/08/20/sb2/.
28. "In Brief: General; Syrian-Iraqi-Palestinian Meetings," *Damascus Home Service—BBC Summary of World Broadcasts,* January 16, 1979 (accessed via LexisNexis).
29. "In Brief: General; Tour of Jordanian-Palestinian Delegation," *Qatar News Agency—BBC Summary of World Broadcasts,* June 19, 1979 (accessed via LexisNexis).
30. "In Brief: General; Arrivals and Departures," *Aden Home Service—BBC Summary of World Broadcasts,* July 27, 1979 (accessed via LexisNexis).
31. "In Brief: General; Tour of Jordanian-Palestinian Delegation," *Qatar News Agency—BBC Summary of World Broadcasts,* October 13, 1979 (accessed via LexisNexis).
32. "In Brief: General; Arafat in PDRY," *Voice of Palestine—BBC Summary of World Broadcasts,* February 10, 1979 (accessed via LexisNexis).
33. "Statements in Kuwait by Palestinian Officials," *Qatar News Agency—BBC Summary of World Broadcasts,* February 13, 1979 (accessed via LexisNexis).
34. "In Brief: Fatah Official in Moscow," *Voice of Palestine—BBC Summary of World Broadcasts,* April 28, 1979 (accessed via LexisNexis).
35. "In Brief: Fatah Leaders in Czechoslovakia," *Voice of Palestine—BBC Summary of World Broadcasts,* May 1, 1979 (accessed via LexisNexis).
36. "In Brief: Fatah Official's Friendship Visit," *Moscow in Arabic—BBC Summary of World Broadcasts,* February 8, 1980 (accessed via LexisNexis).
37. "Palestinian-Soviet Friendship Society Chairman Writes in 'Izvestiya,'" *Telegraph Agency of the Soviet Union—BBC Summary of World Broadcasts,* October 23, 1980 (accessed via LexisNexis).
38. "In Brief: General; PLO Official on Saudi-USSR Relations," *Voice of Palestine—BBC Summary of World Broadcasts,* November 24, 1981 (accessed via LexisNexis).
39. "In Brief: General; Cuba-Palestine Resistance Co-operation Agreement," *Havana Television—BBC Summary of World Broadcasts,* May 1, 1982 (accessed via LexisNexis).
40. Helena Cobban, *The Palestinian Liberation Organisation: People, Power, and Politics* (Cambridge, UK: Cambridge University Press, 1984), p. 269.
41. Website of PA President Mahmoud Abbas, http://presidency.ps/general.aspx?id=42&T=m7.
42. "Other Reports on Lebanon; UAA Foreign Ministry Official Meets PLO Representatives," *Qatar News Agency—BBC Summary of World Broadcasts,* June 11, 1982 (accessed via LexisNexis).
43. Website of PA President Mahmoud Abbas, http://presidency.ps/general.aspx?id=42&T=m7.
44. Jim Zanotti, "The Palestinians: Background and U.S. Relations," Congressional Research Service, August 30, 2011, www.fas.org/sgp/crs/mideast/RL34074.pdf.
45. Hillel Fendel, "Report: Abbas' Holocaust-Denial Dissertation Widely-Taught in PA," *Arutz Sheva,* April 28, 2011, www.israelnationalnews.com/News/News.aspx/143752#.UGHwJhgmai4.
46. Benny Morris, "Exposing Abbas," *National Interest,* May 19, 2011, http://nationalinterest.org/commentary/exposing-abbas-5335.
47. Rafael Medoff, "A Holocaust-Denier as Prime Minister of 'Palestine'?" David S. Wyman Institute for Holocaust Studies, March 2003, translation by the Simon Wiesenthal Center, www.wymaninstitute.org/articles/2003-03-denier.php.

216 STATE OF FAILURE

48. Ibid.
49. Yael Yehoshua, "Abu Mazen: Political Profile," Middle East Media Research Institute, April 29, 2003, www.memri.org/report/en/0/0/0/0/0/0/856.htm.
50. N. Maruani and A. Savyon, "Iranian 'Conference on Hollywoodism and Cinema' Honors Prominent French Holocaust Deniers," Middle East Media Research Institute, February 23, 2012, www.memri.org/report/en/0/0/0/0/0/0/6111.htm.
51. Greg Myre, "Soft-Spoken but Not Afraid to Voice Opinions," *New York Times,* March 11, 2003, www.nytimes.com/2003/03/11/international/middleeast/11ABBA.html.
52. Akiva Eldar, "U.S. Told Us to Ignore Israeli Map Reservations," *Haaretz,* May 28, 2003, www.haaretz.com/print-edition/news/u-s-told-us-to-ignore-israeli-map-reservations-1.8840.
53. Ernest Claassen, "Abbas Tevreden Over Bezoek Aan Nederland," *Nederlandse Omroep Stichting,* July 1, 2011, http://nos.nl/artikel/252894-abbas-tevreden-over-bezoek-aan-nederland.html.
54. "Reaction to Israeli-Palestinian Contacts," *Voice of Palestine—BBC Summary of World Broadcasts,* January 25, 1983 (accessed via LexisNexis).
55. Trudy Rubin, "PLO's Peaceful Offensive: Expand Ties to Israeli Jews," *Christian Science Monitor,* March 10, 1983 (accessed via LexisNexis).
56. "PLO-Israeli CP Meeting in Prague," *Yugoslav News Agency—BBC Summary of World Broadcasts,* March 31, 1983 (accessed via LexisNexis).
57. Abbas, *Through Secret Channels,* p. 17.
58. "Palestine National Council: Statements by Leaders," *Voice of Palestine—BBC Summary of World Broadcasts,* February 15, 1983 (accessed via LexisNexis).
59. Interview with Former Palestinian negotiator, Washington, DC, April 22, 2013.
60. "Fatah Central Committee Decisions," *Voice of Palestine—BBC Summary of World Broadcasts,* August 31, 1983 (accessed via LexisNexis).
61. Website of PA President Mahmoud Abbas, http://presidency.ps/officialresume.aspx.
62. "Fatah Official on Palestinian Threat to US Interests Everywhere," *Algiers Radio—BBC Summary of World Broadcasts,* October 21, 1985 (accessed via LexisNexis).
63. Janet Wallach and John Wallach, *Arafat: In the Eyes of the Beholder* (Secaucus, NJ: Carol Publishing Group, 1990), p. 55.
64. "Full Text of Arafat's Statement to News Conference," Reuters, December 14, 1988, http://articles.latimes.com/1988-12-15/news/mn-379_1_news-conference.
65. "Transcript of Shultz's Remarks on United States' Stance Regarding PLO," *New York Times,* December 15, 1988, www.nytimes.com/1988/12/15/us/transcript-of-shultz-s-remarks-on-united-states-stance-regarding-plo.html.
66. "PLO to Form Delegation for US Visit," *BBC Summary of World Broadcasts,* January 3, 1989 (accessed via LexisNexis).
67. "Jordanian Deputy Premier Talks With Senior PLO Official on Palestinian Issue," Xinhua General Overseas News Service, May 3, 1989 (accessed via LexisNexis).
68. "Briefing on 13th June Relations with PLO," *Tass—BBC Summary of World Broadcasts,* June 27, 1989 (accessed via LexisNexis).
69. Daniel Gavron, "Toledo Dialogue Hopes to Revive 'Golden Age' of Jewish-Arab Friendship," *Jerusalem Post,* July 2, 1989 (accessed via LexisNexis).
70. Michael Deure, "Fatah Committee Elected, Reflects Arafat Views," United Press International, August 9, 1989 (accessed via LexisNexis).
71. "Palestinian Affairs in Brief; Appointments in Fatah leadership," *Radio Monte Carlo—BBC Summary of World Broadcasts,* November 21, 1989 (accessed via LexisNexis).
72. "Abbas, Mahmoud," www.passia.org/palestine_facts/personalities/alpha_a.htm.
73. Barry Rubin, *Revolution Until Victory? The Politics and History of the PLO* (Cambridge, MA: Harvard University Press, 1994), p. 154.
74. Abbas, *Through Secret Channels,* p. 71.
75. "Other Reports; Soviet Deputy Foreign Minister Receives PLO Representative," *Moscow in Arabic—BBC Summary of World Broadcasts,* January 8, 1991 (accessed via LexisNexis).

76. "Palestinian Affairs in Brief; Egyptian Foreign Minister Abd al-Majid Meets PLO and Fatah Officials," *Middle East News Agency—BBC Summary of World Broadcasts*, May 4, 1991 (accessed via LexisNexis).

77. "PLO Executive Committee Member in Czechoslovakia," *Bratislava—BBC Summary of World Broadcasts*, May 30, 1991 (accessed via LexisNexis).

78. "PLO Official: Mideast Conference in Doubt Due to Soviet Instability," Associated Press, August 21, 1991 (accessed via LexisNexis).

79. "Palestinian Affairs in Brief; Abu Mazen on Palestinian Preconditions for Attending Peace Conference," *Voice of Palestine—BBC Summary of World Broadcasts*, September 4, 1991 (accessed via LexisNexis).

80. "PLO Delegation Leaves for Libya to Monitor Arafat Search," Agence France-Presse, April 8, 1992 (accessed via LexisNexis).

81. Ed Blanche, "Arafat's Disappearance Strips PLO of Vital Leadership," Associated Press, April 8, 1992 (accessed via LexisNexis).

82. Patrick Martin, "Deep-Seated Problems Flare in Filling Deputy's Chair PLO Leadership," *Globe and Mail*, May 7, 1992 (accessed via LexisNexis).

83. Mahmoud Abbas, *Through Secret Channels*, p. 210.

84. "Years of Discreet Pay Off for Fatah's Quiet Dove," *Guardian*, September 14, 1993 (accessed via LexisNexis).

85. "Text of Abbas' Remarks," Associated Press, September 13, 1993 (accessed via LexisNexis).

86. "Arafat Adviser Predicts Terrorism Will Disappear," Associated Press, October 15, 1993 (accessed via LexisNexis).

87. Website of PA president Mahmoud Abbas, http://presidency.ps/officialresume.aspx; "Abbas, Mahmoud," www.passia.org/palestine_facts/personalities/alpha_a.htm.

88. Barry Rubin and Judith Colp Rubin, *Yasir Arafat: A Political Biography* (New York: Oxford University Press, 2003), p. 160.

89. Rubinstein, *The Mystery of Arafat*, p. 6.

90. "Arafat Names Head of Committee on Talks With Israel," Agence France-Presse, March 19, 1995 (accessed via LexisNexis).

91. "Abbas, Mahmoud," www.passia.org/palestine_facts/personalities/alpha_a.htm.

92. "Abu Mazen, Possible Arafat Challenger, Returns From Exile," Associated Press, July 13, 1995 (accessed via LexisNexis).

93. Mahmoud Abbas, *Through Secret Channels*, p. 209.

94. "Abbas, Mahmoud," www.passia.org/palestine_facts/personalities/alpha_a.htm.

95. "Palestinians Will Prevent Attacks From Autonomous Territories," Agence France-Presse, January 22, 1997 (accessed via LexisNexis).

96. "Three Men Accused of Planning Attack on Arafat's Deputy," Associated Press, February 24, 1997 (accessed via LexisNexis); "Abbas: Islamists Plotted to Kill Me," Reuters, February 25, 1997 (accessed via LexisNexis).

97. Imad Musa, "Report: Arafat Names Abu Mazen Successor," Associated Press, February 4, 1998 (accessed via LexisNexis).

98. Jean-François Legrain, "The Successions of Yasir Arafat," *Journal of Palestine Studies* 28, no. 4 (Summer 1999): 10.

99. Ibid., p. 190.

100. Interview with former Palestinian negotiator, Washington, DC, April 22, 2013.

101. "Abu Mazen: Had Camp David Convened Again, We Would Take the Same Positions, Part I," Middle East Media Research Institute, August 2, 2001, www.memri.org/report/en/0/0/0/0/0/0/489.htm.

102. Massimo Calabresi and Simon Robinson, "Bush vs. Arafat," *Time*, July 8, 2002, www.time.com/time/magazine/article/0,9171,1002841,00.html.

103. Greg Myre, "Soft-Spoken but Not Afraid to Voice Opinions," *New York Times*, March 11, 2003, www.nytimes.com/2003/03/11/international/middleeast/11ABBA.html.

104. Yehoshua, "Abu Mazen: Political Profile."

105. James Bennet and John Kifner, "6 Men Who Could Be Contenders to Lead the Palestinians If Arafat Goes," *New York Times*, June 14, 2002, www.nytimes.com

/2002/06/14/world/mideast-turmoil-succession-6-men-who-could-be-contenders
-lead-palestinians-if.html.

106. James Bennet, "Palestinians Approve Limited Scope for Premier Post," *New York Times,* March 11, 2003, www.nytimes.com/2003/03/11/world/palestinians-approve
-limited-scope-for-premier-post.html.

107. Greg Myre, "Palestinian Premier Faces Competing Demands Over Cabinet," *New York Times,* April 9, 2003, www.nytimes.com/2003/04/09/world/palestinian
-premier-faces-competing-demands-over-cabinet.html.

108. Rubin and Rubin, *Yasir Arafat,* p. 269.

109. Steven Weisman, "White House Is Pressing Israelis to Take Initiatives in Peace Talks," *New York Times,* April 17, 2003, www.nytimes.com/2003/04/17/world
/white-house-is-pressing-israelis-to-take-initiatives-in-peace-talks.html.

110. James Bennet, "MidEast Peace Proposal: The Peace Plan; U.S. and Partners Present Proposal for MidEast Peace," *New York Times,* April 30, 2003, www.nytimes
.com/2003/05/01/world/mideast-peace-proposal-peace-plan-us-partners-present-
proposal-for-mideast-peace.html.

111. "Bolstering the Palestinian Premier," *New York Times,* June 4, 2003, www.nytimes
.com/2003/06/04/opinion/bolstering-the-palestinian-premier.html.

112. Greg Myre, "Abbas Says He Will Use Persuasion, Not Force, in Dealing with Palestinian Militants," *New York Times,* June 10, 2003, www.nytimes.com/2003/06/10
/world/abbas-says-he-will-use-persuasion-not-force-dealing-with-palestinian
-militants.html.

113. Interview with Ghaith al-Omari, Washington, DC, January 18, 2013.

114. James Bennet, "Abbas in Clash Over His Stance in Peace Talks," *New York Times,* July 8, 2003, www.nytimes.com/2003/07/09/world/abbas-in-clash-over-his-stance
-in-peace-talks.html.

115. Robin Wright, "Bush Gives Abbas Praise and Promises," *Los Angeles Times,* July 26, 2003, http://articles.latimes.com/2003/jul/26/world/fg-abbas26.

116. Jim Zanotti, "The Palestinians: Background and U.S. Relations," Congressional Research Service, August 30, 2011, www.fas.org/sgp/crs/mideast/RL34074.pdf.

117. Interview with Ghaith al-Omari, Washington, DC, January 18, 2013.

118. Steven R. Weisman, "The MidEast Turmoil: White House; The U.S. Option: Staying the Course," *New York Times,* September 7, 2003, www.nytimes.com/2003/09/07
/world/the-mideast-turmoil-white-house-the-us-option-staying-the-course.html.

119. Ibid.

120. Elisabeth Bumiller, "Bush Admits Mideast Plan Is Stalled and Blames Arafat," *New York Times,* September 18, 2003, www.nytimes.com/2003/09/19/world/bush-admits
-mideast-plan-is-stalled-and-blames-arafat.html.

121. Zanotti, "The Palestinians: Background and U.S. Relations," www.fas.org/sgp/crs
/mideast/RL34074.pdf.

122. Aaron Pina, "Palestinian Elections," Congressional Research Service, February 9, 2006, www.fas.org/sgp/crs/mideast/RL33269.pdf.

123. Steven R. Weisman, "Bush Welcomes Abbas as Palestinian Leader," *New York Times,* January 11, 2005, www.nytimes.com/2005/01/10/world/americas/10iht
-diplo.html.

124. John Ward Anderson, "Abbas Seeks Revival of 'Road Map' Peace Plan," *Washington Post,* January 16, 2005, www.washingtonpost.com/wp-dyn/articles/A11464
-2005Jan15.html.

125. Interview with Elliott Abrams, Washington, DC, March 8, 2013.

126. Barry Rubin, "After Arafat," *Middle East Quarterly* 11, no. 2 (Spring 2004), www
.meforum.org/606/after-arafat.

127. Ehud Yaari, "The Morning After," in *After Arafat? The Future of Palestinian Politics,* ed. Robert Satloff (Washington, DC: Washington Institute for Near East Policy, 2001), www.washingtoninstitute.org/uploads/Documents/pubs/PolicyFocus42.pdf.

128. Haim Malka, "One Law, One Army: A Strategy for Palestinian Disarmament," *Oxford Journal on Good Governance* 2, no. 2 (August 2005): 45.

129. Jim Zanotti, "U.S. Security Assistance to the Palestinian Authority," Congressional Research Service, January 8, 2010, www.fas.org/sgp/crs/mideast/R40664.pdf.

CHAPTER 8   THE RISE OF HAMAS

1. Ilene Prusher, "Palestinian 'Third Way' Rises," *Christian Science Monitor,* December 13, 2005, www.csmonitor.com/2005/1213/p06s02-wome.html.
2. "Hamas Landslide Shakes Mideast," CNN, January 26, 2006, www.cnn.com/2006/WORLD/meast/01/26/palestinian.election.1604/index.html.
3. Ibid.
4. Interview with Elliott Abrams, Washington, DC, March 8, 2013.
5. Zaki Chehab, *Inside Hamas: The Untold Story of the Militant Islamic Movement* (New York: Nation Books, 2007), pp. 9–10.
6. Matt Levitt, *Hamas: Politics, Charity and Terrorism in the Service of Jihad* (New Haven, CT: Yale University Press, 2006), p. 24.
7. "Hamas Covenant 1988," The Avalon Project, August 18, 1988, http://avalon.law.yale.edu/20th_century/hamas.asp.
8. Ibid., pp. 33–34.
9. Azzam Tamimi, *Hamas: A History From Within* (Northampton, MA: Olive Branch Press, 2007), p. 189.
10. Boaz Ganor, "Hamas—The Islamic Resistance Movement in the Territories," *Survey of Arab Affairs,* February 2, 1992, http://jcpa.org/jl/saa27.htm; Graham Usher, "The Rise of Political Islam in the Occupied Territories," *Middle East International,* June 25, 1993, p. 20.
11. Michel Jubran and Laura Drake, "The Islamic Fundamentalist Movement in the West Bank and Gaza Strip," *Middle East Policy* 2, no. 2 (May 1993): 13.
12. "FM Peres Reaction to Afula Attack," Israeli Ministry of Foreign Affairs, April 6, 1994, www.mfa.gov.il/MFA/Archive/Speeches/FM%20PERES%20REACTION%20TO%20AFULA%20ATTACK%20-%2006-Apr-94.
13. Amira Hass, *Drinking the Sea at Gaza: Days and Nights in a Land Under Siege* (New York: Metropolitan Books, 1996), p. 77.
14. Clyde Haberman, "Arafat's Forces Arrange a Truce with Militants," *New York Times,* November 20, 1994, www.nytimes.com/1994/11/20/world/arafat-s-forces-arrange-a-truce-with-militants.html.
15. Hass, *Drinking the Sea at Gaza,* p. 84.
16. "Amnesty International Report 1996," Amnesty International, January 16, 2013, http://web.archive.org/web/19971015003230/http://www.amnesty.org/ailib/aireport/ar96/index.html.
17. Haim Malka, "Hamas: Resistance and Transformation of Palestinian Society," in *Understanding Islamic Charities,* ed. Jon B. Alterman and Karin Von Hippel (Washington, DC: Center for Strategic and International Studies, 2007), p. 111.
18. Khaled Abu Toameh, "Abbas: Hamas Planning W. Bank Takeover," *Jerusalem Post,* October 28, 2007, www.jpost.com/MiddleEast/Article.aspx?id=80021.
19. Barry Rubin and Judith Colp Rubin, *Yasir Arafat: A Political Biography* (New York: Oxford University Press, 2003), p. 180.
20. Hass, *Drinking the Sea at Gaza,* p. 76.
21. Chehab, *Inside Hamas,* pp. 6, 113–114, 224.
22. Ali El-Saleh, "Interview with Hamas's Said Siyam," *Asharq al-Awsat,* November 25, 2007.
23. "Arafat Arrests Hamas Leaders: Angered Militants Promise to Resume Bombings," CNN, March 9, 1996, http://web.archive.org/web/20000903184821/http://www2.cnn.com/WORLD/9603/jerusalem_blast/03-09/index.html.
24. Hass, *Drinking the Sea at Gaza,* p. 91.
25. "Palestinian Authority Arrests Hamas Leader Rantisi," CNN, April 9, 1998, http://web.archive.org/web/20010608224324/http://www.cnn.com/WORLD/meast/9804/09/hamas.arrest/.

26. Amira Hass, "Top Hamas Officials Still in PA Custody," *Haaretz*, October 15, 2000.

27. David Schenker, "Palestinian Fictions—Yasser Arafat Stands Alone as the Undisputed Leader of the Palestinian Authority and the Palestinians," *The World and I* 16, no. 11 (November 2001): 26.

28. Dore Gold, *The Fight for Jerusalem: Radical Islam, the West and the Future of the Holy City* (Washington, DC: Regnery Publishing, 2007), p. 5.

29. Chehab, *Inside Hamas*, p. 134.

30. Daniel Sobelman and Amos Harel, "PA Frees Hamas Prisoners," *Haaretz*, October 6, 2000.

31. Amira Hass, "Hamas Blamed for Attacks against Gaza Liquor Stores," *Haaretz*, October 15, 2000.

32. Levitt, *Hamas*, p. 40.

33. Tamimi, *Hamas: A History From Within*, p. 201.

34. Ely Karmon, "Hamas's Terrorism Strategy: Operational Limitations and Political Restraints," *Middle East Review of International Affairs* 4, no. 1 (March 2000), www.offiziere.ch/wp-content/uploads/2000-karmon.pdf.

35. Malka, "Hamas: Resistance and Transformation of Palestinian Society," p. 106.

36. Levitt, *Hamas*, pp. 116–117.

37. "Interviews from Gaza: Palestinian Options Under Siege," *Middle East Policy* 9, no. 4 (December 2002): 118.

38. "Hamas, Fatah to Resume Ceasefire Talks Within Days: Palestinians," Agence France-Presse, December 8, 2002 (accessed via LexisNexis).

39. Lamia Lahoud, "Fatah Threatens Hamas in Leaflet," *Jerusalem Post*, December 11, 2002 (accessed via LexisNexis).

40. Tamimi, *Hamas: A History from Within*, p. 187.

41. James Bennet, "Hamas Leader Tells Muslims to Retaliate If U.S. Attacks," *New York Times*, February 8, 2003, www.nytimes.com/2003/02/08/international/middle east/08MIDE.html.

42. "Hamas Leader Killed in Israeli Air Strike," PBS, March 22, 2004, www.pbs.org /newshour/updates/mideast_03-22-04.html.

43. Ibid.

44. Greg Myre, "In Loss of Leaders, Hamas Discovers a Renewed Strength," *New York Times*, April 25, 2004, www.nytimes.com/2004/04/25/world/in-loss-of-leaders -hamas-discovers-a-renewed-strength.html.

45. Yossi Alpher, "Bankruptcy," Bitterlemons.org, March 29, 2004, www.bitterlemons .org/previous/bl290304ed12.html.

46. Myre, "In Loss of Leaders, Hamas Discovers a Renewed Strength."

47. Mitchell Bard, "Will Israel Return to Gaza?" *inFocus Quarterly* 1, no. 2 (Fall 2007), www.jewishpolicycenter.org/article/60.

48. "Ariel Sharon Describes 'Disengagement Plan,'" Jewish Virtual Library, December 18, 2003, www.jewishvirtuallibrary.org/jsource/Peace/sharon_1203.html.

49. Chehab, *Inside Hamas*, p. 52.

50. Bard, "Will Israel Return to Gaza?"

51. Khaled Abu Toameh, "PA Official Threatens 'Fallujah-Style' Operation Against Hamas," *Jerusalem Post*, January 6, 2005 (accessed via LexisNexis).

52. Michael Eisentstadt, *The Palestinians: Between State Failure and Civil War* (Washington, DC: Washington Institute for Near East Policy, 2007), p. 13, www.wash ingtoninstitute.org/templateC04.php?CID=285.

53. Chehab, *Inside Hamas*, pp. 2–6.

54. Mark Dubowitz, "Terrorist TV in Eurabia," *inFocus Quarterly* 1, no. 3 (Winter 2007), www.jewishpolicycenter.org/92/terrorist-tv-in-eurabia.

55. Khaled Abu Toameh, "The Fallen Hope for Palestinian Press Freedom," *Jerusalem Post*, January 4, 2006 (accessed via LexisNexis).

56. Robert Berger, "VOA News: First Votes Cast in Palestinian Elections," US Fed News—Voice of America, January 21, 2006 (accessed via LexisNexis).

57. Rashid Khalidi, *The Iron Cage: The Story of the Palestinian Struggle for Statehood* (Boston, MA: Beacon Press, 2006), p. 152.

58. Sara Toth, "Hamas TV Campaign Ad Shows Violence Aimed Symbolically at Government Corruption," Associated Press, January 22, 2006 (accessed via LexisNexis).

59. "Hamas Calls for Palestinian Unity," Ma'an News Agency, November 1, 2005, www.maannews.net/eng/ViewDetails.aspx?ID=179066.

60. "Hamas Announces PLC List for Tulkarem District," Ma'an News Agency, December 7, 2005, www.maannews.net/eng/ViewDetails.aspx?ID=180294.

61. "Hamas Leader Hania Lays Out Elections Agenda, Including Three Points," Ma'an News Agency, December 9, 2005, www.maannews.net/eng/ViewDetails.aspx?ID=180394.

62. "Hamas to Enter Qassam Brigades Into PA Security Forces, End 'Bombing Operations,'" Ma'an News Agency, December 19, 2005, www.maannews.net/eng/ViewDetails.aspx?ID=180783.

63. "Hamas Rejects Relating Kidnappings to Resistance," Ma'an News Agency, December 31, 2005, www.maannews.net/eng/ViewDetails.aspx?ID=181261.

64. "Hamas PLC List Begins Campaign in Jenin, Vows to Combat Corruption and Unemployment," Ma'an News Agency, January 7, 2006, www.maannews.net/eng/ViewDetails.aspx?ID=181655.

65. "Popular Resistance Committees Support Hamas List, Announce Joint Operations Room for Armed Resistance Groups," Ma'an News Agency, January 25, 2006, www.maannews.net/eng/ViewDetails.aspx?ID=182377.

66. Aaron Pina, "Palestine Elections," Congressional Research Service, February 9, 2006, www.fas.org/sgp/crs/mideast/RL33269.pdf.

67. "A Crumpling Peace Process and a Greater Public Complaint of Corruption and Chaos Gave Hamas a Limited Advantage Over Fateh, but Fragmentation Within Fateh Turned That Advantage into an Overwhelming Victory," Palestinian Center for Policy and Survey Research, February 15, 2006, http://pcpsr.org/survey/polls/2006/exitplcfulljan06e.html.

68. Khaled Abu Toameh, "Fatah Leaders Reeling From 'The Big Punishment,'" *Jerusalem Post,* January 27, 2006, www.jpost.com/LandedPages/PrintArticle.aspx?id=11391.

69. Chris McGreal, "Palestinian Authority 'May Have Lost Billions,'" *Guardian,* February 5, 2006, www.guardian.co.uk/world/2006/feb/06/israel.

CHAPTER 9   CIVIL WAR

1. Shmuel Rosner, "Bush Urges Abbas to Remain in Office Despite Hamas Win," *Haaretz,* January 26, 2006, www.haaretz.com/print-edition/news/bush-urges-abbas-to-remain-in-office-despite-hamas-win-1.178627.

2. "Despite Negative Evaluation of Palestinian Conditions Since the Election of Abu Mazin, and Despite the Continued Rise in the Popularity of Hamas, Expected Elections' Outcome Gives Fateh 44% and Hamas 33% of the Seats of the Next PLC," Palestinian Center for Policy and Survey Research, June 13, 2005, www.pcpsr.org/survey/polls/2005/p16epressrelease.html; "On the Eve of the Israeli Withdrawal From the Gaza Strip, 84% See It as Victory for Armed Resistance and 40% Give Hamas Most of the Credit for It; But 62% Are Opposed to Continued Attacks Against Israelis From the Gaza Strip, 60% Support Collection of Arms From Armed Groups in Gaza, Fateh's Electoral Standing Improved at Hamas' Expense (47% to 30%), Optimism Prevails Over Pessimism, and 73% Support the Establishment of a Palestinian State in the Gaza Strip That Would Gradually Extend to the West Bank," Palestinian Center for Policy and Survey Research, September 25, 2005, www.pcpsr.org/survey/polls/2005/p17a.html; "Six Weeks Before the Parliamentary Elections: Fateh Makes Further Gains Compared to September 2005 Results,"

Palestinian Center for Policy and Survey Research, December 11, 2005, www.pcpsr .org/survey/polls/2005/p18epressrelease.html.

3. Martin Kramer, "Polls That Hid Hamas," *Sandbox,* January 28, 2006, www.martin kramer.org/sandbox/2006/01/polls-that-hid-hamas/.

4. Interview with Elliott Abrams, Washington, DC, March 8, 2013.

5. Khalid Amayreh, "Palestinian PM Quits After Poll Upset," Al-Jazeera, January 27, 2006, www.aljazeera.com/archive/2006/01/20084914467631187.html.

6. "Black Pages in the Absence of Justice: Report on Bloody Fighting in the Gaza Strip From 7 to 14 June 2007," Palestine Center for Human Rights, October 1, 2007, pp. 11–12, www.pchrgaza.org/files/Reports/English/pdf_spec/Gaza%20Conflict%20-%20 Eng%209%20october.pdf.

7. Ibrahim Barzak, "Fatah, Hamas Gunmen Clash in Gaza," Associated Press, April 23, 2006, www.washingtonpost.com/wp-dyn/content/article/2006/04/22/AR2006 042200481.html.

8. Ibid.

9. "Hamas, Fatah Clash Again in Gaza," Voice of America, May 9, 2006, http:// english.chosun.com/site/data/html_dir/2006/05/10/2006051061003.html.

10. Mohammad Yaghi, "The Growing Anarchy in the Palestinian Territories," Washington Institute for Near East Policy, Policywatch 1103, May 16, 2006, www.washington institute.org/policy-analysis/view/the-growing-anarchy-in-the-palestinian-territo ries.

11. Taghreed al-Khodary, "Gaza: Life Under Hamas Rule," *Arab Reform Bulletin* 5, no. 9 (November 2007), www.carnegieendowment.org/files/novemberkhodary1.pdf.

12. Taghreed al-Khodary, "Hamas Police Force Recruits Women in Gaza," *New York Times,* January 18, 2008, www.nytimes.com/2008/01/18/world/middleeast/18gaza .html.

13. "Black Pages in the Absence of Justice," p. 13.

14. Ibid.

15. "Black Pages in the Absence of Justice," pp. 12–15.

16. "Hamas Accuses Fatah Over Attack," Al-Jazeera, December 15, 2006, www.al jazeera.com/news/middleeast/2006/12/200852513152100682.html.

17. "Fragile Ceasefire Holds in Gaza," Al-Jazeera, December 18, 2006, www.aljazeera .com/news/middleeast/2006/12/200852513816270213.html.

18. Ali El-Saleh, "Interview With Hamas's Said Siyam," *Asharq al-Awsat,* November 25, 2007.

19. Michael Eisentstadt, "The Palestinians: Between State Failure and Civil War," Washington Institute for Near East Policy, Policy Focus 78, December 2007, www .washingtoninstitute.org/templateC04.php?CID=285.

20. "Black Pages in the Absence of Justice," pp. 16–19.

21. Alfred B. Prados and Christopher M. Blanchard, "Saudi Arabia: Terrorist Financing Issues," Congressional Research Service, December 8, 2004, www.fas.org/irp /crs/RL32499.pdf.

22. "Text of Palestinians' Mecca Agreement," Agence France-Presse, February 9, 2007, www.lebanonwire.com/0702MLN/07020923AF.asp.

23. "Black Pages in the Absence of Justice," pp. 20–22.

24. Ibid.

25. "Occupied Palestinian Territories Torn Apart by Factional Strife," Amnesty International, October 24, 2007, www.amnesty.org/en/library/asset/MDE21/020/2007 /en/6609e419-d363-11dd-a329-2f46302a8cc6/mde210202007en.html.

26. "Black Pages in the Absence of Justice."

27. Shlomo Shamir, "Arabs Thwart PA UN Bid to Condemn Hamas," *Haaretz,* November 18, 2007, www.haaretz.com/print-edition/news/arabs-thwart-pa-un-bid-to -condemn-hamas-1.233428.

28. Steven Erlanger, "Hamas Seizes Broad Control in Gaza Strip," *New York Times,* June 14, 2007, www.nytimes.com/2007/06/14/world/middleeast/14mideast.html.

29. Cam Simpson and Neil King Jr., "Hamas to Show an Improved Hand," *Wall Street Journal,* July 30, 2007, http://online.wsj.com/article/SB118575064310581669.html.

CHAPTER 10   BACKSLIDE

1. Interview with Aaron David Miller, Washington, DC, March 11, 2013.
2. "Former Palestinian Oil Board Chief Arrested for Graft," Agence France-Presse, January 4, 2006 (accessed via LexisNexis).
3. "Palestinian Attorney General Vows to Fight Corruption," Xinhua, February 5, 2006 (accessed via LexisNexis).
4. Greg Myre, "Israel Makes Payment to Palestinians, but Says It Could Be the Last," *New York Times,* February 6, 2006, www.nytimes.com/2006/02/06/international/middleeast/06mideast.html.
5. Khaled Abu Toameh, "Boycotts Bring Paralysis to PA Embassies Worldwide," *Jerusalem Post,* April 11, 2006 (accessed via LexisNexis).
6. "Palestinian Ambassador in Romania to Be Investigated After Accusing Fatah of Corruption," Ma'an News Agency, July 11, 2006, www.maannews.net/eng/ViewDetails.aspx?ID=187928.
7. Khaled Abu Toameh, "Abbas Sues Prominent Palestinian Editor for Libel," *Jerusalem Post,* May 22, 2006 (accessed via LexisNexis).
8. Khaled Abu Toameh, "Fatah's Change of Focus," *Jerusalem Post,* June 16, 2006 (accessed via LexisNexis).
9. Khaled Abu Toameh, "If You Can't Beat 'em Join 'em," *Jerusalem Post,* August 27, 2006 (accessed via LexisNexis).
10. Khaled Abu Toameh, "Fatah Central Committee Authorizes Unity Gov't," *Jerusalem Post,* August 27, 2006 (accessed via LexisNexis).
11. Khaled Abu Toameh, "Fatah Activists Threaten Abbas With 'Intifada,'" *Jerusalem Post,* August 29, 2006 (accessed via LexisNexis).
12. "Dismissed Leaders Urge Fatah to Investigate All Cases of Corruption in the Movement," Ma'an News Agency, April 29, 2007, www.maannews.net/eng/ViewDetails.aspx?ID=195480.
13. "Fatah Fighters Demand Reformation of Movement and an End to Corruption," Ma'an News Agency, April 14, 2007, www.maannews.net/eng/ViewDetails.aspx?ID=195082.
14. Ibid.
15. Interview with Michael Singh, Washington, DC, March 29, 2013.
16. "Corruption in Gaza Power Company Revealed by Deputy Chair of Palestinian Power Authority," Ma'an News Agency, August 21, 2007, www.maannews.net/eng/ViewDetails.aspx?ID=198425.
17. Khaled Abu Toameh, "PA Arrests TV Station Owner for Showing Haniyeh Press Conference," *Jerusalem Post,* November 11, 2007 (accessed via LexisNexis).
18. Khaled Abu Toameh, "Abbas's Latest Headaches," *Jerusalem Post,* March 28, 2008 (accessed via LexisNexis).
19. Khaled Abu Toameh, "Released Fatah Member Aims to Reform Faction," *Jerusalem Post,* September 1, 2008 (accessed via LexisNexis).
20. "PA Says Ministry Employees Took Bribes, Admitted Corruption," Ma'an News Agency, October 21, 2008, www.maannews.net/eng/ViewDetails.aspx?ID=205775.
21. Khaled Abu Toameh, "Ramattan News Agency Shuts Down in Response to Raids," *Jerusalem Post,* December 1, 2008 (accessed via LexisNexis).
22. "Journalists: PA Censoring Dissent in Media Crackdown," Ma'an News Agency, December 16, 2008, www.maannews.net/eng/ViewDetails.aspx?ID=207033.
23. "Palestine Investment Fund Moved Under President," Wikileaks, February 8, 2006, http://wikileaks.org/cable/2006/02/06JERUSALEM585.html.

24. Email correspondence with PIF representative, May 10, 2013.

25. Interview with Jim Prince, Washington, DC, May 10, 2013.

26. Correspondence with PIF representative, May 10, 2013.

27. Interview with Jim Prince, Washington, DC, May 10, 2013.

28. "FACTBOX: Proposed Changes at Palestinian Investment Fund," Reuters, April 28, 2009, www.reuters.com/article/2009/04/28/us-palestinians-aid-rules-factbox -sb-idUSTRE53R2HL20090428.

29. Correspondence with PIF representative, May 10, 2013.

30. Interview with Jim Prince, Washington, DC, May 10, 2013.

31. "FACTBOX: Proposed Changes at Palestinian Investment Fund."

32. Adam Entous, "Exclusive-Debate over Control of Palestinian Investment Fund," Reuters, April 28, 2009, www.reuters.com/article/2009/04/28/idUSLQ581028.

33. Interview with Palestinian businessman, Ramallah, September 8, 2011.

34. Mark Perry, "Dayton's Mission: A Reader's Guide," Al-Jazeera, January 25, 2011, www.aljazeera.com/palestinepapers/2011/01/2011125145732219555.html.

35. "Palestinian Group Accuses Hamas, Fatah of Abusing Human Rights," Reuters, May 27, 2008, www.ynetnews.com/articles/0,7340,L-3548506,00.html.

CHAPTER 11   CRUSHING POLITICAL CHALLENGERS

1. Lawahez Jabari, Ranna Khalil, and Dave Copeland, "Resistance Through Reality TV? Young Palestinians Battle to Become 'President,'" NBC News, May 6, 2013, http://worldnews.nbcnews.com/_news/2013/05/06/18017544-resistance-through -reality-tv-young-palestinians-battle-to-become-president?lite.

2. "Profile: Mohammed Dahlan," Al-Jazeera, August 11, 2009, www.aljazeera.com /news/middleeast/2009/08/200981184622781846.html.

3. Khaled Abu Toameh, "Fatah Hamas Trade Threats to Assassinate Each Other's Leaders. Hundreds of Thousands Rally in Support of Abbas," *Jerusalem Post,* January 8, 2007 (accessed via LexisNexis).

4. Khaled Abu Toameh, "PA Security Forces Remain Idle During 'Pogrom' in Ramallah," *Jerusalem Post,* January 9, 2007 (accessed via LexisNexis).

5. Khaled Abu Toameh, "Hamas, Fatah Leaders in Mecca for 'Do or Die' Talks on Unity," *Jerusalem Post,* February 7, 2007 (accessed via LexisNexis).

6. Avi Issacharoff, "Barghouti, Fatah Execs Urge Dahlan Removal," *Haaretz,* June 19, 2007, www.haaretz.com/print-edition/news/barghouti-fatah-execs-urge-dahlan -removal-1.223542.

7. Khaled Abu Toameh, "Dahlan: I Predicted Hamas Takeover of Strip. Former Gaza Strongman Slams Qatar Iran for Funding Movement," *Jerusalem Post,* June 28, 2007 (accessed via LexisNexis).

8. Avi Issacharoff, "Mohammed Dahlan Resigns Following Fatah's Gaza Defeat," *Haaretz,* July 26, 2007, www.haaretz.com/news/mohammed-dahlan-resigns-fol lowing-fatah-s-gaza-defeat-1.226286.

9. Khaled Abu Toameh, "Abbas Resists US Pressure to Name Dahlan His Deputy," *Jerusalem Post,* October 22, 2007 (accessed via LexisNexis).

10. Khaled Abu Toameh, "Where There's Smoke . . . ," *Jerusalem Post,* August 1, 2008 (accessed via LexisNexis).

11. Jack Khoury and Avi Issacharoff, "Abbas Tells Sixth Fatah Convention in Bethlehem: Peace Is Our Choice, Resistance Our Right," *Haaretz,* August 5, 2009, www .haaretz.com/print-edition/news/abbas-tells-sixth-fatah-convention-in-bethlehem -peace-is-our-choice-resistance-our-right-1.281405; "Fatah Congress: Preliminary Central Committee Results Arrive," Wikileaks, August 11, 2009, http://wikileaks .org/cable/2009/08/09JERUSALEM1394.html#.

12. Khaled Abu Toameh, "Lights Out for Fatah Station That Aimed to Counter Hamas," *Jerusalem Post,* December 18, 2009 (accessed via LexisNexis).

13. Khaled Abu Toameh, "Abbas Fears Dahlan Trying to Take His Place," *Jerusalem Post,* December 5, 2010, www.jpost.com/MiddleEast/Article.aspx?id=198141.

14. Avi Issacharoff, "PA Suspects Former Fatah Strongman in Gaza Recruiting for New Armed Militia," *Haaretz,* December 17, 2010, www.haaretz.com/print-edition /news/pa-suspects-former-fatah-strongman-in-gaza-recruiting-for-new-armed -militia-1.331029.

15. Abu Toameh, "Abbas Fears Dahlan Trying to Take His Place."

16. Maher Abukhater, "Onetime Fatah Strongman Dahlan Struggling to Get Out of a Quagmire," *Los Angeles Times,* December 29, 2010, http://latimesblogs.latimes .com/babylonbeyond/2010/12/west-bank-fatah-strongman-dahlan-struggling-to -get-out-of-a-quagmire.html.

17. Khaled Abu Toameh, "Dahlan Denies Coup to Overthrow Abbas," *Jerusalem Post,* January 5, 2011, www.jpost.com/MiddleEast/Article.aspx?id=202255.

18. Khaled Abu Toameh, "Fatah to Probe Reports Dahlan Aiding Gaddafi," *Jerusalem Post,* April 6, 2011, www.jpost.com/MiddleEast/Article.aspx?id=215324.

19. Khaled Abu Toameh, "Abbas Shuts Down Web Sites Run by Dahlan Supporters," *Jerusalem Post,* June 11, 2011, www.jpost.com/MiddleEast/Article.aspx?id=224539.

20. "Fatah Central Committee Expels Dahlan," WAFA, June 12, 2011, http://english .wafa.ps/index.php?action=detail&id=16419.

21. "Former Top PA Security Chief Muhammad Dahlan Attacks PA President Mahmoud Abbas: He Can Take the Decision to Fire Me and Shove It," Middle East Media Research Institute, June 13, 2011, www.memritv.org/clip_transcript/en/2993.htm.

22. Khaled Abu Toameh, "Palestinian Security Forces Nab Mohammed Dahlan Supporters," *Jerusalem Post,* July 26, 2011, www.jpost.com/MiddleEast/Article.aspx ?id=230978.

23. "Palestinian Police Raid Home of President's Rival, Arrest 23 Guards," Associated Press, July 28, 2011, www.haaretz.com/news/diplomacy-defense/palestinian -police-raid-home-of-president-s-rival-arrest-23-guards-1.375754.

24. Khaled Abu Toameh, "Abbas 'Feels He's Above the Law,' Charges Dahlan," *Jerusalem Post,* July 31, 2011, www.jpost.com/MiddleEast/Article.aspx?id=231686.

25. "Fatah: Ex-Gaza Strongman Mohammed Dahlan Poisoned Arafat," Associated Press, August 8, 2011, www.haaretz.com/news/middle-east/fatah-ex-gaza-strong man-mohammed-dahlan-poisoned-arafat-1.377635.

26. Khaled Abu Toameh, "PA Commission of Inquiry: Dahlan Helped Poison Arafat," *Jerusalem Post,* August 7, 2011, www.jpost.com/MiddleEast/Article.aspx?ID =232834.

27. "Fatah Ratifies Dahlan's Final Sacking Decision," WAFA, August 14, 2011, http:// english.wafa.ps/index.php?action=detail&id=16988.

28. "Dahlan Lacks Parliamentary Legitimacy," *Palestine Today,* January 10, 2012, http://paltoday.ps/ar/index.php?act=post&id=127502.

29. "Mohammad Dahlan," Facebook, January 30, 2012, www.facebook.com/moham mad.dahlan2/posts/287628904624572.

30. "Anti-Corruption Chief Going After Foreign Accounts," Ma'an News Agency, January 2, 2012, www.maannews.net/eng/ViewDetails.aspx?ID=449451.

31. Khaled Abu Toameh, "Jordan Seizes Assets of Mohammed Dahlan," *Jerusalem Post,* January 11, 2012, www.jpost.com/MiddleEast/Article.aspx?id=253088.

32. Yazid Sayigh, *Armed Struggle and the Search for State: The Palestinian National Movement, 1949–1993* (Oxford: Clarendon Press, 1997), p. 604.

33. William A. Orme Jr., "Palestinian Investment Fund, No Longer Secret, Will Close," *New York Times,* July 7, 2000, www.nytimes.com/2000/07/07/world/palestinian -investment-fund-no-longer-secret-will-close.html.

34. Ronen Bergman and David Ratner, "The Man Who Swallowed Gaza," *Haaretz,* April 4, 1997, www.mfa.gov.il/mfa/archive/articles/1997/the%20man%20who %20swallowed%20gaza%20-%2004-apr-97.

35. Orme, "Palestinian Investment Fund, No Longer Secret, Will Close."

36. Phone interview with former PA advisor, June 4, 2012.

37. Deborah Sontag and Jane Perlez, "Arab-Israeli Negotiations Turn on the Chemistry of the Central Players," *New York Times,* July 16, 2000, www.nytimes

.com/2000/07/16/world/arab-israeli-negotiations-turn-on-the-chemistry-of-the
-central-players.html.

38. "Abu Mazen: Had Camp David Convened Again, We Would Take the Same Positions, Part II," Middle East Media Research Institute, August 6, 2001, www.memri
.org/report/en/0/0/0/0/0/0/0/490.htm.

39. Phone interview with former PA negotiator, April 22, 2013.

40. Daoud Kuttab, "Mohammad Rashid: The Ugly Rich Man of Palestine," website of Daoud Kuttab, January 12, 2003, www.daoudkuttab.com/?p=172.

41. Ibid.

42. Arnon Regular, "Mysteries Multiply Over Yasser Arafat's Missing Monies," *Haaretz*, November 8, 2004, www.haaretz.com/print-edition/news/mysteries-mult
iply-over-yasser-arafat-s-missing-monies-1.139575.

43. Khaled Abu Toameh, "Abbas Orders Probe of 'Corrupt' Judges Tied to Arafat," *Jerusalem Post*, February 15, 2012 (accessed via LexisNexis).

44. Karin Laub, "Officials: Abbas Envoys, Hamas Head Meet," Associated Press, January 13, 2007, www.washingtonpost.com/wp-dyn/content/article/2007/01/13
/AR2007011300333_pf.html.

45. Avi Issachroff, "Mohammed Rashid to Advise Abbas on Palestinian Unity," *Haaretz*, January 14, 2007, www.haaretz.com/print-edition/news/mohammed-ras
hid-to-advise-abbas-on-palestinian-unity-1.209949.

46. "Former Arafat Aide Under Investigation for Embezzling Funds From PA," Ma'an News Agency, March 26, 2008, www.maannews.net/eng/ViewDetails
.aspx?ID=201831.

47. Khaled Abu Toameh, "Arafat Adviser Demands Extradition of PA Official," *Jerusalem Post*, February 15, 2011, www.jpost.com/MiddleEast/Article.aspx?id=208369.

48. Khaled Abu Toameh, "Fatah to Probe Reports Dahlan Aiding Gaddafi," *Jerusalem Post*, April 6, 2011, www.jpost.com/MiddleEast/Article.aspx?id=215324.

49. Karin Laub and Mohammed Daraghmeh, "Arafat's Moneyman Targeted in Corruption Probe," Associated Press, May 16, 2012, http://news.yahoo.com/arafats
-moneyman-targeted-corruption-probe-173916721.html.

50. Ibid.

51. "Interpol 'Refuses to Help' in Arafat Adviser Case," Ma'an News Agency, May 18, 2012, www.maannews.net/eng/ViewDetails.aspx?ID=487029.

52. "Habash Launches Scathing Attack on Mohammad Rachid," *Palestine Press*, May 25, 2012, www.palpress.co.uk/arabic/?action=detail&id=49399.

53. Khaled Abu Toameh, "Former Arafat Advisor Sentenced to 15 Years in Jail," *Jerusalem Post*, June 7, 2012, www.jpost.com/MiddleEast/Article.aspx?id=273086.

54. Mohammed Daraghmeh, "Arafat Moneyman Gets 15 Years for Corruption," Associated Press, June 7, 2012, http://bigstory.ap.org/article/arafat-moneyman-gets
-15-years-corruption.

55. "Abbas Plans to Sequester Abed Rabbo," *Palestine Today*, December 14, 2011, http://paltoday.ps/ar/index.php?ajax=preview&id=125290.

56. "Abed Rabbo Dismisses Reports of Feud With Abbas," Ma'an News Agency, December 28, 2011, www.maannews.net/eng/ViewDetails.aspx?ID=448187.

57. "Palestinian National Authority—The PA Ministerial Cabinet List April 2003—October 2003," Jerusalem Media & Communication Centre, September 27, 2007, http://web.archive.org/web/20070927220148/http://www.jmcc.org/politics/pna
/newpagov03.htm.

58. "Abed-Rabbo Appointed as PLO Secretary General," IMEMC, December 10, 2006, www.imemc.org/article/23137.

59. "Fayyad Refused to Carry Abbas' Message to Netanyahu," *Al-Quds Al-Arabi*, April 19, 2012, www.alquds.co.uk/index.asp?fname=data20120404-1919qpt962
.htm.

60. Avi Issacharoff, "Top Palestinian Leaders Abbas, Fayyad Reportedly Cut All Contact With Each Other," *Haaretz*, April 23, 2012, www.haaretz.com/news

/diplomacy-defense/top-palestinian-leaders-abbas-fayyad-reportedly-cut-all
-contact-with-each-other-1.425999.

61. "Abbas Sacks Supervisor of Official Palestinian Media," Xinhua, April 24, 2012,
http://news.xinhuanet.com/english/world/2012-04/24/c_131548780.htm.

62. "Palestinian President Sacks Abed Rabbo from Media Position," *Al-Quds Al-
Arabi,* April 25, 2012, www.alquds.co.uk/index.asp?fname=today25z500.htm
&arc=data20120404-2525z500.htm.

63. Avi Issacharoff, "Revealed: Netanyahu's Secret Talks with the Palestinians,"
Times of Israel, May 13, 2013, www.timesofisrael.com/revealed-netanyahus-secret
-talks-with-the-palestinians/

64. "Jailed Intifada Leader Registers Rival Fatah List," Agence France-Presse, December 14, 2005 (accessed via LexisNexis).

65. Khaled Abu Toameh, "Fatah Activists Blame Their Leaders," *Jerusalem Post,* January 27, 2006 (accessed via ProQuest).

66. "Palestinian Legislative Elections: Day After Election Day SITREP #1," Wikileaks, January 26, 2006, http://wikileaks.org/cable/2006/01/06JERUSALEM366
.html.

67. "Leading Fatah Member Demands Resignation of Fatah Central Committee," *Ramattan News Agency—BBC World Monitoring,* January 27, 2006 (accessed via
LexisNexis).

68. Khaled Abu Toameh, "PA Commission of Inquiry: Dahlan Helped Poison Arafat," *Jerusalem Post,* August 7, 2011, www.jpost.com/MiddleEast/Article.aspx?ID
=232834.

69. "Fatah Central Committee Expels Member of Revolutionary Council Mashharawi," WAFA, January 30, 2012, http://english.wafa.ps/index.php?action=detail
&id=18863.

70. "Exclusive: Fatah Decides to Expel Samir Mashharawi," *Palestine Press,* February
15, 2012, www.palpress.co.uk/arabic/?action=detail&id=37520.

71. "Fatah Officials Criticize Abbas' Said Intention to Rescind Official's Immunity,"
Palestinian Information Centre—BBC Worldwide Monitoring, January 12, 2012
(accessed via LexisNexis).

72. "Mohammad Dahlan," Facebook, January 30, 2012, www.facebook.com/moham
mad.dahlan2/posts/287425087978287.

73. Thomas L. Friedman, "Green Shoots in Palestine," *New York Times,* August 4,
2009, www.nytimes.com/2009/08/05/opinion/05friedman.html.

74. "PA Minister of Finance Dr. Salam Fayyad Resigns," Ma'an News Agency, November 19, 2005, www.maannews.net/eng/ViewDetails.aspx?ID=179478.

75. Khaled Abu Toameh, "Abbas to Receive Monthly Salary of $10,000," *Jerusalem
Post,* November 24, 2005 (accessed via LexisNexis).

76. Khaled Abu Toameh, "PA Economy Minister Charged with Corruption," *Jerusalem
Post,* November 29, 2011, www.jpost.com/MiddleEast/Article.aspx?id=247466.

77. "Anti-Corruption Committee: Minister to Face Court," Ma'an News Agency, August 24, 2011, http://maannews.net/ENG/ViewDetails.aspx?ID=415389.

78. Lena Dirbashi, "Farmers Defend Embattled Agriculture Minister," Ma'an News
Agency, September 19, 2011, http://maannews.net/eng/ViewDetails.aspx?ID=4216
80.

79. Dan Ephron, "Palestine's Split Over Statehood," *Daily Beast,* July 14, 2011, www.the
dailybeast.com/articles/2011/07/14/mahmoud-abbas-and-salam-fayyad-disagree
-on-palestinian-u-n-representation.html.

80. "Palestine: Ending the Occupation, Establishing the State," *Palestinian National Authority,* August 2009, www.americantaskforce.org/palestinian_national
_authority_ending_occupation_establishing_state.

81. Taylor Luck, "Politics Not Ripe for Palestinian Statehood Bid—Fayyad," *Jordan
Times,* December 5, 2011, www.americantaskforce.org/daily_news_article/2011
/12/05/1323061200_8.

82. "Salam Fayyad Signals He May Resign 'For Sake of Palestinian Unity,'" Reuters, November 14, 2011, www.haaretz.com/news/diplomacy-defense/salam-fayyad -signals-he-may-resign-for-sake-of-palestinian-unity-1.395549.

83. Avi Issacharoff, "Fayyad to Haaretz: I Will Not Lead a Palestinian Unity Government," *Haaretz,* December 2, 2011, www.haaretz.com/print-edition /news/fayyad-to-haaretz-i-will-not-lead-a-palestinian-unity-government-1.399065.

84. Adel Zaanoun, "Hundreds of Thousands Join Fatah Rally in Gaza," Agence France-Presse, January 4, 2013, www.google.com/hostednews/afp/article/ALeqM5hchLm DQQYEPh84Hctkttwx9ytUZg?docId=CNG.d8019c30b155d3174b08eae5cb97 5567.171.

85. "Thousands Chanted 'Dahlan Is the President,'" *Palestine Now,* January 5, 2013, http://paltimes.net/new/ar/prints/news/30833.

86. "Fatah Rally in Gaza Looks Toward Unity With Hamas," Associated Press, January 4, 2013, www.usatoday.com/story/news/world/2013/01/04/gaza-palestinian/18 08493/.

87. Khaled Abu Toameh, "Fatah Reinstates Plans for Gaza Anniversary Event," *Jerusalem Post,* December 28, 2012, www.jpost.com/MiddleEast/Article.aspx?id=297 666.

88. "Dahlan Is Back to Fatah by Forming and Supporting the Electoral Lists for Municipal and Village Councils in the West Bank," *Al-Quds Al-Arabi,* October 9, 2012, www.alquds.co.uk/index.asp?fname=data%5C2012%5C10%5C10-09%5C09 x85.htm.

89. See https://www.facebook.com/mohammad.dahlan2; www.youtube.com/user/Moh madDahlan; https://twitter.com/mohammad_dahlan; www.dahlan.ps/. Others believed to be associated with him include: Amad, Fatah Voice, Firas Press, InLight Press, Karama Press, Kofia Press, Milad News and Palestine Beituna.

90. "Dahlan Launches Scathing Attack on Abbas," *Palestine Today,* November 3, 2012, http://paltoday.ps/ar/index.php?ajax=preview&id=150501.

91. "The Calm May Not Last Forever," *The Economist,* June 30, 2012, www.econo mist.com/node/21557812.

92. Karin Laub and Mohammed Daraghmeh, "Palestinian Government Debt Hurts Private Sector," Associated Press, August 18, 2012, http://bigstory.ap.org/article /palestinian-government-debt-hurts-private-sector.

93. Dia al-Kahlout, "Possibility of Reconciliation Between Abbas and Dahlan Closer," Al-Safir, March 4, 2013, www.assafir.com/MulhakArticle.aspx?EditionId=2401 &MulhakArticleId=1177262&MulhakId=5456.

94. "High Court Sets a Date for Appeal Against the Decision to Lift Dahlan's Immunity," Ma'an News Agency, March 5, 2013, www.maannews.net/arb/ViewDetails .aspx?ID=571648.

95. "Palestine Court Rejects Ex-Fatah Member Appeal Against Lifting Immunity," Xinhua, March 28, 2013, http://news.xinhuanet.com/english/world/2013-03/28/c_13 2269390.htm.

96. Ali Sawafta, "Palestinian Prime Minister Fayyad Offers Resignation: Sources," Reuters, April 10, 2013, www.reuters.com/article/2013/04/10/us-palestinians-fayyad -abbas-idUSBRE93917I20130410?feedType=RSS&feedName=worldNews.

97. "US Believes Palestinian PM Not Resigning," Agence France-Presse, April 11, 2013, www.globalpost.com/dispatch/news/afp/130411/us-believes-palestinian-pm-not -resigning.

98. "Obama: Israel Has 'True Partners' in Peace in Abbas, Fayyad," Real Clear Politics, March 21, 2013, www.realclearpolitics.com/video/2013/03/21/obama_israel_has _true_partners_in_peace_in_abbas_fayyad.html.

99. Nasouh Nazzal, "Mohammed Mustafa Expected as Next Palestinian PM," Gulf News, April 7, 2013, http://gulfnews.com/news/region/palestinian-territories/mo hammad-mustafa-expected-as-next-palestinian-pm-1.1167818.

100. "Palestinian Prime Minister Salam Fayyad Resigns," BBC, April 13, 2013, www .bbc.co.uk/news/world-middle-east-22139517.

CHAPTER 12   QUASHING CRITICAL MEDIA AND PROTESTERS

1. "Amended Basic Law," website of the US Agency for International Development, March 26, 2012, www.usaid.gov/wbg/misc/Amended_Basic_Law.pdf.
2. Email correspondence with George Hale, April 27, 2013.
3. "PA Arrests Palestinian Cartoonist," Al-Haq, April 19, 2012, www.alhaq.org /documentation/weekly-focuses/562-pa-arrests-palestinian-cartoonist-.
4. Khaled Abu Toameh, "Palestinian Journalists Decry Threats Assaults by Hamas Fatah," *Jerusalem Post,* August 27, 2007 (accessed via LexisNexis).
5. Khaled Abu Toameh, "Fatah Forces Beat Students Reporters at Hebron University Hamas Event," *Jerusalem Post,* September 10, 2007 (accessed via LexisNexis).
6. Khaled Abu Toameh, "PA Arrests TV Station Owner for Showing Haniyeh Press Conference," *Jerusalem Post,* November 11, 2007 (accessed via LexisNexis).
7. Khaled Abu Toameh, "Hamas Bans Fatah-Affiliated Newspapers. Death Threats, Arrests Are Being Used to Intimidate Palestinian Journalists," *Jerusalem Post,* July 29, 2008 (accessed via LexisNexis).
8. "Journalists: PA Censoring Dissent in Media Crackdown," Ma'an News Agency, December 16, 2008, www.maannews.net/eng/ViewDetails.aspx?ID=207033.
9. Khaled Abu Toameh, "Ramattan News Agency Shuts Down in Response to Raids," *Jerusalem Post,* December 1, 2008 (accessed via LexisNexis).
10. "Monthly Report on Violations of Human Rights and Freedoms in the PNA-Controlled Territory," Independent Commission for Human Rights, January 2009, www.ichr.ps/pdfs/eMRV-1-09.pdf.
11. Khaled Abu Toameh, "PA Holding Six Palestinian Journalists Without Trial," *Jerusalem Post,* February 16, 2009 (accessed via LexisNexis).
12. Khaled Abu Toameh, "PA Security Forces Summon Palestinian Journalist Who Criticized Leadership," *Jerusalem Post,* January 10, 2012, www.jpost.com/Middle East/Article.aspx?id=252914.
13. "Report of the Special Rapporteur on the Promotion and Protection of the Right to Freedom of Opinion and Expression, Frank La Rue," United Nations, June 12, 2012, http://unispal.un.org/unispal.nsf/47d4e277b48d9d3685256ddc00612265/6 8a8430f7c1ae73285257a1c00512d46?OpenDocument&reason=0.
14. Email correspondence with George Hale, April 27, 2013.
15. "Palestinians Ban Al-Jazeera for Airing Arafat Conspiracy Allegations," Reuters, July 15, 2009, www.haaretz.com/news/palestinians-ban-al-jazeera-for-airing-arafat -conspiracy-allegations-1.280060.
16. Khaled Abu Toameh, "PLO Calls Estranged Leader Qaddoumi 'Deranged,'" *Jerusalem Post,* July 15, 2009, www.jpost.com/MiddleEast/Article.aspx?id=148684.
17. Khaled Abu Toameh, "PA Issues Arrest Warrant for Shabaneh," *Jerusalem Post,* February 11, 2010, www.jpost.com/MiddleEast/Article.aspx?id=168375.
18. "The Palestine Papers," Al-Jazeera, www.aljazeera.com/palestinepapers/ (accessed July 5, 2012).
19. Robert Mackey, "Palestinian Police Are Said to Have Participated in Protest Against Al Jazeera," *New York Times,* January 25, 2011, http://thelede.blogs.ny times.com/2011/01/25/palestinian-police-are-said-to-have-participated-in-protest -at-al-jazeera/.
20. Khaled Abu Toameh, "Facebook Slight of Mahmoud Abbas Lands Palestinian Journalist in Jail. 2 Bethlehem Men Arrested Under 1960 Jordanian Law, Then Freed," *Jerusalem Post,* January 21, 2011 (accessed via LexisNexis).
21. Ibid.
22. Khaled Abu Toameh, "PA Bans Journalists From Reporting on Damning Human Rights Violation Report," *Jerusalem Post,* June 9, 2011, www.jpost.com/Middle East/Article.aspx?id=224143.
23. Khaled Abu Toameh, "Award-Winning Palestinian Journalist Forced Into Hiding," *Jerusalem Post,* August 7, 2011, www.jpost.com/NationalNews/Article.aspx ?id=232720.

24. "AG Sees 'No Problem' With Journalist's Arrest," Ma'an News Agency, April 1, 2012, www.maannews.net/eng/ViewDetails.aspx?ID=473160.

25. Khaled Abu Toameh, "PA to Try Local Journalist for Criticizing Medical Services," *Jerusalem Post,* September 14, 2011, www.jpost.com/MiddleEast/Article.aspx?id=237862.

26. "Palestinian Security Forces Question 2 Journalists," Associated Press, February 1, 2012, http://cnsnews.com/news/article/palestinian-security-forces-question-2-journalists.

27. Yousef al-Shayeb, "Palestinian Mission in France Accused of Spying," *Al-Ghad,* January 30, 2012, www.alghad.com/index.php/article/527034.html.

28. Khaled Abu Toameh, "PA Detains Journalist Critical of Mission to France," *Jerusalem Post,* March 26, 2012, www.jpost.com/MiddleEast/Article.aspx?id=263490.

29. "Ramallah Court Extends Arrest of Palestinian Reporter," Ma'an News Agency, March 28, 2012, www.maannews.net/eng/ViewDetails.aspx?ID=471992.

30. "AG Sees 'No Problem' With Journalist's Arrest," Ma'an News Agency.

31. "MADA Calls for an End to the Policy of Arrest of Journalists," Palestinian Center for Development and Media Freedoms, March 29, 2012, www.madacenter.org/report.php?lang=1&id=1149&category_id=6&year=2012.

32. Khaled Abu Toameh, "PA Arrests Man for Facebook Anti-Corruption Drive," *Jerusalem Post,* April 7, 2012, www.jpost.com/MiddleEast/Article.aspx?id=265181.

33. "AG Sees 'No Problem' With Journalist's Arrest."

34. Khaled Abu Toameh, "PA Steps up Crackdown on Journalists," *Jerusalem Post,* April 1, 2012, www.jpost.com/MiddleEast/Article.aspx?id=264261.

35. "Security Official Says There Is No Control Over Media," WAFA, April 9, 2012, http://english.wafa.ps/index.php?action=detail&id=19507.

36. "AG Sees 'No Problem' with Journalist's Arrest."

37. George Hale, "Palestinian Media Clampdown Spreads to the Web," Ma'an News Agency, April 23, 2012, www.maannews.net/eng/ViewDetails.aspx?ID=478726.

38. "Journalists: PA Censoring Dissent in Media Crackdown," Ma'an News Agency, December 16, 2008, www.maannews.net/eng/ViewDetails.aspx?ID=207033.

39. "Mahmoud Abbas Launches Attack Against InLightPress," Israellycool, January 30, 2012, www.israellycool.com/2012/01/30/mahmoud-abbas-launches-attack-against-inlightpress/.

40. "Report: Mahmoud Abbas Monitoring Phones of Top Palestinian Figures," Israellycool, January 20, 2012, www.israellycool.com/2012/01/20/report-mahmoud-abbas-monitoring-phones-of-top-palestinian-figures/.

41. "InLightPress Slams Mahmoud Abbas Over Hacking Attack," Israellycool, February 1, 2012, www.israellycool.com/2012/02/01/inlightpress-slams-mahmoud-abbas-over-hacking-attack/.

42. "Mahmoud Abbas Orders Another Attack on InLightPress," Israellycool, February 3, 2012, www.israellycool.com/2012/02/03/mahmoud-abbas-orders-another-attack-on-inlightpress/.

43. "Palestinian Authority Blocks Access to InLightPress," Israellycool, February 9, 2012, www.israellycool.com/2012/02/09/palestinian-authority-blocks-access-to-inlightpress/.

44. "Palestinian Intelligence Ordered the Telecommunications Company to Block Amad," *Amad,* February 12, 2012, www.amad.ps/arabic/?action=detail&id=76964.

45. Hale, "Palestinian Media Clampdown Spreads to the Web."

46. "Palestinian Communications Ministers Admits to Targeting InLight Press," InLight Press, February 14, 2012, http://inlightpress.com/index.php?option=com_content&view=article&id=9094:2012-02-14-10-02-03&catid=3:2011-07-04-18-39-20&Itemid=304.

47. Hale, "Palestinian Media Clampdown Spreads to the Web."

48. George Hale, "PalTel: No Choice in Web Censorship Orders," Ma'an News Agency, April 25, 2012, www.maannews.net/eng/ViewDetails.aspx?ID=479638.

49. Khaled Abu Toameh, "PA Minister Resigns Amid Censorship Row," *Jerusalem Post,* April 26, 2012, www.jpost.com/MiddleEast/Article.aspx?id=267666.
50. George Hale and Wajde al-Jafari, "Abbas Lifts Ban on Critical Websites," Ma'an News Agency, May 5, 2012, www.maannews.net/eng/ViewDetails.aspx?ID=482586.
51. "Palestinian President to Meet Israeli Vice PM: Official," Reuters, June 28, 2012, www.reuters.com/article/2012/06/28/us-palestinians-israel-idUSBRE85R07820120628.
52. "PA Security Clash With Protesters in Ramallah," Ma'an News Agency, June 30, 2012, www.maannews.net/eng/ViewDetails.aspx?ID=500066.
53. "Injuries, Arrests Reported at New Ramallah Demo," Ma'an News Agency, July 1, 2012, www.maannews.net/eng/ViewDetails.aspx?ID=500424.
54. "PA Police Crush New Ramallah Demo," Ma'an News Agency, July 1, 2012, www.maannews.net/eng/ViewDetails.aspx?ID=500441.
55. "PCHR Strongly Condemns the Use of Force Against Peaceful Demonstrations in Ramallah," Palestine Center for Human Rights, July 2, 2012, www.pchrgaza.org/portal/en/index.php?option=com_content&view=article&id=8591:pchr-strongly-condemns-the-use-of-force-against-peaceful-demonstrations-in-ramallah-&catid=36:pchrpressreleases&Itemid=194.
56. "PA Police Crush New Ramallah Demo."
57. "PCHR Strongly Condemns the Use of Force Against Peaceful Demonstrations in Ramallah."
58. "Activists Call for Ramallah Police Director Dismissal," Ma'an News Agency, July 2, 2012, www.maannews.net/eng/ViewDetails.aspx?ID=500566.
59. "PCHR Strongly Condemns the Use of Force Against Peaceful Demonstrations in Ramallah."
60. "MADA: Attacks against Journalists in Ramallah a Flagrant Violation of Palestinian Law," Palestinian Center for Development and Media Freedoms, July 2, 2012, www.madacenter.org/report.php?lang=1&id=1184&category_id=6&year=2012.
61. "Union Condemns Police Attack on Palestinian Journalist," Ma'an News Agency, July 1, 2012, www.maannews.net/eng/ViewDetails.aspx?ID=500449.
62. "Palestinian Security Forces Assault Journalists at Protests," Committee to Protect Journalists, July 2, 2012, www.cpj.org/2012/07/palestinian-security-forces-assault-journalists-co.php.
63. "Ashrawi Condemns Violence Against Ramallah Protesters," Ma'an News Agency, July 2, 2012, www.maannews.net/eng/ViewDetails.aspx?ID=500745.
64. "Interior Minister Orders Investigation Into Ramallah Clashes," Ma'an News Agency, July 2, 2012, www.maannews.net/eng/ViewDetails.aspx?ID=500488.
65. "Live Report: Ramallah Protests," Maan News Agency, July 3, 2012, www.maannews.net/eng/ViewDetails.aspx?ID=501059.
66. "High Ranking Officials Ordered Suppression of Ramallah Protests," Ma'an News Agency, August 27, 2012, www.maannews.net/eng/ViewDetails.aspx?ID=514925&reason=0.
67. "Palestinian Authority: Hold Police Accountable for Ramallah Beatings," Human Rights Watch, August 27, 2012, www.hrw.org/news/2012/08/27/palestinian-authority-hold-police-accountable-ramallah-beatings.
68. "PA Slams Rights Report," Ma'an News Agency, August 28, 2012, www.maannews.net/eng/ViewDetails.aspx?ID=515236.
69. "Abbas: Media Should Be Free," Ma'an News Agency, July 2, 2012, www.maannews.net/eng/ViewDetails.aspx?ID=500597.
70. "Violations of Media Freedoms in the OPT During July 2012," Palestinian Center for Development and Media Freedoms, November 2, 2012, www.madacenter.org/report.php?lang=1&id=1199&category_id=13&year=.
71. Itamar Marcus and Nan Jacques Zilberdik, "'Palestinian Spring' Unfolds: PA TV Mutes Broadcast When Citizens Criticize PA Leaders," Palestinian Media Watch, September 12, 2012, www.palwatch.org/main.aspx?fi=157&doc_id=7428.

72. "Violations of Media Freedoms in OPT During September 2012," Palestinian Center for Development and Media Freedoms, November 2, 2012, www.mada center.org/report.php?lang=1&id=1223&category_id=13&year=2012.

73. "PA Summons Palestinian Columnist for Interrogation," Ma'an News Agency, October 31, 2012, www.maannews.net/eng/ViewDetails.aspx?ID=532780.

74. Jihad Harb, "Presidential Decisions Are Made in a Coffee Shop," *Shasha,* August 25, 2012, www.shasha.ps/more.php?id=36156#.UJPZOG9_CIO.

75. "PA Summons Palestinian Columnist for Interrogation," Ma'an News Agency, October 31, 2012, www.maannews.net/eng/ViewDetails.aspx?ID=532780; Khaled Abu Toameh, "West Bank: What the West Is Funding," Gatestone Institute, November 2, 2012, www.gatestoneinstitute.org/3429/palestinian-authority-free-speech.

76. Khaled Abu Toameh, "PA Gives Man 1 Year Prison for Criticizing Leaders," *Jerusalem Post,* February 7, 2013, www.jpost.com/NationalNews/Article.aspx?id=3024 11.

77. "Court Upholds Jail Sentence for Reporter Accused of Insulting Abbas," Ma'an News Agency, March 28, 2013, www.maannews.net/eng/ViewDetails.aspx?ID=57 9849.

78. "Palestinian Journalist Pardoned for Insulting President," Committee to Protect Journalists, April 2, 2013, http://cpj.org/2013/04/palestinian-journalist-pardoned -for-insulting-pres.php.

79. Email correspondence with George Hale, April 27, 2013.

80. "PCHR Is Concerned Over the Security Officers' Violent Dispersal of Two Peaceful Sit-ins Organized by Hizbut-Tahrir in Tulkarm," Palestinian Center for Human Rights, April 30, 2013, www.pchrgaza.org/portal/en/index.php?option=com_con tent&view=article&id=9461:pchr-is-concerned-over-the-security-officers-violent -dispersal-of-two-peaceful-sit-ins-organized-by-hizbut-tahrir-in-tulkarm&catid=36 :pchrpressreleases&Itemid=194.

81. "Fayyad: Press Freedom Essential for Palestinian State," Ma'an News Agency, May 13, 2013, www.maannews.net/eng/ViewDetails.aspx?ID=594833.

CHAPTER 13   UNILATERALISM

1. "Full Text of Pres. Mahmoud Abbas' Statement to the UN General Assembly," Voice of America, November 29, 2012, www.voanews.com/content/mahmoud -abbas-speech-to-united-nations-general-assembly/1556084.html.

2. "United Nations Latin American and Caribbean Meeting in Support of Israel-Palestinian Peace Concludes in Montevideo, Uruguay," United Nations, March 31, 2011, www.un.org/News/Press/docs/2011/gapal1193.doc.htm.

3. "Venezuelan-Palestinian Ties Forged," Al-Jazeera, April 28, 2009, www.aljazeera .com/news/americas/2009/04/2009427234224190396.html.

4. "Abbas Concludes South America Tour," Ma'an News Agency, November 29, 2009, www.maannews.net/eng/ViewDetails.aspx?ID=243116.

5. "Brazilian President: I Dream of Free Palestine," WAFA, March 17, 2010, http:// english.wafa.ps/index.php?action=detail&id=13894.

6. "Brazil Says It Recognizes Palestinian State," Associated Press, December 4, 2010, www.jpost.com/International/Article.aspx?id=197908.

7. "Brazil, Argentina, Uruguay Recognize Palestinian State," Agence France-Presse, December 6, 2010, www.google.com/hostednews/afp/article/ALeqM5j6LW4hivgK RMW-N8S1xV6P9AwVew; "Bolivia Recognizes Palestinian State," Ma'an News Agency, December 17, 2010, www.maannews.net/eng/ViewDetails.aspx?ID=3429 77; "Ecuador Recognizes Palestinian State," Agence France-Presse, December 25, 2010, www.ynetnews.com/articles/0,7340,L-4004103,00.html.

8. "Brazil, Argentina, Uruguay Recognize Palestinian State," Agence France-Presse, December 6, 2010, www.google.com/hostednews/afp/article/ALeqM5j6L W4hivgKRMW-N8S1xV6P9AwVew.

9. "Abbas Lays Brazil Embassy Cornerstone," Agence France-Presse, December 31, 2010, www.ynetnews.com/articles/0,7340,L-4007250,00.html.

10. Eva Vergara, "Chile Says It Recognizes a Palestinian State," Associated Press, January 8, 2011, http://abcnews.go.com/International/wireStory?id=12566957.

11. "Peru Recognizes Palestinian State," Reuters, January 24, 2011, www.reuters.com /article/2011/01/24/us-palestinians-peru-idUSTRE70N5ZW20110124; "Paraguay Recognizes 'Palestine' with Pre-1967 Borders," *Jerusalem Post,* January 29, 2011, www.jpost.com/International/Article.aspx?id=205690; "Guyana Becomes 7th South American State to Recognize Palestinian Independence," *Haaretz,* January 14, 2011, www.haaretz.com/news/diplomacy-defense/guyana-becomes-7th-south-ameri can-state-to-recognize-palestinian-independence-1.336944.

12. "Suriname Recognizes Palestinian State," Ma'an News Agency, February 1, 2011, www.maannews.net/eng/ViewDetails.aspx?ID=356264.

13. "Uruguay Recognizes Palestinian State," Reuters, March 15, 2011, http://ca.reuters .com/article/topNews/idCATRE72F0SA20110316.

14. "France Upgrades Its Diplomatic Relations With the Palestinians," *European Jewish Press,* July 27, 2010, www.ejpress.org/article/45147.

15. "Portugal Upgrades Palestinian Representation," Ma'an News Agency, October 14, 2010, www.maannews.net/eng/ViewDetails.aspx?ID=324060; Marianne Stigset, "Norway Calls for Palestinian State, Gives Diplomatic Mission Embassy Rank," Bloomberg, December 15, 2010, www.bloomberg.com/news/2010-12-15/norway -calls-for-palestinian-state-gives-diplomatic-mission-embassy-rank.html; "Obama Sees Enormous Hurdles in Mideast Peace Talks," Reuters, September 10, 2010, www .reuters.com/article/2010/09/10/us-obama-mideast-idUSTRE6893JY20100910.

16. "In for a Pound," *Monocle,* 4, no. 37 (October 2010).

17. "Erdogan Pledges Support for '67 State," Ma'an News Agency, December 6, 2010, www.maannews.net/eng/ViewDetails.aspx?ID=339326.

18. "Erekat Demands UN Intervention," Ma'an News Agency, November 27, 2010, www.maannews.net/eng/ViewDetails.aspx?ID=336454.

19. "Hammad: We Will Go to the World for Recognition of a Palestinian State," WAFA, December 5, 2010, www.wafa.ps/arabic/index.php?action=detail&id=92334.

20. "Cyprus Upgrades Palestinian Delegation," Agence France-Presse, May 6, 2011, www.maannews.net/eng/ViewDetails.aspx?ID=385370; "Denmark to Upgrade Status of Palestinian Representation to 'Mission,'" *Haaretz,* March 9, 2011, www.haaretz.com/news/international/denmark-to-upgrade-status-of-palestinian -representation-to-mission-1.348168; Bruno Waterfield, "Ireland Upgrades Palestinian Diplomatic Delegation to a Mission," *Telegraph,* January 25, 2011, www.telegraph.co.uk/news/worldnews/europe/ireland/8281760/Ireland-upgrades -Palestinian-diplomatic-delegation-to-a-mission.html; "Foreign Secretary Announces Upgrading of the Palestinian Delegation to London," Foreign & Commonwealth Office, March 8, 2011, www.fco.gov.uk/en/news/latest-news/?id=562006582 &view=News; "Greece Upgrades Palestinian Representation Status," Agence France-Presse, February 15, 2011, www.naharnet.com/stories/en/3078-greece-upgrades -palestinian-representation-status.

21. Khaled Abu Toameh, "Spain Will Recognize Palestinian State on 1967 Lines," *Jerusalem Post,* May 30, 2011, www.jpost.com/MiddleEast/Article.aspx?ID =222873&R=R1; "Shaath: Slovenia to Recognize Palestine Before September," Ma'an News Agency, May 17, 2011, www.maannews.net/eng/ViewDetails.aspx?ID =388711; "Report: Iceland Backs Recognition of Palestinian State," Ma'an News Agency, June 7, 2011, www.maannews.net/eng/ViewDetails.aspx?ID=402842.

22. "Dominican Republic Supports Palestine's Statehood, Honors Abbas," Xinhua, October 7, 2011, http://news.xinhuanet.com/english2010/world/2011-10 /08/c_131179157.htm; "Peru Recognizes Palestinian State," Reuters, January 24, 2011, www.reuters.com/article/2011/01/24/us-palestinians-peru-idUSTRE70N5Z W20110124.

23. David Sheen, "Norway's Ambassador: Palestinian Appeal to UN Legitimate in Lieu of Treaty with Israel," *Haaretz,* July 28, 2011, www.haaretz.com/news /diplomacy-defense/norway-s-ambassador-palestinian-appeal-to-un-legitimate-in -lieu-of-treaty-with-israel-1.375761; "Bulgaria Unexpectedly Rebuffs Israel Over Palestinian UN Bid," Agence France-Presse, July 7, 2011, www.maannews.net/eng /ViewDetails.aspx?ID=403329; Ronen Medzini, "Who Will Endorse Palestine?" Ynet News, August 27, 2011, www.ynetnews.com/articles/0,7340,L-4114432,00 .html.

24. "EU States Divided on Palestinian Statehood Bid," Reuters, September 2, 2011, www .reuters.com/article/2011/09/02/us-eu-palestinians-idUSTRE7816AJ20110902.

25. Barak Ravid, "Merkel: Unilateral Recognition of Palestinian State May Not Push Peace Forward," *Haaretz,* April 7, 2011, www.haaretz.com/news/diplomacy -defense/merkel-unilateral-recognition-of-palestinian-state-may-not-push-peace -forward-1.354676.

26. "Window of Opportunity for Peace Is Closing," *La Gazzetta del Mezzogiorno,* May 23, 2011, www.lagazzettadelmezzogiorno.it/notizia.php?IDNotizia=429222.

27. "Sarkozy: 'Netanyahou Doit Prendre le Risque de la Paix,'" *L'Express,* May 5, 2011, www.lexpress.fr/actualite/monde/sarkozy-netanyahou-doit-prendre-le-risque -de-la-paix_989485.html.

28. Herb Keinon, "Spanish FM Signals Support for PA at UN, Drawing," *Jerusalem Post,* August 21, 2011, www.jpost.com/DiplomacyAndPolitics/Article.aspx ?id=234739.

29. "Portugal Upgrades Palestinian Representation," Ma'an News Agency, October 14, 2010, www.maannews.net/eng/ViewDetails.aspx?ID=324060; Marianne Stigset, "Norway Calls for Palestinian State, Gives Diplomatic Mission Embassy Rank," Bloomberg, December 15, 2010, www.bloomberg.com/news/2010-12-15/norway -calls-for-palestinian-state-gives-diplomatic-mission-embassy-rank.html; "Obama Sees Enormous Hurdles in Mideast Peace Talks," Reuters, September 10, 2010, www .reuters.com/article/2010/09/10/us-obama-mideast-idUSTRE6893JY20100910.

30. "Palestinians Seek Support for UN Recognition," Associated Press, June 27, 2011, www.guardian.co.uk/world/feedarticle/9716026.

31. "Promised Donor Aid Not Arriving: Palestinian PM," Agence France-Presse, May 31, 2011, www.google.com/hostednews/afp/article/ALeqM5g-4YX650HUS_8yrN pFQerIxiG0HA?docId=CNG.836b5e3d9530f1a41a32f2a2dc8f9d11.3b1.

32. Ora Coren and Nadan Feldman, "In Response to UN Vote, Israel Unlikely to Rescind Economic Accords with PA," *Haaretz,* December 2, 2012. www.haaretz .com/business/in-response-to-un-vote-israel-unlikely-to-rescind-economic-accords -with-pa.premium-1.481812.

33. "Palestinians Plan Mass Demonstrations Against Israel on Eve of UN Vote," Associated Press, August 1, 2011, www.haaretz.com/news/diplomacy-defense /palestinians-plan-mass-demonstrations-against-israel-on-eve-of-un-vote-1.376457.

34. "Officials Set Date for 'Palestine 194' March," Al-Jazeera, August 1, 2011, www .aljazeera.com/news/middleeast/2011/08/201181185654921787.html.

35. "Barghouti Urges Palestinian March to Back UN Statehood Bid," Reuters, July 20, 2011, www.jpost.com/Headlines/Article.aspx?id=230195.

36. Tom Perry and Ali Sawafta, "Abbas Urges Palestinian Protest to Support U.N. Bid," Reuters, July 27, 2011, www.reuters.com/article/2011/07/27/us-palestinians -israel-abbas-idUSTRE76Q3IH20110727.

37. Daoud Kuttab, "The Palestinian Third Way," *Jerusalem Post,* July 16, 2011, www .jpost.com/Opinion/Op-EdContributors/Article.aspx?id=229648.

38. Khaled Abu Toameh, "70% of Palestinians Expect Third Intifada If Talks Fail," *Jerusalem Post,* May 17, 2011, www.jpost.com/MiddleEast/Article.aspx?ID=22 0974.

39. "Apple Drops iPhone 'Intifada' App That Encourages Users to Launch Violence Against Israel," *Daily Mail,* June 23, 2012, www.dailymail.co.uk/news/article

-2007174/Apple-drops-iPhone-intifada-app-encourages-users-launch-violence
-Israel.html#ixzz2KjmzSBz1.

40. "MK Mofaz: Reserves Likely to Be Mobilized in September," *Ynet News*, August 2, 2011, www.ynetnews.com/articles/0,7340,L-4103383,00.html.

41. "Full Transcript of Abbas Speech at UN General Assembly," *Haaretz*, September 23, 2011, www.haaretz.com/news/diplomacy-defense/full-transcript-of-abbas -speech-at-un-general-assembly-1.386385.

42. "Abbas Receives Rousing Reception in Ramallah," Al-Jazeera, September 25, 2011, www.aljazeera.com/news/middleeast/2011/09/2011925104155882960.html.

43. Ibid.

44. Tovah Lazaroff, Yaakov Katz, and Khaled Abu Toameh, "Obama Opposes With-holding Funds to the PA," *Jerusalem Post*, October 4, 2011, www.jpost.com /DiplomacyAndPolitics/Article.aspx?id=240434.

45. "Limitation on Contributions to the United Nations and Affiliated Organizations," *New York Times*, June 20, 2012, http://graphics8.nytimes.com/packages/pdf /world/PLO-UN-legislation.pdf.

46. Luisa Blanchfield, "The UNESCO World Heritage Convention: Congressional Is-sues," *Congressional Research Service*, July 20, 2011, www.fas.org/sgp/crs/row /R40164.pdf.

47. Dan Perry and Don Melvin, "Europe Set for Key Palestine Role," *Associated Press*, May 25, 2011, www.boston.com/news/world/europe/articles/2011/05/25 /europe_set_for_key_palestine_role/.

48. "UNESCO Executive Board Recommends Palestinian Membership," UNESCO, September 27, 2011, www.unesco.org/new/en/media-services/single-view/news /moving_unesco_into_the_21st_century/.

49. Scott Shane and Steven Erlanger, "Palestinians Win a Vote on Bid to Join UNESCO," *New York Times*, October 5, 2011, www.nytimes.com/2011/10/06/world/middle east/palestinians-win-initial-vote-on-unesco-bid.html.

50. "Palestinians Get UNESCO Seat as 107 Vote in Favour," BBC, October 31, 2011, www.bbc.co.uk/news/world-middle-east-15518173.

51. Barak Ravid, "Netanyahu Mulls Gestures Toward Palestinians to Keep Peace Talks Going," *Haaretz*, January 10, 2012, www.haaretz.com/print-edition/news/netan yahu-mulls-gestures-toward-palestinians-to-keep-peace-talks-going-1.406357.

52. "Bustling UN Security Council Welcomes Five New Members," *Agence France-Presse*, January 1, 2012, www.france24.com/en/20120101-united-nations-diplo macy-countries-join-arab-spring-un-security-council.

53. Barak Ravid, "Palestinians Plan Diplomatic Steps to Put Israel Under 'International Siege,'" *Haaretz*, January 2, 2012, www.haaretz.com/print-edition/news/palestin ians-plan-diplomatic-steps-to-put-israel-under-international-siege-1.404973.

54. "Abbas Wants Jordan Meeting to Be Last," Ma'an News Agency, January 25, 2012, www.maannews.net/eng/ViewDetails.aspx?ID=455209.

55. "Palestine to Call for Vote on UN Membership, Says Foreign Minister," WAFA, January 25, 2012, http://english.wafa.ps/index.php?action=detail&id=18814.

56. "Ashrawi to Ashton: Europe's Commitment to Peace Is Being Tested," WAFA, Jan-uary 26, 2012, http://english.wafa.ps/index.php?action=detail&id=18825.

57. "Netanyahu Says Abbas 'Shunned Peace,'" *Sky News*, February 14, 2012, www .skynews.com.au/world/article.aspx?id=718110&vId=.

58. "Abbas to Ask Arab League for Peace Conference," *Jerusalem Post*, February 12, 2012, www.jpost.com/MiddleEast/Article.aspx?id=257503.

59. "Erekat: We Agreed With Qatar on a Plan to Move Towards the United Nations," *Palestine Press*, March 22, 2012, www.palpress.co.uk/arabic/?action=detail&id =42475.

60. "President Abbas: If You Do Not See Any Development With the Peace Process We Will Go to the United Nations," *Palestine Press*, April 30, 2012, www.palpress .co.uk/arabic/?action=detail&id=46491.

61. "Abbas to Resume Statehood Bid in UN: Official," Xinhua, May 16, 2012, http://news.xinhuanet.com/english/world/2012-05/16/c_131592189.htm.

62. "Authority in a State of Frustration," Ma'an News Agency, May 26, 2012, www.maannews.net/arb/ViewDetails.aspx?ID=489409.

63. Asher Zieger, "Israel to Fight PA Request for Statehood Status at UN Conference," Times of Israel, May 10, 2012, www.timesofisrael.com/israel-to-fight-pa-request-for-state-status-at-un-conference/.

64. "Palestinians Seek Full Representation at Rio+20," Agence France-Presse, June 16, 2012, www.google.com/hostednews/afp/article/ALeqM5jPnTNLQH-Qt2Z8svfDHLAPKAF0uw?docId=CNG.57af47f3cbe2260c211d864cfe7f5c93.6d1.

65. "Obtaining Non-Member Status Eliminates Legitimacy of the Settlements," Okaz (Saudi Arabia), June 10, 2012, www.okaz.com.sa/new/Issues/20120610/Con20120610509549.htm.

66. Allison Good, "Palestinians Deny U.S. Aid Threat," Foreign Policy, July 19, 2012, http://thecable.foreignpolicy.com/posts/2012/07/19/palestinians_deny_us_aid_threat.

67. "Decision to Go to the United Nations to Request Membership for Palestine Is Incomplete Without a Date," Al-Hayat, July 23, 2012, http://mobile.alhayat.com/content/1343059495414844500/Politics.

68. "Palestinians Debate Whether to Seek UN Recognition of 'Palestine' Before or After US Vote," Associated Press, August 2, 2012, www.washingtonpost.com/world/middle_east/palestinians-brace-for-us-israeli-repercussions-if-they-seek-un-recognition-document-shows/2012/08/02/gJQAG0DXRX_story.html.

69. William Bigelow, "Palestinians Seek Statehood Before U.S. Election," Breitbart, August 3, 2012, www.breitbart.com/Big-Peace/2012/08/03/Palestinians-seek-statehood-while-obama-can-help-them.

70. Raphael Ahren, "Israel Says It Will Free Prisoners, Let Palestinians Exploit Gaza Gas Field, If Abbas Abandons UN Statehood Bid," Times of Israel, August 5, 2012, www.timesofisrael.com/jerusalem-intensifies-carrot-and-stick-efforts-to-prevent-palestinian-un-statehood-bid/.

71. "Report: Netanyahu to Release Prisoners If UN Bid Scrapped," Ma'an News Agency, August 6, 2012, www.maannews.net/eng/ViewDetails.aspx?ID=510272.

72. "Abbas Says Going to UN Even If It Conflicts With Others' Interests," Ma'an News Agency, August 8, 2012, www.maannews.net/eng/ViewDetails.aspx?ID=510868.

73. Elior Levy, "Arab League to Present UN With New PA Bid?," Ynet News, August 14, 2012, www.ynetnews.com/articles/0,7340,L-4268555,00.html.

74. "Palestinian's UN Recognition Quest on Hold," Associated Press, August 28, 2012, www.foxnews.com/world/2012/08/28/palestinian-un-recognition-quest-on-hold/.

75. Khaled Abu Toameh, "PA's Abbas to Delay Pursuit of UN Statehood," Jerusalem Post, August 31, 2012, www.jpost.com/DiplomacyAndPolitics/Article.aspx?ID=283327.

76. "Abbas Says Has Backing for New UN Upgrade Push," Reuters, September 5, 2012, www.maannews.net/eng/ViewDetails.aspx?ID=517620.

77. "FM: Arab States to Back UN Bid at General Assembly," Ma'an News Agency, September 6, 2012, www.maannews.net/eng/ViewDetails.aspx?ID=517937.

78. "Fatah Leadership Affirms UN Bid," Ma'an News Agency, September 17, 2012, www.maannews.net/eng/ViewDetails.aspx?ID=520797.

79. Jodi Rudoren, "Year After Effort at U.N., New Aim for Palestinians," New York Times, September 20, 2012, www.nytimes.com/2012/09/21/world/middleeast/palestinians-aim-for-nonmember-state-status-at-united-nations-general-assembly.html.

80. Joel Greenberg, "Abbas Set for Scaled-Down Bid at U.N.," Washington Post, September 24, 2012, www.washingtonpost.com/world/middle_east/abbas-set-for-scaled-down-bid-at-un/2012/09/24/b660cbca-0677-11e2-a10c-fa5a255a9258_story.html.

81. "Statement by H.E. Mr. Mahmoud Abbas," United Nations, September 27, 2012, http://gadebate.un.org/sites/default/files/gastatements/67/PS_en.pdf.

82. "Erekat: Consultations Underway Over UN Resolution," Ma'an News Agency, October 1, 2012, www.maannews.net/eng/ViewDetails.aspx?ID=525011.

83. "Newspapers Review: Israeli Foreign Minister's Attack on Abbas Dominates Dailies," WAFA, October 1, 2012, http://english.wafa.ps/index.php?action=detail&id=20774.

84. "U.S. Says Palestinian Status Bid Jeopardizes Peace Process," Reuters, October 15, 2012, www.reuters.com/article/2012/10/15/us-palestinians-status-usa-idUSBRE89E15P20121015.

85. "Abbas to Obama: Talks With Israel After U.N. Statehood Vote," Agence France-Presse, October 16, 2012, www.naharnet.com/stories/en/57309.

86. Noah Browning, "Abbas Says Ready for Peace Talks If U.N. Recognition Bid Succeeds," Reuters, October 24, 2012, www.reuters.com/article/2012/10/24/us-palestinians-israel-negotiations-idUSBRE89N12C20121024.

87. Noah Browning and Ali Sawafta, "Palestinians Lobby for Convincing Win in U.N. Vote," Reuters, October 30, 2012, www.reuters.com/article/2012/10/30/us-palestinians-un-statehood-idUSBRE89T11H20121030.

88. "Mohammad Shtayyeh Goes on an Official Visit to Scandinavia," Ma'an News Agency, October 31, 2012, www.maannews.net/arb/ViewDetails.aspx?ID=532792.

89. Mohammed Daraghmeh, "Palestinians Campaign for UN Recognition," Associated Press, October 31, 2012, www.boston.com/news/world/middle-east/2012/10/31/palestinian-threatens-quit-over-cash-crunch/6os134YxJ0o4MUhlXpf2dJ/story.html.

90. Nabil Sha'ath, "Britain Must Atone for Its Sins in Palestine," *Telegraph*, October 31, 2012, www.telegraph.co.uk/news/worldnews/middleeast/palestinianauthority/9645925/Britain-must-atone-for-its-sins-in-Palestine.html.

91. Barak Ravid, "Senior Israeli Ministers to Discuss 'Retaliatory Actions' against Palestinians Over UN Bid," *Haaretz*, November 6, 2012, www.haaretz.com/news/diplomacy-defense/senior-israeli-ministers-to-discuss-retaliatory-actions-against-palestinians-over-un-bid.premium-1.475606.

92. "Abbas Congratulates Obama for Winning Presidential Election," WAFA, November 7, 2012, http://english.wafa.ps/index.php?action=detail&id=21001.

93. "Erakat Hopes for Palestinian Statehood in 4 Years," Agence France-Presse, November 8, 2012, http://dailynewsegypt.com/2012/11/08/erakat-hopes-for-palestinian-statehood-in-4-years/.

94. "Palestinians Circulate Resolution That Would Raise Status at UN to Non-Member Observer State," Associated Press, November 8, 2012, www.foxnews.com/world/2012/11/08/palestinians-circulate-resolution-that-would-raise-status-at-un-to-non-member/.

95. "Official: 51 States 'Undecided' Over Palestinian UN Bid," Ma'an News Agency, November 9, 2012, www.maannews.net/eng/ViewDetails.aspx?ID=535506.

96. Chris McGreal, "Palestinians Warn: Back UN Statehood Bid or Risk Boosting Hamas," *Guardian*, November 27, 2012, www.guardian.co.uk/world/2012/nov/27/palestinians-un-statehood-bid-hamas.

CHAPTER 14   RIGHTING THE SHIP

1. "Arab League Chief to Brief PA on Financial 'Safety Net,'" Ma'an News Agency, December 25, 2012, www.maannews.net/eng/ViewDetails.aspx?ID=550983.

2. "Fayyad: Arab States Evading Commitments to PA," Ma'an News Agency, December 23, 2012, www.maannews.net/eng/ViewDetails.aspx?ID=550522.

3. "PLO Official: US Pressuring Arab Countries to Withhold PA Aid," Ma'an News Agency, December 21, 2012, www.maannews.net/eng/ViewDetails.aspx?ID=549998.

4. "Palestinian Govt May Take Loans From National Investment Fund," Xinhua, December 31, 2012, www.shanghaidaily.com/article/article_xinhua.asp?id=116606.

5. Correspondence with PIF representative, May 10, 2013.

6. "Group: PA Losing Millions of Dollars Due to Border Inefficiency," Ma'an News Agency, February 8, 2013, www.maannews.net/eng/ViewDetails.aspx?ID=5627 70.

7. "Palestinian Watchdog: Corruption Continues," Associated Press, April 24, 2013, http://bigstory.ap.org/article/palestinian-watchdog-corruption-continues.

8. Jillian C. York, "Make Fun of Mahmoud Abbas at Your Peril," Al-Jazeera, February 13, 2013, www.aljazeera.com/indepth/opinion/2013/02/201321261532152376 .html.

9. George Hale, "Occupied Palestinian Territory: Linking Censorship and Corruption," Global Information Society Watch 2021, pp. 186–189, www.giswatch.org /sites/default/files/gisw_12_cr_o_palestinian_territory.pdf.

10. David Keyes, "Palestine's Democratic Deficit," New York Times, February 12, 2013, www.nytimes.com/2013/02/12/opinion/palestines-democratic-deficit.html?_r=0.

11. "Financial Crisis in the West Bank," New York Times, January 10, 2013, www .nytimes.com/2013/01/11/opinion/financial-crisis-in-the-west-bank.html?_r=0.

12. Faine Greenwood, "Palestinian Authority's Name Changed to State of Palestine," Global Post, January 4, 2013, www.globalpost.com/dispatch/news/reg ions/middle-east/israel-and-palestine/130104/palestinian-authorits-name-chang ed-st.

13. Hugh Naylor, "State of Palestine Title Is Symbolic but a Political Risk," The National, January 8, 2013, www.thenational.ae/news/world/middle-east/state-of -palestine-title-is-symbolic-but-a-political-risk#ixzz2HKIb7w6H.

14. Raphael Ahren, "Abbas Changes Name of Palestinian Authority to State of Palestine," Times of Israel, January 4, 2013, www.timesofisrael.com/abbas-changes -name-of-palestinian-authority-to-state-of-palestine/.

15. "Palestine Regained? The PA Gets Renamed Following UN Status Upgrade," Al-Bawaba, January 7, 2013, www.albawaba.com/news/state-of-palestine-461933.

16. "PECDAR Begins Using State of Palestine on Official Documents," Ma'an News Agency, January 7, 2013, www.maannews.net/eng/ViewDetails.aspx?ID =554279&utm_source=twitterfeed&utm_medium=twitter.

17. "Information Ministry to Use 'State of Palestine' on Press Cards," WAFA, January 8, 2013, http://english.wafa.ps/index.php?action=detail&id=21470.

18. "PLO's Central Council to Discuss Changes, Says Official," WAFA, January 5, 2013, http://english.wafa.ps/index.php?action=detail&id=21457.

19. Khaled Abu Toameh, "Mahmoud Abbas' Empty Threats," Gatestone Institute, November 1, 2011, www.gatestoneinstitute.org/2553/mahmoud-abbas-empty-thre ats.

20. "Financial Crisis in the West Bank," New York Times, Jan 10, 2013, www.nytimes .com/2013/01/11/opinion/financial-crisis-in-the-west-bank.html?_r=0.

21. Roger Cohen, "Fayyad Steps Down, Not Out," New York Times, May 3, 2013, www.nytimes.com/2013/05/04/opinion/global/Roger-Cohen-Fayyad-Steps-Down -Not-Out.html?pagewanted=all.

22. "Fayyad Denies Statement in New York Times Article," WAFA, May 4, 2013, http://english.wafa.ps/index.php?action=detail&id=22289.

23. Roger Cohen, Twitter, https://twitter.com/NYTimesCohen/status/331354357801 054208.

24. Nathan J. Brown, "Are Palestinians Building a State?," Carnegie Endowment, July 1, 2010, www.carnegieendowment.org/2010/07/01/are-palestinians-building -state/1du.

25. Interview with Dennis Ross, Washington, DC, April 19, 2013.

26. Interview with Aaron David Miller, Washington, DC, March 11, 2013.

27. Interview with Dennis Ross, Washington, DC, April 19, 2013.

28. David Rose, "Hooded, Hanged and Left in Agony for Hours on End," Daily Mail, March 30, 2013, www.dailymail.co.uk/news/article-2301682/Hooded-hanged-left

-agony-hours-end-Palestinian-security-chief-tells-tormented-suspects-MI6s-knowl edge—reveals-Britain-helps-pay-33m-foreign-aid.html.
29. Interview with Michael Singh, Washington, DC, March 29, 2013.
30. Osamah Khalil, "Who Are You? The PLO and the Limits of Representation," Al-Shabaka, March 18, 2013, http://al-shabaka.org/node/585.
31. Interview with US Treasury official, Washington, DC, February 14, 2013.

INDEX